THE
PLAY
OF THE
EYES

ALSO BY ELIAS CANETTI

Elias Canetti

THE PLAY of the EYES

Translated from the German by Ralph Manheim

FARRAR STRAUS GIROUX
NEW YORK

Library of Congress Cataloging-in-Publication Data
Canetti, Elias.
The play of the eyes.
Translation of: Das Augenspiel.
1. Canetti, Elias.   —Biography.
2. Authors, Austrian—20th century—Biography.
I. Title.
PT2605.A58Z46313   1986   833'.912 [B]   86–2088

Portions of this book originally appeared in The New Yorker.

Contents

PART ONE
The Wedding

Büchner in the Desert

Kant Catches Fire, as the novel was then titled, had left me ravaged. I could not forgive myself for burning the books. I believe I had got over my regrets about Kant (later Kien). He had been treated so cruelly while I was writing the book, I had gone to such lengths repressing my pity for him, hiding the relief, the sense of liberation I felt at the thought of ending Kant's life.

But the books had been sacrificed to this liberation, and when *they* went up in flames, I felt that the same thing had happened to me. I felt that I had sacrificed not only my own books but also those of the whole world, for the sinologist's library included everything that was of importance to the world, the books of all religions, all thinkers, all Eastern literatures, and those of the Western literatures that were still in any sense alive. All that had burned, I had let it happen, I had made no attempt to save any part of it; what remained was a desert, and I myself was to blame. For what happens in that kind of book is not just a game, it is reality; one has to justify it, not only against criticism from outside but in one's own eyes as well. Even if an immense fear has compelled one to write such things, one must still ask oneself whether in so doing one has not helped to bring about what one so vastly fears.

Catastrophe had taken root in me and I could not shake it off. Seven years before, the seed had been sown by Karl Kraus's book *The Last Days of Mankind.* But now the thought of catastrophe had taken a personal form that stemmed from the constants of my life—fire, whose connection with crowds I had recognized July 15, and books, which

I lived with day after day. Different as the protagonist of the novel was from me, what I had put into him was something so essential that after it had served its purpose I could not take it back with impunity.

The desert I had created for myself began to cover everything. Never have I felt the threat to the world in which we live more intensely than after Kien's death. The unrest into which I had relapsed was like the earlier state in which I had planned my "Human Comedy of Madmen," with the difference that something crucial had happened in the meantime and that I felt guilty. The cause of my unrest was not unknown to me. At night, and by day as well, I ran through the same streets. There was no question of my undertaking any new novel, let alone one of the series I had planned. My enormous undertaking had been stifled in the smoke of the burning books, and in its place, wherever I happened to be, I saw nothing that was not threatened by a catastrophe that might descend at any moment.

Every conversation I overheard in passing seemed the last. What has to be done in last moments was being done under terrible, merciless pressure. But the fate of those threatened was closely bound up with themselves. They had brought themselves into a situation from which there is no escape. They had taken the most extraordinary pains to be the kind of people who *deserve* their ruin. Every pair of interlocutors I listened to seemed to me as guilty as I had been when I kindled that fire. But though this guilt, like some special sort of ether, so permeated everything that nothing was free of it, in other respects people remained exactly as they had been. The situations they were in were unmistakably their own, independent of the man who perceived them and assimilated them. His only contribution was to give them direction and fuel them with his own anxiety. Every breathtaking scene, which he took in with the passion of the perceiver, whose only reason for being had become perception, ended in catastrophe.

He wrote at a headlong pace and in gigantic letters— graffiti on the walls of a new Pompeii. His writing was a preparation for a volcanic eruption or earthquake: you know that it's coming soon, that nothing can stop it, and you write what went before, what people, separated by their activities and circumstances, did before, not suspecting that their doom was close at hand, inhaling the stifling atmosphere with their daily breath and for that very reason, before the catastrophe has actually begun, breathing a little more hectically and insistently. I wrote scene after scene, each stood by itself, none was connected with any other, but all ended with an immense catastrophe, which alone connected it with the others. When I now look at what has remained of them, they seem to have been engendered by the night bombings of the world war that was yet to come.

Scene upon scene, written on the run, in frantic haste— each ended in catastrophe, and immediately after it there began a new scene, enacted among different people and having nothing in common with those that preceded it but the *deserved* catastrophe with which they all ended. Each resembled an indiscriminate, all-embracing judgment, and the most severely punished was he who presumed to pass judgment on others. For he who wished to avert the judgment brought it about. It was he who saw through these people's lovelessness. He grazed them in passing, saw them and left them, heard their phrases, which lingered in his ears, joined them with others that were equally loveless, and when his head threatened to burst with remembered self-seeking phrases, he was driven to record the most urgent of them.

The worst torment in those weeks was my room in Hagenberggasse. For over a year I had lived there with my prints of the Isenheim altar. The most merciless details of the crucifixion had penetrated my flesh and blood. As long as I was working on the novel, my prints seemed to be in the right place, they spurred me on in one and the same direction, a merciless goad. I *wanted* the suffering they gave me, I got used to them, I never let them out of my sight, they became converted into something which, apparently, had nothing to do with them; for who would have been presumptuous or foolish enough to liken the sinologist's sufferings to those of Christ? And yet a kind of connection had established itself between the prints on my walls and the chapters of my book. I needed the pictures so badly that I would never have put anything else in their place. Nor did I let myself be put off by the horror expressed by my infrequent visitors.

But then, when library and sinologist had gone up in flames, something strange and unexpected happened. Grünewald recovered his old force. Once I stopped working on the novel, the painter was there independently, and in the desert I had made for myself he alone held power. When I came home, I was terrified by the walls of my room. Grünewald intensified my sense of menace.

In that period reading was no help to me. I had lost my right to books, because I had sacrificed them for the sake of my novel. When forcing myself to fight back my feeling of guilt I reached out for one of my books, as though it were still there, not burned, not destroyed, and then forced myself to read it, it soon disgusted me, and those I knew best, those I had loved longest, disgusted me the most. I remember the evening when I picked up Stendhal, who every day for a year had encouraged me to work, and dropped him in anger, not on the table but on the floor. Such was my despair at my disappointment that I didn't even pick him up but left him lying there. On another occasion I had the absurd idea of trying Gogol. Even "The Overcoat" struck me as silly and arbitrary, and I wondered why I had ever been moved by it. None of the familiar works out of which I had developed appealed to me. Perhaps by burning those books I had indeed destroyed all that was old. The volumes still seemed to be there, but their content was *destroyed*, none of it was left within me. Every attempt to resurrect what had burned infuriated me and aroused my resistance. After several pathetically unsuccessful attempts, I ceased to pick up books. My shelf of "great" works, those I had read innumerable times, remained untouched; it was as though they were no longer there; I no longer saw them, I no longer reached out for them, the desert around me had become total.

Then one night, in a state of mind that could not have been more desolate, I found salvation in something unknown, which had long been on my shelf but which I had never touched. It was a tall volume of Büchner bound in yellow linen and printed in large letters, placed in such a way that it could not be overlooked, beside four volumes of Kleist in the same edition, every letter of which was familiar to me. It will sound incredible when I say that I had never read Büchner, yet that is the truth. Of course, I knew of his importance, and I believe I also knew that he would someday mean a great deal to me. Two years may have gone by since I had caught sight of the Büchner volume at the Vienna bookshop in Bognergasse, taken it home and placed it next to Kleist.

Delayed encounters have played an extraordinary role in my life. These have been with places, people or pictures as well as books. There are cities I yearn for as if I had been predestined to spend my whole life there. I resort to all kinds of subterfuges to avoid visiting them, and every new opportunity I neglect to take advantage of increases their importance for me enough to make it appear that I lived for them alone and would have perished long ago if no such places existed. There are persons I so much enjoy hearing about that I seem to know more about them than they do themselves, yet I avoid looking at pictures of them and make no attempt to find out what they look like. And there are persons whom I see for years in the same street whom I think about, whom I look upon as enigmas that I have been appointed to elucidate, and yet I don't address a word to them, I pass them by in silence, as they do me; we exchange questioning looks, yet we both keep our lips firmly sealed. And I conjure up our first conversation in my mind, eagerly anticipating the many surprises in store for me. Finally, there are persons I have loved for years without their suspecting it; I grow older, and the prospect of my ever telling them so becomes more and more illusory, though I never cease to think of that glorious moment. Without these elaborate preparations for things to come, I should find it impossible to live, and I know for sure that they are no less important to me than the sudden surprises that come from nowhere and overwhelm me on the spot.

I wouldn't think of naming the books for which I am still preparing myself, including some of the most famous in all world literature whose greatness—attested by a consensus of those whose opinions I have valued down through the years—I have no reason to doubt. It seems evident that after twenty years of expectation an encounter with such a work will be a tremendous experience, and perhaps this is the only way of achieving the spiritual rebirth that saves one from routine and decay. Be that as it may, at the age of twenty-six I had known the name of Büchner for a long time, and for two years I had had a very conspicuous volume of his work in my bookcase.

One night, in a moment of extreme despair—I was sure I would never again write anything, sure I would never again *read* anything—I picked up the yellow volume and opened it at random—to a scene from *Wozzeck*, as the name was then written, the scene in which the doctor speaks to Wozzeck. It was as if I had been struck by lightning; I read that scene, I read all the rest of the fragment, I read the whole fragment over and over, how often I cannot say, innumerable times it must have been, for I read all that night, I read nothing else in the yellow volume, I read *Wozzeck* over and over from beginning to end. I was so excited that I left the house before six in the morning and ran to the Stadtbahn. I took the first train to the city, rushed to Ferdinandstrasse and woke Veza out of a deep sleep.

The chain was not fastened and I had the key to her apartment. We had made this arrangement in case some emergency should drive me to her early in the morning. In the six years of our love this had never happened, so that now when Büchner sent me running to her she was understandably alarmed.

The end of the ascetic year during which I was writing my novel had come as a great relief to her, and I doubt if any subsequent reader of the novel could have been as relieved as she was when the gaunt sinologist went up in flames. She had feared new vicissitudes, further adventures. Before writing the last chapter, "The Red Rooster," I had stopped working for a week, and she had interpreted my pause as *doubt*, as dissatisfaction with my ending. As she saw it, Georges would be assailed by misgivings on the return journey to Paris. Suddenly he would understand his brother's true condition. How could he have left him alone! At the next station he gets out and takes the train back. He forces his way into the house, packs up Peter's things and carries him off to Paris. There Peter becomes one of his brother's patients, an unusual patient, to be sure, resisting treatment with all his strength. But in vain; little by little he too finds his master in Georges.

Something told her that I was seriously tempted to prolong the struggle between the two brothers, the covert dialogue begun in that long last chapter but by no means exhausted. When she heard that "The Red Rooster" had finally been written, that the sinologist had carried out his plan, her first reaction was one of disbelief. She thought I was trying to set her mind at rest, for she knew that I knew how worried she had been about the life I was leading. The third part of the novel had affected her deeply, and she felt sure my own mind would be endangered if I persisted in digging deeper into the sinologist's persecution mania. Thus nothing could have been more natural than her relief when I read her the last chapter. She persuaded herself that the worst was over, when in fact I was entering on my most abysmal period, the period I have called my "desert."

Yet it soon became evident to her that now more than ever I was avoiding her and everyone else, that though I was not doing anything particular, I found little time for her or for my few friends. When I did see her, I was monosyllabic and morose. There had never been *this* kind of silence between us. Once she lost control and cried out: "Now that he's dead, your book character has taken possession of you. You're just like him. Maybe that's your way of grieving for him." She was infinitely patient with me, but I resented her relief over Kant's death. Once when she said: "Too bad Theresa isn't an Indian widow, she'd have thrown herself into the fire," I countered bitterly: "He had better companions than a woman, he had his books; they knew what was fitting and proper and they went up in flames with him."

After that she kept expecting me to turn up one night or one morning with the news that she feared above all, that I'd changed my mind, that the last chapter wasn't right, that for one thing the style jarred with the rest of the book, so I'd *torn it up*. Kant had come back to life, the whole thing was going to start in again, there would be a second volume of the same novel, and it would keep me busy for at least a year.

She was terrified when I woke her up on that Büchner morning. "Aren't you surprised to see me so early? I've never done this before." "No," she said. "I've been expecting you." She was already looking desperately for a way of deterring me from going on with the novel.

But I started right in with Büchner. Had she read *Wozzeck*? Of course she had read *Wozzeck*. Who hadn't? She spoke impatiently, she was still waiting for the unwelcome truth, the real reason for my coming. There was something disparaging in her tone—I felt offended for Büchner.

"And you don't think much of it?" There was anger, menace, in my voice. Suddenly she caught on.

"What?! Who doesn't think much of it? Why, I think it's the greatest play ever written in German."

I couldn't believe my ears. I stammered the first thing that came into my head: "But it's only a fragment."

"A fragment? You call it a fragment? What's missing from it is better than what's present in any other play. We could do with more such fragments."

"You never mentioned it to me. Have you known Büchner long?"

"Longer than I've known you. I read him long ago. I came across Büchner at the same time as Hebbel's *Journals* and Lichtenberg."

"But you never said a word about him. You often showed me passages from Hebbel and Lichtenberg. But not a word about *Wozzeck*. Why?"

"I even hid it. You could never have found my Büchner."

"I read it all night. *Wozzeck*. Over and over from beginning to end. I couldn't believe that such a work exists. I still can't believe it. I came here to bawl you out. First I thought you'd never heard of it. But I realized that was impossible. For you with your great love of literature. So you must have read Büchner, but you've kept him away from me. For six years we've talked about everything under the sun. But you've never once uttered the name of Büchner in my presence. And now you tell me you hid the book from me. I can't believe it. I know your room inside out. Prove it. Show me the book. Where have you hidden it? It's a big yellow book. How can it be hidden?"

"It's neither big nor yellow. It's an India-paper edition. See for yourself."

She opened the cabinet where she kept her favorite books. I remembered when she had shown me that cabinet for the first time. I knew it well. How could she possibly have hidden Büchner in it? She took out several volumes of Victor Hugo. Behind them, flat against the back wall, lay the Insel Verlag edition of Büchner. She held it out to me. I didn't like seeing Büchner in that reduced format. I still had the big letters of the night before my eyes, that was how I wanted to see Büchner.

"Have you hidden any other books from me?"

"No. This is the only one. I knew you wouldn't touch Victor Hugo, I know you don't read him, behind him Büchner was safe. Incidentally, he translated two of Victor Hugo's plays."

She pointed them out to me. That annoyed me and I handed back the volume.

"But why? Why did you hide him from me?"

"Be glad you hadn't read him. Do you think you could have written anything if you had? He's the most modern of writers. He could be living today, except that there's no one like him. No modern writer can take him as a model. A modern writer can only hide his head and say: 'Why am I writing? I should hold my tongue.' I didn't want you to hold your tongue. I believe in you."

"In spite of Büchner?"

"Let's not go into that now. Some things are bound to be unattainable. But you mustn't let the unattainable crush you. Now that you've finished your novel, there's something else of his that I want you to read. Another fragment, a story, *Lenz*. Read it now."

I sat down without another word and read the most wonderful piece of prose. My night of *Wozzeck* was followed by a morning of *Lenz*, without a moment's sleep in between. My novel that I'd been so proud of crumbled into dust and ashes.

It was a hard blow, but fortunate. After listening to the chapters of *Kant Catches Fire*—I had read them all to her— Veza thought of me as a playwright. She had lived in fear that I would never find my way out of my novel. She had seen how deeply I had entangled myself in it and how much it had taken out of me. She was aware of my unfortunate tendency to undertake tasks that would drag on for years, and she hadn't forgotten my plans for a "Human Comedy of Madmen"; I had often spoken to her about it. The view of the Steinhof insane asylum had impressed her at first, but she had soon come to detest it. It seemed to her that my fascination with madmen and misfits had increased during my work on the novel. My friendship with Thomas Marek troubled her too. I took his part violently, aggressively. Once when I went so far as to say that this paralytic was more important than any empty-headed ingrate walking on two legs, she ridiculed my fanaticism.

She was really worried about me. My profession of love, in the "Madhouse" chapter of the novel, for all those regarded as insane, convinced her that I had crossed a perilous threshold. She was seriously alarmed by my reclusiveness, by my admiration for individuals who were totally different, by my desire to break off all ties with a degraded mankind. In speaking to her, I had represented the manias of some people I knew as perfect works of art, and tried to give her a step-by-step account of how a mania of my own invention had come into being. She had often objected, partly on aesthetic grounds, to the exhaustiveness of my account of a case of persecution mania. I would point out that such cases could not be described in any other way, that every detail, every trifling step was important. I tried to convince her that earlier literary accounts of madness were unreliable. She replied that it must be possible to describe such states succinctly, in such a way as to bring out their development. With this I radically disagreed; that sort of writing, I argued, threw more light on the author's vanity than on the subject in point; madness, it should finally be realized, was not something shameful, but a phenomenon with its own meanings and implications, which were different in every particular case. This she denied and—though she believed nothing of the kind and took this position solely out of concern for me—defended the prevailing psychiatric classifications. She displayed a special weakness for the concept of "manic-depressive insanity," though she was rather more reserved in her use of "schizophrenia," which was then becoming fashionable.

Her intention in all this—to steer me away from this kind of novel—was clear to me. I was fiercely determined not to let myself be influenced by anyone, not even by her, and cited my, as I believed, successful novel in defense of my position. Though I myself felt guilty of arson and suffered severely under my guilt, this, I felt, did not detract from the value of my novel, which I did not doubt for one moment. Though, once it was finished, all my plans had been concerned with the theater, it does not seem impossible that after a period of exhaustion I would have started a novel of no lesser length, dealing with some other mania.

But the night when I picked up *Wozzeck*, and the following morning when *Lenz* hit me in my state of fatigue and hyperexcitation, were decisive. In a few pages I found everything that could be said about Lenz's specific condition; to expand this into a full-length novel would be unthinkable. My obstinate pride had been defeated. I did not start another novel and months went by before I regained my confidence in *Kant Catches Fire*. By that time I was possessed by *The Wedding*.

It may sound pretentious when I say that I owe *The Wedding* to the impact of *Wozzeck* that night. But I cannot sidestep the truth just to avoid giving that impression. The visions of catastrophe that I had conceived up until then were still colored by Karl Kraus. Only the worst things happened, they happened all at once and for no reason at all. These happenings were witnessed by a writer and denounced. He denounced them *from outside,* holding a whip over each scene of the catastrophe. His whip gave him no rest, it drove him headlong, he paused in his course only when there was something to whip, and no sooner was the punishment administered than his whip drove him on. Essentially, the same thing happened over and over again: people engaged in their daily activities spoke the most banal words, stood unsuspecting on the brink of disaster. Then came the whip and drove them over the edge; all fell into the same abyss. Nothing could have saved them. For their statements never changed; their statements were appropriate to their persons, and the man who had framed them was one and the same, the writer with the whip.

Through *Wozzeck* I discovered something for which I found a name only later: self-denunciation. The characters (apart from the protagonist) who make the strongest impression introduce themselves. The doctor and the drum major strike blows. They attack, but in such different ways that one hesitates to use the same word "attack" in both cases. But an attack it is, for that is its effect on Wozzeck. Their words, which are not interchangeable, are directed against him and have the gravest consequences. But that is only because they portray the speaker, who with them delivers a hard blow, a blow that will never be forgotten, by which one would recognize him anywhere and at any time.

These characters, I say, present themselves. They have not been whipped into place. As though it were the most natural thing in the world, they denounce themselves, and in their self-denunciation there is more vainglory than condemnation. They are, in every case, present before a moral statement has been made about them. We think of them with horror, but our horror is mixed with approval, because in presenting themselves they are unaware of the horror they arouse. There is a kind of innocence in their self-denunciation; no juridical net has yet been prepared for them (though perhaps such a net will be thrown over them later on), but no indictment even by the most powerful satirist could be as powerful as this self-indictment, for it encompasses the whole man, his rhythm, his fear, his breath.

Another reason for the strength of these characters is no doubt that they are given the full value of the word "I," which a pure satirist grants to no one except himself. There is enormous vitality in this direct and by no means parenthetical "I." It has more to say about itself than has any judge. A judge speaks largely in the third person; even the direct address in which the judge says his worst is usurped. Only when the judge relapses into his "I" is he present in the full horror of his function, but then he himself has become a character who unsuspectingly presents himself, the giver of judgment, in *his* self-denunciation.

The captain, the doctor, the bellowing drum major step forward, as it were, of their own accord. No one has lent them their voice, they speak their selves and with these selves strike out at one and the same object, namely, Wozzeck; it is in striking him that they come into being. He serves them all, he is their center. Without him they would not exist, but of this they are no more aware than he is, one might even say that he infects his tormentors with his innocence. They cannot be other than they are, and it is in the essence of self-denunciation that they make this impression. The strength of these characters, of all characters, is their innocence. Should we hate the captain, should we hate the doctor because they could be different if only they wanted to be? Should we hope for their conversion? Should the play be a mission school, which such characters should attend until they can be written *differently?* A satirist *expects* people to change. He whips them as if they were schoolboys. He prepares them to appear before moral authorities at some future date. He even knows in what way they should be improved. Where does he get his unshakable certainty? Without it, he could not even begin to write. He starts by being as dauntless as God. Without actually saying so, he stands in for God and feels comfortable about it. The thought that he may not be God doesn't trouble him for a moment. For since such a supreme authority exists, one can always set oneself up as His deputy.

But there is a very different attitude, which sides with the creature and not with God, which defends the creature against Him and may even go so far as to disregard God altogether and concentrate on humankind. One who takes the attitude that human beings cannot be changed, though he would like to see them different. Human beings cannot be changed by hatred or punishment. They accuse themselves by representing themselves as they are, and this is self-indictment, it does not come from someone else. A writer's justice cannot consist in condemning them. He can invent their victim and show the marks they make on him as if they were fingerprints. The world is swarming with such victims, but it is very hard to take one as a character and make him speak in such a way that the marks remain recognizable instead of being blurred and made to look like accusations. Wozzeck is such a character, we see what is done to him while it is being done, and not a word of accusation is added. Through him, the marks of self-denunciation become recognizable. Those who have struck him are present, and when it's all over with him they are still alive. The fragment does not show the *manner* of his ending, it shows what he *does*, shows *his* self-denunciation after that of the others.

Eye and Breath

My relationship with Hermann Broch was foreshadowed, more than is usually the case, by the circumstances of our first meeting. It had been arranged that I should read my *Wedding* at the house of Maria Lazar, a Viennese writer with whom we were both, independently of each other, acquainted. A few guests had been invited. Among them were Ernst Fischer and his wife, Ruth, who the others were I don't remember. Broch had said he was coming, he was late and we waited some time for him. I was about to begin when he turned up with Brody, his publisher. There was time only for brief introductions; we had not yet spoken to each other when I started reading *The Wedding*.

Maria Lazar had told Broch how much I admired *The Sleepwalkers*, which I had read during the summer of 1932. He had seen nothing of mine, nor could he have, since nothing had been published. I had been enormously impressed by *The Sleepwalkers* and even more by *Huguenau;* I regarded him as a great writer, while in his eyes I was a young man who admired him. It must have been mid-October, I had completed *The Wedding* seven or eight months before. I had read the play to a few friends who expected great things of me—but never to more than one at a time.

Broch, on the other hand, and this is the crux of the matter, was exposed to the full force of *The Wedding* before knowing anything else of mine. I read the play with passion, the characters were clearly differentiated by their acoustic masks, and now, years later, I still hear them the same way. I read the play without stopping and it took more than two hours. The atmosphere was tense, there may have been a dozen people there in addition to Veza and myself, but I felt their presence so keenly that there seemed to be many more.

I had a good view of Broch, I was struck by the way he sat there. His bird's head seemed to sink slightly between his shoulders. During the "caretaker" scene, the last of the prologue, which now strikes me as the strongest in the whole play, I noticed his eyes. I think it was during the dying Mrs. Kokosch's sentence—"Listen, husband, there's something I have to . . ." which she has to start over and over again and is unable to finish—that I encountered Broch's eyes. If eyes could breathe, they would have held their breath. They waited for the sentence to be completed and this expectant pause was filled with Kokosch's quotation of Samson. It was a twofold reading; the spoken dialogue, which was hardly dialogue, because Kokosch wasn't listening to the dying woman's words, was accompanied by a secret exchange between Broch's eyes, which had taken the dying woman under their protection, and myself, as I began time and again to say her sentence, which kept being interrupted by the caretaker's lines from the Bible.

This was the situation in the first half hour of my reading. Then came the actual wedding, and it began with great indecency, which did not embarrass me at the time because I hated it so. I may not have fully realized at the time how true to life these repellent scenes are. One source for them was Karl Kraus, another was George Grosz, whose *Ecce Homo* I had admired and detested. But most of the material was supplied by my own observation.

In reading the sordid middle section of *The Wedding*, I never gave a thought to the people around me. I was possessed, I felt I was gliding through the air, carried by these horrible, sordid speeches which had nothing to do with me, which inflated me and forced me to fly with them, rather in the manner of a shaman, though I wouldn't have known it at the time.

But that night it was different. Throughout the middle part I felt Broch's presence. His silence was more penetrating than that of the others. He checked himself as though holding his breath, I'm not sure exactly what he did, but I felt it had something to do with breath and I believe I was aware at the time that he breathed differently from all the others. His silence withstood the terrible uproar my characters were making. There was something physical about it, it was produced by him, it was a silence that he *created*, and today I know it was connected with his way of breathing.

In the third part of the play, the catastrophe and dance of death, I lost all contact with my surroundings. My exertion had worn me down, I was so caught up in the rhythm that is crucial to this section that I couldn't have said what impression I was making on any of my listeners, and by the time I had finished I wasn't even aware of Broch's presence. Something had happened in the meantime; it was as though I were still waiting for his arrival. But then he spoke, he said that if he had known my play, he wouldn't have written his. (He was evidently working on a play at the time, most likely the one that was later produced in Zurich.)

Then he said something that I do not want to repeat here, though it showed a remarkable insight into the genesis of my play. Without knowing him, I was sure he was really moved. All through the reading, Brody, his publisher, had an amiable grin on his face; I didn't like it at all. *He* had not been moved; it seems possible that my attack on bourgeois morality had ruffled him, and that he grinned to hide his displeasure. Or possibly that was his nature, perhaps nothing moved him. What he and Broch had in common—for undoubtedly they were friends—is more than I can say.

The two of them didn't stay long, they were expected somewhere else. Though Broch had turned up with his publisher—which suggested a kind of self-assurance—he struck me, by the end of my reading, as vulnerable—in an attractive sort of way, meaning that he was easily affected by events, by the ups and downs in human relationships. This may have struck most people as weakness, and I have no objection to calling it weakness because to me weakness at that level of intelligence is a distinction, a virtue. But when members of the business world in which he moved or of any similar social group speak today of his "weakness," I want to slap their faces.

It is not without misgiving that I speak of Broch, for I'm not sure of being able to do him justice. I expected so much; from the start I courted him, though he did his best to stop me; blindly I admired everything about him, such as his beautiful eyes, in which I read everything imaginable, excepting any sign of calculation. There is hardly a noble trait that I did not find in him, and how naïvely, how heedlessly I succumbed to my fascination, making no secret of my immense ignorance. For though I was really open and eager to learn, my thirst for knowledge had as yet borne no fruit. As I see it today, I had thus far learned very little and in any case nothing in what was his chosen branch of knowledge: contemporary philosophy. His library was largely philosophical; unlike me, he did not shy away from the world of abstract ideas; he was addicted to ideas as other men are to nightclubs.

He was the first "weakling" I had met; victory or conquest was of no interest to him, and he was certainly not boastful. He was not a man to proclaim lofty purposes, whereas every second sentence of mine was: "I mean to write a book about that." I couldn't express a thought or perhaps even a mere observation without adding: "I mean to write a book about that." But this was no vain boast, for I had written a long book, *Kant Catches Fire;* it existed in manuscript, few people knew of it, and I was projecting another, which I regarded as my lifework, a work about "crowds." Thus far my preparations for it amounted to little more than personal experiences (but they went very deep) and wide, voracious reading, which, I believed, had a bearing on "crowds"—but was actually related in no lesser degree to *everything* else. My whole life was geared to a great work, I took the idea so seriously that I was capable of saying unsmilingly: "But it will take decades." He could not help recognizing my tendency to include *everything* in my plans and ambitions as an authentic passion. What repelled him was my zealotic, dogmatic way of making the improvement of mankind dependent on chastisement and without hesitation appointing myself executor of this chastisement. I had learned that from Karl Kraus, I didn't imitate him *deliberately,* I wouldn't have dared, but a good part of his being had gone into mine, especially, in the winter of 1931–32 while I was working on *The Wedding,* his rage.

In reading my play I presented myself to Broch with this rage, which through the play had become my own. It overpowered him, but it was the only emotion of mine that had that effect on him. Apart from that, the only influence I had on him was of an entirely different nature, which I did not understand until much later—to be exact, after his death. When Broch could not resist someone else's impulses or intentions in any other way, he simply took them over.

Broch always gave way; he assimilated by giving way. It was a complicated process, it was his nature, and I believe I was right in relating it to his manner of breathing. But among the numerous items he assimilated, there were some that were too powerful to rest in peace. Sooner or later, troublesome ideas, which upset him and met with his moral disapproval, became his own initiatives. I am certain that years later, when as a refugee in America he went in for the psychology of crowds, he had not forgotten our conversations on the subject. But the content, the substance of what I had said, had made no impression on him. My *ignorance*, my innocence of the prevailing philosophical terminologies, led Broch to overlook completely the content of what I had said, though it was not without originality. What impressed him was the *force* of my intention, of my call for a new science which would be developed *someday* but which thus far only existed in pathetic beginnings—this intention he construed as a command and let it work in him as though it had been addressed to him. When in his presence I spoke of what I intended to do, what he heard was: "Do it!"—though he was not immediately aware of the pressure these words put on him. He was left with the germ of a project, which burgeoned later on, in new surroundings, but bore no fruit.

I have got ahead of myself, so blurring the history of our relationship. But now, after all these years, I feel that I must try to gain a true picture of what happened between us from the start, though neither of us was aware of it, he no more than I.

In the course of his hurried comings and goings Broch often dropped in on us on Ferdinandstrasse. I saw him as a big, beautiful bird with clipped wings. He seemed to remember a time when he could still fly, and he had never got over what had happened to him. I would have liked to question him about it, but didn't dare at the time. His faltering manner was deceptive, perhaps he would not have been unwilling to talk about himself. But he reflected before speaking. From him I could not expect fluent confessions such as I heard from most of the people I knew in Vienna. He wouldn't have spared himself, he was inclined to self-criticism, there was not a trace of complacency in him, he seemed unsure of himself, but this lack of assurance, it seemed to me, was *acquired*. My *positive* manner of speaking irritated him, but he was too kind to show it. I noticed it, though, and when he had left me, I felt ashamed. I blamed myself for what I thought was his dislike of me. He would have liked to teach me self-doubt, perhaps he was making cautious attempts at just that, but if so he did not succeed. I thought highly of him, I was very much taken with *The Sleepwalkers*, because in it he did what I was incapable of doing. The atmospheric element in literature had never interested me, I thought it belonged to the province of painting. But Broch's way of handling it made me receptive to it. I admired it, because I admired everything that was denied me. It didn't shake my confidence in my own intentions, but I was amazed to see that there was an entirely different sort of writing, which had its own justification and which, as I read it, liberated me from myself. Such transformations in reading are indispensable for a writer. It is after being strongly drawn to others that he really finds his way back to himself.

Whenever Broch published anything, he brought it straight to Ferdinandstrasse. He attached special importance to his writings in the *Frankfurter Zeitung* and the *Neue Rundschau*. It would never have occurred to me that he attached any importance to my opinion. It was not until some years later, when his letters were published, that I realized how much approval meant to him. Though irritated by my *assertive* manner of speaking, he welcomed my categorical judgments when they favored him and even quoted them in letters to others.

At that time I had an almost mythical interpretaion of Broch's hurried movements. This big bird had never resigned himself to the clipping of his wings. No longer able to fly up into the freedom of the empyrean, the *one* atmosphere transcending all humankind, he sought out the particular atmospheres surrounding individuals. Other writers collected people, he collected the atmospheres around them, which contained the air that had been in their lungs, the air they had exhaled. From this collected air he deduced their particularity; he characterized people on the basis of the atmospheres they gave off. This struck me as utterly new, it was something I had never before encountered. I knew about writers in whom the visual and others in whom the acoustic element was dominant. I had never dreamed of a writer who might be characterized by his way of breathing.

He was extremely reserved and, as I said before, seemed unsure of himself. Whatever his eyes fell on, he assimilated—but rhythmically this assimilation was not a devouring but a breathing. He didn't jostle anything, everything remained as it was, immutable, preserving its particular aura. He seemed to assimilate all manner of things in order to preserve them. He distrusted violent speeches, and whatever good intentions may have inspired them, he suspected evil behind them. To his mind, *nothing* was beyond good and evil, and one thing I liked about him from the start was that in speaking he took a responsible attitude from first to last and was not ashamed of it. This sense of responsibility was evident also in his reluctance to pass judgment, in what I began at an early date to call his "faltering."

I accounted for his "faltering"—his long pauses before

speaking, though one could see that he was thinking the matter over carefully—by his unwillingness to impose on anyone. It embarrassed him to think of his advantage. I knew that he came from a family of industrialists; his father had owned a spinning mill in Teesdorf. Broch had wanted to become a mathematician and had gone to work in the factory against his will. When his father died, he had to take it over, not for his own sake but because he had to look out for his mother and other members of his family. A kind of defiance had led him to take up the study of philosophy and persist in it; when I first met him, he was attending the philosophical seminar at the University of Vienna, which he evidently took very seriously. His commercial background inspired the same deep distaste in him as mine did in me and he fought against it in every available way. For him, it was a hard fight, because of the years spent running his father's factory. He was strongly drawn to the exact sciences and did not mind seeing them presented in academic form. I thought of this man of richly active mind as a student. If he was wise enough to be uncertain, how could he find certainty in seminars? What he wanted was dialogue, but he conducted himself as though he were always the learner. I felt sure that this could seldom be the case, for it was obvious that he usually knew more than the persons he conversed with. It was his kindness, I therefore decided, which deterred him from *shaming* anyone.

I made the acquaintance of Broch's mistress Ea von Allesch at the Café Museum. I had met Broch somewhere else. He told me he had an appointment with Ea and had promised to bring me along. He seemed somehow constrained, he didn't talk in his usual way and he was *very* late. "She has been waiting a long time for us," he said. He walked faster and faster, and in the end he seemed to fly through the revolving door, pulling me into the café after him. "We're late," he said meekly, before introducing me. Then he said my name. The apprehension had gone out of his voice when he added: "And this is Ea Allesch."

He had mentioned her to me a few times. Both parts of her name, the "Allesch" and especially the "Ea," had struck me as unusual and even mysterious. I hadn't asked him where this name "Ea" came from and never made any attempt to find out. She was no longer young, she must have been in her fifties. She had the head of a lynx, but a velvet one, and reddish hair. She was beautiful, and it appalled me to think how beautiful she must have been. She spoke softly and gently, but so penetratingly that I couldn't help feeling somewhat afraid of her. She seemed, without meaning to, to dig her claws into one. But I had this impression only because she was always contradicting Broch. She found fault with everything he said. She asked what had kept us so long, she had thought we would never come, she had been sitting there for an hour. Broch told her where we had been. But though he included me, as though citing me as a witness, she listened with an air of not believing a word he said. She made no direct statement but she wasn't convinced, and after we had been sitting there for some time she reverted to the subject in a sentence shot through with her doubt, as though this doubt had already entered into history and she merely wanted to show us that she was filing it away with all her other doubts.

A literary conversation started up. Wishing to divert her from our offense, Broch recalled how he had gone to see her on Peregringasse just after my reading of *The Wedding* and had spoken to her about it. He seemed to be asking her to take me seriously. She did not deny what had happened on that occasion but immediately turned it against him. According to her, he had felt crushed; he had wailed that he wasn't a playwright; oh, why had he

ever written a play? he had had a good mind to get it
back from the Zurich theater that had it. Broch, she went
on, had lately taken it into his head that he had to become
a writer. Who could have talked him into that? A woman
most likely. Her words sounded gentle, almost ingratiating, but since there was no one present she had any desire
to ingratiate herself with, they were devastating. For she
went on to say that she was a graphologist and that she
had told him after looking at his handwriting that he was
not a writer; one had only to compare his handwriting
with Musil's to know that Broch was no writer.

I found this so embarrassing that I jumped at the
diversion offered by Musil and asked her if she knew him.
Yes, she had known him for years, from her Allesch
period and even before, yes, she had known him even
longer than she had known Broch. *He* was a writer, her
tone changed completely when she said that, and when
she went so far as to add that Musil didn't think so much
of Freud and was not easily bamboozled, I understood
that her animosity was directed against everything connected with Broch while Musil stood untarnished in her
eyes. She had seen a good deal of him in the days of her
marriage with Allesch, who was Musil's best friend, and
now, years after the breakup of that marriage, she still
saw him occasionally. Her being a graphologist meant
something to her, and she also had her views on psychology. "I'm an Adlerian," she said, pointing to herself,
and, pointing at Broch, "he's a Freudian." And indeed,
he believed almost religiously in Freud. I don't mean that
he had become a zealot like so many people I knew at
the time, but that he was permeated by Freud as by a
mystical doctrine.

It was typical of Broch that he didn't conceal his
difficulties. He didn't put up a front. I don't know why
he introduced me to Ea so soon. He had always known
that she wasn't nice to him when others were present.

Possibly he wanted to counter her harsh rejection of his writing with my admiration; if so, I was unaware of it at the time. I discovered only little by little that Broch had been regarded as a patron of the arts, an industrialist to whom the life of the spirit meant more than his factory and who was always glad to help artists. His generosity was still there, but it was easy to see that he was no longer a rich man. He didn't complain of poverty but of lack of time. All who knew him would have liked to see him more often.

He induced me to speak of myself, to talk myself into a lather and go on and on. I mistook this for a special interest in my person, my plans and purposes, my great designs. I failed to realize that this interest went out to *every* person, though I might have gathered as much from *The Sleepwalkers*. Actually it was his way of listening that captivated people. One expanded in his silence, one encountered no obstacles. There was nothing one could not have said, he rejected nothing. One felt ill at ease only as long as one had not expressed oneself fully. While in other such conversations there comes a point where one suddenly says to oneself: "Stop. This far and no further," where one senses the danger of relinquishing too much—for how does one find the way back to oneself, and how after that can one bear to be alone?—with Broch there was never such a point or such a moment, one never came up against warning signs, one staggered on, faster and faster, as though drunk. It is devastating to discover how much one has to say about oneself; the further one ventures, the more one loses oneself, the faster the words flow; the hot springs rise from underground, one becomes a field of geysers.

This sort of eruption was not unknown to me. Others had spoken to me in this way. The difference was that I usually *reacted* to others. I was driven to reply, I could not keep silent, and in speaking I took a position, judged, advised, showed approval or disapproval. In the same situation, Broch, quite to the contrary, *kept still*. His was not the cold or imperious silence known to us from psychoanalysis, where one individual surrenders irretrievably to another, who *must not* harbor any feeling for or against him. Broch's listening was punctuated by short, hardly perceptible breaths, which showed not only that one had been listened to but that what one had said had also been *welcomed,* as though with every sentence uttered one had stepped into a house and made oneself elaborately at home. The little breathing sounds were the host's words of welcome: "Whoever you are and whatever you may have to say, come in, be my guest, stay as long as you like, come again, stay forever!" The little breathing sounds were a minimum reaction. Fully formed words and sentences would have implied a judgment, would have amounted to taking a position before the visitor had settled in with all the baggage a man carries around with him. The host's eyes were always directed at the visitor and at the same time at the interior of the rooms into which he was inviting him. Though his head resembled that of a great bird, his eyes were never intent on prey. They looked into the distance, which usually took in the other's vicinity, and the host's innermost thought was at once far and near.

It was this mysterious welcome that drew people to Broch. I could think of no one who did not long for it. This welcome carried no signature or evaluation; where women were involved, it resulted in love.

The Beginning of a Conflict

In the course of the five and a half years during which Broch was present in my life, I grew aware only gradually of something which today, since it is a dire threat to all life, has come to be regarded as self-evident, namely, the *nakedness* of *breath*. The main sense through which Broch apprehended the world around him was his breath. While others must unceasingly see and hear, and rest from the exercise of these senses only at night when they withdraw into sleep, Broch was always at the mercy of his breath which he could not turn off and merely attempted to structure by means of the barely perceptible sounds that I called his breath-punctuation. I soon realized that he was incapable of getting rid of anyone. I never heard him say No, though he could in a pinch write a No, if the person to whom it was addressed was not sitting and breathing face to face with him.

If a stranger had come up to him on the street and taken him by the elbow, I'm sure he would have followed that stranger without resistance. I never saw this happen, but I could picture such an incident, and I asked myself where he would have followed the stranger. The answer: to a place determined by the stranger's breath. In him what is commonly called curiosity took a special form, which might be called breath-lust. By observing him, I came to realize that the differentiation of atmospheres is something we do not think about, that one can live for years without becoming aware of it. Anyone who breathed, that is, anyone at all, could captivate Broch. The *defense-lessness* of a man of his age, who had lived as long as he had, who had wrestled with heaven knows what problems, was something stupendous. Every meeting was for him a peril because once he met somebody he couldn't get away from that person. To get away, he had to have someone waiting for him somewhere else.

He established bases all over town; they could be far apart. When he arrived somewhere, at Veza's on Ferdinandstrasse, for instance, he went straight to the phone and called Ea Allesch. "I'm at the Canettis'," he would say. "I won't be long." He knew he was expected and gave a plausible reason for his lateness. But this was only the surface reason for his phone call, motivated by Ea's hostile attitude. Ea wasn't the only person he phoned—if he had just come from Ea's and she knew quite well where he was going, then he would ask Veza, who had just welcomed him: "May I make a phone call?" And proceed to tell someone else where he was. The person he called was always the person who was expecting him, and this seemed reasonable since he had to apologize for his invariable lateness. In reality, I believe these phone calls served an entirely different purpose. He was securing his trajectory from base to base, laying the groundwork for having to leave soon. No assault, no capture would stop him.

When one chanced to meet him on the street, his only defense was his manifest hurry. The first thing he said— and it sounded quite friendly, though it took the place of a greeting—would be "I'm in a hurry"; he would move his arms, his clipped wings, as though trying to take flight, flap them a few times, and then let them sink in discouragement. I felt sorry for him at such times and thought: Poor fellow, what a pity he can't fly! Always having to run like that! It was a flight in two senses: on the one hand, he had to tear himself away from whomever he was with, for he was expected somewhere and en route, and on the other hand, he had to escape from all those he might run into and who might try to hold him fast. I sometimes looked after him as he disappeared down the street: His cape flapped in the breeze like wings. He wasn't really moving very fast, he only seemed to be; the bird's head and the cape made an impression of hampered flight, but it never looked ugly or undignified; it had become second nature, a natural mode of locomotion.

I have begun by speaking about what was *incomparable* in Broch, of what distinguished him from all other people I have known, but that is not the whole story. For quite aside from the mysterious respiratory phenomena that conditioned his appearance and physical reactions, I had conversations with him that gave me food for thought and that I would have liked to prolong. I came to him with an unspent eagerness to admire. A storm of opinions, convictions, and projects beat down on him, but whatever I said, whatever I did to win his favor, nothing could efface the powerful impression I made on him with my two hours' reading of *The Wedding*. This impression was at the bottom of everything he said to me for the next few years, but he was too kind a man to let me notice it. He never said anything to suggest that I made him feel uneasy.

In *The Wedding* the house caved in and all perished. Of course, he recognized the despair that had led me to write it. In those years, many including Broch himself had experienced this same despair. But it disturbed him to see it expressed in this merciless form, as though I myself were a part of what was threatening us all. I don't believe that he came to any conclusion about it. Karl Kraus, whom because Broch was nineteen years my senior he had read long before me, and who was much more violent than I was, had meant a good deal to him. Kraus seldom figured in our conversations, but he never mentioned the name without respect. I'm sure I never saw Broch at any of Karl Kraus's lectures, for I wouldn't have forgotten a head like his. Possibly he stayed away from the lectures after he himself began to write; or perhaps he had come to find them stifling. In that case he was bound to be appalled by a work like *The Wedding*, motivated by similar apocalyptic terrors. But these are conjectures, I shall never know for sure what was behind Broch's secret antagonism; it may have been nothing more than my assiduous courtship of him, which he tried to evade as he did all courtship.

My first conversations with him, at the Café Museum, took place at lunchtime, but neither of us ate. They were animated conversations in which he held up his end. (It was only later that I was struck by his silences.) But our talks did not last long, perhaps an hour. Regularly, just when our exchange had become so interesting that I'd have given anything to go on, he would suddenly stand up and say: "I must go to Dr. Schaxl's now." Dr. Schaxl was his analyst, and since he always arranged to meet me just before his appointments with her, I had the impression that he went to his analysis every day. I felt as if he had hit me on the head; the more freely and openly I had spoken—every word of his had added to my élan— the wiser and more penetrating were his answers, the more deeply his announcement wounded me; moreover, I took the ridiculous name of Schaxl as an insult.

Here are two people conversing; and now one of them, Broch, for whose words I'm thirsting, the man who wrote *The Sleepwalkers*, stands up, cuts himself off in midsentence with a view to confiding, as he did every day (or so I thought), in a woman whose name is Schaxl and who is an analyst. I was filled with consternation. I felt ashamed for him; I hardly dared picture him lying down on a couch to tell her things that no one else would ever hear and that perhaps he would never even write. One would have to know the earnestness, the dignity, the beauty with which he sat listening, to understand why it struck me as so demeaning that he should lie down and speak to someone whose face he could not see.

Yet today it seems quite possible that Broch was running away from my verbal avalanche, that he could not have borne a longer conversation with me and that was why he arranged to meet me just before his analysis.

Be that as it may, he was so addicted to Freud that he did not hesitate to employ Freudian terms in their commonly accepted meanings in serious conversation, as though their validity were beyond question. This was bound to distress me in one who had read so much philosophy, for it implied that he regarded Freud as the equal of Plato, Spinoza and Kant, whom he so greatly revered. He said things which had become platitudes in the Vienna of those days in the same breath as insights hallowed by centuries-long admiration, including his own.

A few weeks after our first meeting Broch asked me if I would care to give a reading at the Popular University in Leopoldstadt. He himself, he said, had read there a few times and would be glad to introduce me. Feeling very much honored, I accepted. My reading was scheduled for January 23, 1933. Before the turn of the year, I brought Broch the manuscript of *Kant Catches Fire*. A few weeks later, he asked me to go and see him on Gonzagagasse, where he lived.

"What do you mean by this?"

Those were his first words. With a vague gesture he indicated the manuscript that was lying beside him on his desk. I was so taken aback that I could think of nothing to say. That was the last question I would have expected of him. How could the meaning of a novel be summed up in a few sentences? Feeling that I had to make some answer, I stammered something more or less unintelligible. He apologized and withdrew his question.

"If you knew, you wouldn't have written the novel. That was a bad question."

Seeing I was unable to formulate my ideas, he tried to narrow the field by excluding everything that could not be regarded as the purpose of my book.

"You weren't just trying to write the story of a fool?

That can't have been your real purpose. And you weren't simply trying to portray an eccentric figure in the manner of E. T. A. Hoffmann or Edgar Allan Poe?"

I replied in the negative and he did not question my answers. I brought up Gogol. Since Broch had been struck by the grotesqueness of my characters, I thought I would cite a model on whom I had actually drawn.

"I was influenced more by Gogol, I wanted the most extreme characters, at once ludicrous and horrible, I wanted the ludicrous and the horrible to be indistinguishable."

"You're terrifying. Do you want to terrify people?"

"Yes. Everything around us is terrifying. There is no longer a common language. No one understands anyone else. I believe no one *wants* to understand. What impressed me so much in your *Huguenau* was that the characters are so confined within their different value systems that no understanding between them is possible. Huguenau is very much like my characters. This is not apparent in his manner of speaking. He still converses with other people. But there is a document at the end of the book, Huguenau's letter stating his demand on the widow Esch. This is written in his very own language: the language of the pure businessman. You drew a radical distinction between this man and everyone else in the book. That is exactly what I have in mind. That is what I tried to do throughout, with every character and in every passage of my book."

"But then they cease to be real people. They become abstractions. Real people are made up of many components. They have contradictory, conflicting impulses. If you don't take account of that, how can you give a faithful picture of the world? Have you a right to distort people to such a degree that they cease to be recognizable as human beings?"

"They are characters. People and characters are not the same thing. The novel as a literary genre began with characters. The first novel was *Don Quixote*. What do you think of the protagonist? Does he strike you as too extreme to be credible?"

"Those were different times. In a day when chivalric romances were all the rage, he was a credible character. Today we know more about man. Today we have modern psychology, which gives us insights that we simply can't ignore. Literature must operate on the intellectual level of its day. If it lags behind the times, it becomes a kind of kitsch, subservient to purposes unrelated to literature."

"You seem to imply that *Don Quixote* means nothing to us today. To my mind it is not only the first novel, it is and remains the greatest of novels. To my mind it lacks nothing; no modern insight is absent from it. I'd even go so far as to say that it *avoids* certain errors of modern psychology. The author does not undertake to investigate man, he does not try to show all the possible components of an individual, he creates characters, whom he delineates sharply and opposes to one another. Their interaction is the source of what he has to say about man."

"But much of what concerns and torments us today could not be expressed."

"Of course not; things that didn't exist at that time could not be expressed. But today new characters can be devised; and a writer who knows how to operate with them can express our present preoccupations."

"But in art as in other fields there must be new methods. In the age of Freud and Joyce everything can't remain as it was."

"I too believe that the novel must be *different*, but not because we are living in the age of Freud and Joyce. The *substance* of our times is different, and that can be shown only through characters. The more they differ from one another, the more extreme their characters, the greater will be the tensions between them. The nature of these tensions is all-important. They frighten us, and we recognize this fear as our own. They help us *rehearse* our fear. In psychological investigation we also encounter fear and take note of it. Then new methods, or methods which at least seem new to us, are devised to liberate us from it."

"That is not possible. What can liberate us from fear? Maybe it can be diminished, but no more. What you have done in your novel and in *The Wedding* as well is to *heighten* fear. You rub people's noses in their wickedness, as though to punish them for it. I know your underlying purpose is to make them repent. You make me think of a Lenten sermon. But you don't threaten people with hell, you paint a picture of hell in this life. You don't picture it objectively, so as to give people a clearer consciousness of it; you picture it in such a way as to make people feel they are in it and scare them out of their wits. Is it the writer's function to bring more fear into the world? Is that a worthy intention?"

"You have a different method of writing novels. In *Huguenau* you have used it consistently. You contrast different value systems, good ones and bad ones. The religious world of the Salvation Army lass is confronted with Huguenau's business world. Thus you bring in a compromise and partly alleviate the fear you have created with your portrayal of Huguenau. I read your trilogy without stopping, it filled me, it created new areas within me; they have endured and now, six months later, they are still there. I can say beyond the shadow of a doubt that you have broadened and enriched me with it. But you have also *comforted* me. Insight gives comfort. But is that the only function of insight?"

"You believe in alarming people to the point of panic. In *The Wedding* you've undoubtedly succeeded. After it came only destruction and disaster. Do you want this disaster? I suspect that you want the exact opposite. You would gladly help to show a way out. But you do nothing of the kind; in both *The Wedding* and the novel, you end cruelly, mercilessly, with destruction. In that there is an uncompromising quality that I have to respect. But does this mean that you've given up hope? Does it mean that you yourself have not found a way out or that you doubt the existence of a way out?"

"If I did, if I had really given up hope, I couldn't bear to go on living. No, I just think we *know* too little. I have the impression that you like to talk about modern psychology because it originated in your own back yard, so to speak, in a particular segment of Vienna society. It appeals to a certain local patriotism in you. Maybe you feel that you yourself might have invented it. Whatever it says, you find in yourself. You don't have to look for it. This modern psychology strikes me as totally inadequate. It deals with the individual, and in that sphere it has undoubtedly made certain discoveries. But where the masses are concerned, it can't do a thing, and that's where knowledge would be most important, for all the new powers that are coming into existence *today* draw their strength from crowds, from the masses. Nearly all those who are out for political power know how to operate with the masses. But the men who see that such operations are leading straight to another world war don't know how to influence the masses, how to stop them from being misled to the ruin of us all. The laws of mass behavior can be discovered. That is the most important task confronting us today, and so far nothing has been done toward the development of such a science."

"Nothing can be done. In this field everything is vague and uncertain. You are on the wrong road. You can't discover the laws of mass behavior, because there aren't any. You'd be wasting your time. You've told me several times that you regard this as your true lifework, that you are resolved to spend years on it, your whole life if need be. You'd be wasting your life. Better stick to your plays.

You're a writer. You can't devote yourself to a science that isn't science and never will be."

We had this conversation about the study of mass behavior more than once. Broch, as I've said, always treated his interlocutor gently, as though he might damage him in some way if he expressed himself too forcefully. What interested him most was always the other's individuality and the premises on which it functioned. Consequently our arguments were seldom violent; he couldn't bear to humiliate anyone, and for that reason he took care not to be too much in the right.

All the more conspicuous were the occasions when we did clash violently. He was irrevocably opposed to the name I had given the central character in my novel, who in the manuscript I gave him to read was still called Kant. The title *Kant Catches Fire* also infuriated him; as though I had wished to imply that the philosopher Kant was a cold, unfeeling creature, who in my cruel book was forced to catch fire. He never said this in so many words, but he did say that the use of this name, which he so highly revered, struck him as unseemly. And indeed his first word of criticism was "You'll have to change the name." In this he remained uncompromising and almost every time we met he asked: "Have you changed the name?"

He wasn't satisfied when I said that name and title had always been provisional, that I had decided, even before meeting him, to change both in the event of publication. "Then why not now?" he insisted. "Do it in the manuscript." That provoked my resistance. It wasn't like Broch to give orders, but this sounded like an order. I wanted to keep my original title, provisional or not, as long as possible. I left the manuscript just as it was and waited for the time to come when I would make the change because I wanted to and not under pressure.

The second point Broch insisted on was the impossibility

of developing a psychology of the masses. Here his opinion made no impression on me. Much as I admired him as a writer and a man, much as I (vainly) courted his affection, I wouldn't have dreamed of giving in on this point. On the contrary, I tried to convince him that new discoveries could be made, that there were relationships in this field that, strange to say, had never been considered. He usually smiled at my observation and seemed to take little interest, but he listened. He only grew indignant when I criticized certain Freudian conceptions. Once I tried to make it clear that a distinction must be made between panic and mass flight. It was true, I said, that a crowd disintegrates when it panics. But, as is shown by fleeing herds of animals, a crowd can take flight without disintegrating; it can, moreover, develop a collective feeling in the course of flight. "How do you know?" he asked. "Were you ever a gazelle in a fleeing herd?"

There was one thing, I soon discovered, that always impressed him: the word "symbol." When I spoke of "crowd symbols," he pricked up his ears and made me explain exactly what I meant. I had been thinking at the time about the connection between fire and crowds and since, like everyone else in Vienna, he remembered July 15, 1927, he pondered my words and brought them up from time to time. But what really appealed to him was what I had said about the sea and the drops of water in it. I said that I felt a kind of pity for the drops of water on my hand, because they had been separated from the great body to which they belonged. Intrigued by what he saw as an approach to religious feelings, and in particular by my "pity" for the poor isolated drops of water, he began to find something religious in my "psychology of the masses" project and to speak of it in this light. This attitude I resisted, for I regarded it as a reduction of my idea, but little by little I stopped discussing the matter with him.

The Conductor

He compressed his lips to make sure no praise would escape them. He attached the greatest importance to accurate memorizing. At an early age, in straitened circumstances, he attacked difficult texts and mastered them bit by bit in his few free moments. At the age of fifteen he made his living playing the fiddle in a café. Pale and drawn from lack of sleep, he kept a volume of Spinoza hidden under his music and in brief pauses learned the *Ethics* by heart, sentence by sentence. His study was unrelated to his work and was simply an independent step in his education. There were many such oddities in his development, and there was no real connection between his inner and outward lives apart from the exertion that both cost him. The essential was his indestructible will; it needed new obstacles to contend with and found them throughout his life. Even in his old age his will was dominant; it was an inexhaustible appetite, but because of his constant preoccupation with music, it became a rhythmic appetite.

The love of study, with the help of which he improved himself as a young man, stayed with him all his life, side by side with his professional activity. In the face of great difficulties, he became a conductor at an early age, but that was not enough for him. He never found total fulfillment in conducting, and that may be why he never became a really great conductor. He kept looking for what was *different*, because it offered him something more to learn. The many different schools that had come into being in this period of musical renewal were for him a godsend. Every school, provided it was new, set him new tasks and tackling new tasks was what he was best at and wanted most. But no task, however challenging, could claim all his attention. He took on many, he dug his teeth into them, none could be too difficult. What interested him above all was to study and master a new composition and—most important—to put it over, in other words, to present it as perfectly as possible to a public that had no related experience, to whom such music was unfamiliar, repellent and ugly. With him it was a question of power. First he had to coerce the musicians, compel them to play this music as he wanted it played. Once he had the musicians in hand, the resistance of the public—the greater, the better—remained to be broken down.

What distinguished him from other conductors and gave him his special sort of freedom was that his power was always exerted for the sake of something new. He did not confine himself to any one friend, but took up any that offered him a difficult task. Then he would be first to introduce a totally unfamiliar brand of music to the public, its discoverer, so to speak. He was intent on accumulating discoveries, he wanted to see more and more of them, and since his appetite grew with their number and variety, he could not always content himself with music. He was drawn to extend the sphere of his power, to include the theater, for example. Thus he resolved to organize festivals devoted to new theater as well as new music. It was in such a moment of his career that I met him.

Hermann Scherchen was always in quest of *novelty*. When he arrived in a city where he was going to conduct for the first time, he made it his business to find out who was being spoken of. When a name seemed to be associated with the shocking and unexpected, he did his best to make contact with its bearer. He invited the man to a rehearsal and made sure that his new "discovery" would find him in such a welter of activity that there was barely time to shake hands. Conversations with his new "friend"— in whom, as he had let him know, he was "interested"— would have to wait until next time, though it was not certain that he would have more time then. Nevertheless, the new "friend" felt honored, because the go-between had told him how extremely eager the conductor had been to meet him. The first reception had been cold, but that may have been due to lack of time, anyone could see how exacting a task the conductor had set himself, especially in a city like Vienna, well known for its resolutely conservative taste in music. One couldn't possibly take it amiss that a pioneer should concentrate on his work; one could only be grateful to him for suggesting a second meeting at a more favorable time. Amid all the fuss and bustle, the new recruit could see that the conductor expected something of him, and since he was interested only in new things, it was clear that he expected something new. Thus, even before one had a chance to open one's mouth one felt included among those entitled to regard themselves as new men. Several more occasions might go by without a conversation developing; and the more often it was postponed, the more importance one attached to it.

But when a woman who interested Scherchen was among the intermediaries, the process was not so long-drawn-out. Then he and his retinue would come straight to the Café Museum after a rehearsal and listen to the candidate in silence. He would force the candidate to talk about what was dearest to his heart, usually a composition, in my case a play, always taking care not to say a single word about it himself. What one first noticed on such an occasion was his thin, compressed lips. He seemed so unresponsive one could doubt that he was listening; his face was smooth and self-possessed; not the slightest sign of approval or disapproval. He carried his head erect on a rather thick neck and rigid shoulders. The more effectively he kept silent, the more his interlocutor talked; before he knew it, he was forced into the role of a petitioner pleading with a potentate, who reserved his decision as long as possible, perhaps forever.

Yet Hermann was not really a silent man. When you got to know him better, you were amazed at how volubly he could talk. Mostly in self-praise. Hymns of triumph, one might say, if it didn't sound so dull and colorless. Then there were times when he would suddenly blurt out anything that entered his head, stating the most fanciful ideas with an air of absolute authority. For instance: "The year 1100 B.C. witnessed an explosion in the history of mankind." He meant an explosion of artistic inspiration, he had a weakness for the word "explosion." We had been to a museum together; as was his wont, he had made his way rather quickly past objects of widely divergent origin, Cretan, Hittite, Syrian, Babylonian. In reading the notices he had been struck by the recurrence of the date 1100 B.C., and with his usual self-assurance he was quick to conclude: "The year 1100 B.C. witnessed an explosion in the history of mankind."

He was silent, however, relentlessly silent, in the company of anyone whom he thought of discovering or helping. He would sooner have bitten his tongue off than let any word of praise escape him. At such times his determination to waste no words and bestow no praise gave him a very special facial expression.

It was H. who sent me to Anna Mahler with a letter. He left no stone unturned. He had known her in her early days, when she was married to Ernst Krenek. At that time he hadn't progressed far enough in his career to expect much attention from her. Besides, he thought she was wasting herself by submitting to Krenek, whom she helped in his work. Krenek composed quickly, he was always composing, and she sat huddled beside him copying

what he composed. That was her purely musical period.
She had learned to play seven or eight instruments and
she still practiced them by turns. She was impressed by
productivity—to her mind prolific, incessant, uninter-
rupted composition was a proof of genius. This cult of
superabundant inspiration stayed with her all her life. All
her admiration was reserved for those she regarded as
creative artists. When she turned from music to literature,
it was long novels that aroused her enthusiasm; no sooner
had she finished one than she began another. In her
Krenek years her fertility cult was confined to music, and
she seemed content to serve the young creative genius.

Krenek was one of the first in H.'s gallery of discoveries.
He must have noticed Anna then, but in her role as
Krenek's handmaiden she was of no interest to him. Later
he turned up in Vienna with high-flown plans, and as
usual he renewed his old connections. He was invited to
the mansion on Maxingstrasse, which belonged to the
publisher Paul Zsolnay, and there he found the golden-
haired Anna, now the lady of an opulent household. She
had blossomed out as a sculptress in her own right. He
may also have visited her in her studio, but that is unlikely.
He undoubtedly saw her at a reception at the Zsolnays'.
Her mother, whose power in the musical life of Vienna
he was well aware of, had a poor opinion of him, but that
didn't deter him from cultivating the daughter. He put
out feelers, wrote Anna a letter of courtship, and asked
me to bring it to her in her studio.

He was well disposed to me in his way. He had been
impressed by a reading of *The Wedding* at the home of
Bella Band, an ideal setting, upper rather than lower
middle class, but otherwise the same sort of people as in
the play. Not that he said a single word; after two hours
of drunken wedding celebration and the final catastrophe,
he was as silent as the tomb. As usual, his features
remained cold and inexpressive, his lips tightly sealed.

Still, I saw a change in him. It seemed to me that he had almost imperceptibly shrunk. When the reading was over, he did not utter a single domineering word. He took no refreshment and soon left the house.

It was his way to leave abruptly. He stood up and went, saying no more than was indispensable under the circumstances. He extended his hand, but not very far, even in that he did not choose to be accommodating. He not only kept his hand close to his body, he also held it high; you had to raise yours to get at it. In giving you his hand he was bestowing a favor, and with it went a brief command, an order to call on him at such and such a time. Since there were always people around him, you felt this to be a distinction and at the same time a humiliation. In these leave-takings, all trace of a smile vanished from his face. He seemed lifeless and grave; an act of state was being performed by a jerkily but powerfully moving statue. Then he would abruptly turn around and a moment after his final command, his order to call on him at such and such a time, you were looking at his broad back, which set itself resolutely but not too quickly in motion. Though as a conductor he was used to expressing himself with his back, the movements of his back lacked variety. It was no more expressive than his face; determination, arrogance, judgment, coldness were all he wished to reveal of himself.

Silence was his surest instrument of domination. He soon realized that where music was concerned I had little to offer. A teacher-pupil relationship such as he excelled in was out of the question, I played no instrument, I was not a member of any orchestra, and I was not a composer. So he would have to subjugate me in some other way. He thought of including theater in some of the modern music festivals he was interested in organizing. As I've said, he listened to my *Wedding*, and turned to ice. He would have been silent in any case. But what deepened his silence in this case was that he left immediately, a little more quickly than usual. If I had known him better at the time, I would have inferred that he didn't quite know what to think.

I assumed that the atmosphere of the house repelled him, the hostess with her dark, Oriental bulk spread out on a sofa barely long enough to hold her, but overflowing at the sides. I didn't feel at all comfortable while reading the part of Johanna Segenreich in her presence. Though Bella Band came of an entirely different, upper-middle-class background and wouldn't have honored Segenreich with so much as a glance if she had found herself in a room with her, every one of Segenreich's words told me they were birds of a feather. Still, I don't think she felt they had anything to do with her; she listened because she was the hostess; the reading had been arranged by her son, who was a friend of mine. Insofar as any notice was taken of modern music in Vienna, its only representative to be honored with an invitation was H., who was known as a pioneer, but nothing more. The female bulk on the couch behaved exactly the same way, she didn't run away, she lay there to the end, but she smiled no more than H. himself, she favored him with no glance of any kind, it would have been impossible to say what went on in that flesh during the catastrophe scenes; I am certain that she experienced no fear, but I also doubt that H. was frightened by the earthquake.

Some other young people were present. They too probably felt protected by H.'s coldness and Bella Band's unswerving readiness for love. Thus during the reading I was probably the only one to feel *afraid*. I have never been able to read *The Wedding* aloud without feeling afraid. As soon as the chandelier begins to sway, I feel the end approaching and it is beyond me how I manage to maintain my composure through all the Dance of Death scenes—which amount, after all, to a third of the play.

At the end of June 1933 I received a letter from H., who was then in Riva. In it he informed me that he had

read *The Wedding* again and been horrified by the atmosphere of hopeless, icy abstraction in which all this happened. He was overwhelmed, he said, by the power the
writer had at his command and the use this power made
of him. "Come and see me soon, preferably after July 23,
in Strasbourg and we will fight our way through it
together."

He said he believed the writer to be capable of great
things, but that never had he seen so much depend so
utterly on the man himself as in my case. To be capable
of something so new, to master so somnambulistically sure
a technique, to be driven by the powers of the resonant,
as well as the cogitated, word was a great challenge. I
must, he said, live up to it.

He asked me to deliver a letter to "Anni," as he called
her, and be sure to put it into her own hands. "Can you
do anything with the enclosed prospectus? Give it publicity. Cordially, H. Sch."

It costs me an inner struggle to cite the approximate
content of this letter. But I cannot pass it over in silence,
because it played a crucial role in my life. That letter took
me to Strasbourg, and if it were not for the people I met
there, my novel would not have been published. It also
provides a succinct characterization of H., of his way of
winning people over, of binding them, usurping them
and making use of them.

There was more than calculation in his approach to me
and more than a command. His horror at helpless, icy
abstraction was not feigned. He said more about it than
I have quoted and *meant* it. But he could never content
himself with meaning it. Having exalted me, he orders
me to Strasbourg, to his modern-music festival, where I
really have no business, to which he has ordered countless
others, who, however, are musicians, whose works he is
going to perform for the first time. "Come and see me
soon," he says. But exactly what for? "So we can fight our
way through it together." What monstrous presumption!

What can he fight through with a writer? He wants to have me in Strasbourg, someone he can represent as promising, a sideshow for his circus of promising musicians. What sort of fight has he in mind? To justify his summons—though he knows that even if this joint fight of ours made sense he wouldn't have a moment's time— he issues a pretentious judgment, which he instantly revokes with his reference to the supposed danger facing me. In the end, after all this buffeting this way and that, one thing at least becomes clear to me: how much I need H. A secret letter is being sent to "Anni." She too is being ordered somewhere, for other purposes. Not to mention the enclosed prospectus for the festival and the order to "give it publicity."

I'd give a good deal to see some of his letters to other people who were ordered to that festival. The musicians came, they had good reason to. The five widows of famous composers, whom H. wanted to corral for the festival, were a special inspiration. I can remember only three of the five who were invited: the widows of Mahler, Busoni and Reger. None came. Instead came one who didn't belong in those surroundings at all, Gundolf's freshly baked widow, all in black, as cheerful and communicative as could be.

Trophies

I had been several times at the house on Hohe Warte;* Anna had received me privately through the back door

* A hill on the outskirts of Vienna. (Trans.)

before she decided to introduce me to her mother. We were both curious, but for different reasons: she because she had never heard of me, thought poorly of her daughter's judgment of people and wanted to assure herself that I was not dangerous; I because all Vienna was talking about Alma Mahler.

I was led across an open courtyard—between the flag-stones of which grass was allowed to grow with deliberate naturalness—to a kind of sanctum where Mama received me. A large woman, overflowing in all directions, with a sickly-sweet smile and bright, wide-open, glassy eyes. Her first words sounded as if she had heard *so much* about me and had long been waiting for this meeting. "Annerl has told me," she said at once, so diminishing† her daughter from the start; not for a moment did she leave it in doubt who was important here and in general.

She seated herself; a look of complicity gave me to understand that I was to sit beside her. I obeyed hesitantly; after one look at her I was aghast; everyone talked of her beauty; the story was that she had been the most beautiful girl in Vienna and had so impressed Mahler, much older than herself, that he had courted her and taken her for his wife. The legend of her beauty had endured for over thirty years. And now she stood there, now she sat heavily down, a slightly tipsy woman, looking much older than her age. She had gathered all her trophies around her.

The small room in which she received me was so arranged that the most important items of her career were within reach. She herself was the guide in this private museum, and she allowed nothing to be overlooked. Less than six feet from her stood the vitrine in which the score of Mahler's unfinished tenth symphony lay open. My attention was called to it, I stood up, went over and read the dying man's cries of distress—it was his last work—to

† Diminishing because Annerl is a Viennese diminutive. (Trans.)

his wife, his "Almshi, beloved Almshi," and more such intimate, desperate cries; it was to these most intimate pages that the score had been opened. This was no doubt a standard means of impressing visitors. I read these words in the handwriting of a dying man and looked at the woman to whom they had been addressed. Twenty-three years later, she took them as if they were meant for her now. From all who looked at this showpiece she expected the look of admiration due to her for this dying man's homage, and she was so sure of the effect of his writing in the score that the vapid smile on her face expanded into a grin. She had no suspicion of the horror and disgust I felt. I did not smile, but she misinterpreted my gravity as the piety due to a dying genius, and since all this was happening in the memorial chapel she had erected to her happiness, she took my piety as one more homage to herself.

Then it was time for the picture that hung on the wall directly across from her, a portrait of her, painted a few years after the composer had spoken his last words. I had noticed it immediately; it held me fast from the first moment, it had a dangerous, murderous quality. In my consternation over the open music score, my vision grew blurred and I saw the picture as a portrait of the composer's murderess. I had no time to reject this thought, for she stood up, took three steps toward the wall, stationed herself beside me and pointed at the picture, saying: "And this is me as Lucrezia Borgia, painted by Kokoschka." It was a painting from his great period. From Kokoschka himself, who was still living, she distanced herself at once by adding in a tone of commiseration: "Too bad he never got anywhere!" He had turned his back on Germany, he was a "degenerate painter," he had gone to Prague, where he was painting the portrait of President Masaryk. Giving way to my surprise at her contemptuous remark, I asked: "What do you mean he never got anywhere?" She replied: "Because there he is in Prague, a poor refugee. He hasn't painted anything decent since." And with a glance at Lucrezia Borgia: "He had real ability then. That picture really frightens people." I had indeed been frightened, and now on learning that Kokoschka had never got anywhere, I was even more so. He had served his purpose by painting several pictures of "Lucrezia Borgia," and now, what a pity, he was a failure, because the new masters of Germany were not pleased with him and there was no future in doing the portrait of President Masaryk.

But the widow didn't give much time to the second trophy, for she was already thinking of the third, which was not in the sanctuary. She clapped her pudgy hands briskly and cried out: "Where's my pussycat?"

Hardly a moment later a gazelle came tripping into the room, a light-footed, brown-haired creature disguised as a young girl, untouched by the splendor into which she had been summoned, younger in her innocence than her probable sixteen years. She radiated timidity even more than beauty, an angelic gazelle, not from the ark but from heaven. I jumped up, thinking to bar her entrance into this alcove of vice or at least to cut off her view of the poisoner on the wall, but Lucrezia, who never stopped playing her part, had irrepressibly taken the floor:

"Beautiful, isn't she? This is my daughter Manon. By Gropius. In a class by herself. You don't mind my saying so, do you, Annerl? What's wrong with having a beautiful sister? Like father, like daughter. Did you ever see Gropius? A big handsome man. The true Aryan type. The only man who was racially suited to me. All the others who fell in love with me were little Jews. Like Mahler. The fact is, I go for both kinds. You can run along now, pussycat. Wait, go and see if Franzl is writing poetry. If he is, don't bother him. If he isn't, tell him I want him."

With this commission Manon, the third trophy, slipped

out of the room, as untouched as she had come; her errand didn't seem to trouble her. I was greatly relieved at the thought that nothing could touch her, that she would always remain as she was and never become like her mother, the poisoner on the wall, the glassy, blubbery old woman on the sofa.

(I didn't know how tragically my prophecy would be borne out. A year later the light-footed maiden was a paralytic; when her mother clapped her hands, she would be pushed in in a wheelchair. A year after that she was dead. Alban Berg dedicated his last work "To the memory of an angel.")

In one of the upper rooms stood Werfel's desk, at which he wrote standing. Anna had once showed me this attic room when I visited her upstairs. Her mother didn't know that I had already met him at a concert I went to with Anna. There she sat between the two of us, and during the music I felt an eye staring at me, his. He was leaning far to the right to get a better look at me, and the better to observe the expression of his eyes, my left eye had turned almost as far to the left. Our two staring eyes met; for a moment, feeling caught in the act, they retreated but finally, as their mutual interest could not be concealed, they got on with their business. I don't know what was being played; if I had been Werfel, that would have been my first thought, but I wasn't a social lion, I was in love with Anna and that was all. She was not ashamed of me, though I was wearing knickers and was hardly dressed for a concert, as she hadn't told me until the last moment that she had an extra ticket. She was sitting on my left, and it seemed to me that I kept darting furtive glances at her, but in the same direction I collided with Werfel's jutting right eye. It occurred to me that he had a mouth like a carp's, to which his right pop eye was excellently suited. Soon my left eye was behaving just like his right. This was our first meeting, enacted during music between two eyes which, separated by Anna, could not get closer together. Her eyes, her best feature, eyes that no one they had once looked at ever forgot, remained aloof from this play of eyes—though to speak of "play" is grotesque misrepresentation, considering how inexpressive, how utterly lusterless Werfel's eyes and mine were. But words, in the passionate flow of which he was a master, were also inactive, since we were sitting silently in a concert hall. (Friedl Feuermaul* was the name given him by Musil, the greatest of his contemporaries.) Nor was I ordinarily (in Anna's presence, for instance) tongue-tied. Yet both of us were silent, intent on the concert, and possibly it was this first meeting that decided our enmity, which seriously affected my life, his hostility and my dislike.

But for the present I'm still sitting with Alma among her trophies, and she, knowing nothing of the concert, has just sent her third trophy to summon her fourth—whose name is Franzl—if he isn't writing at the moment. It seems that he was writing poetry, for he did not appear on that occasion, and that suited me, for I was suffering under the corrosive impression of the immortal widow and her other trophies. I clung to that impression, I wanted to preserve it, none of Werfel's "O Man!" rubbish was going to stop me. I don't remember how I made my getaway, how I took my leave; in my memory I'm still sitting beside the immortal widow, still listening to her talk about "little Jews like Mahler."

---

* Firemouth. (Trans.)

Strasbourg 1933

I don't know what Hermann Scherchen thought was to be gained by my attending his modern-music festival. I couldn't possibly have contributed anything to the ample program. Concerts were given twice daily at the Conservatory. Musicians from all over the world had come, some stopped at hotels, most were invited to stay with townspeople.

My host was Professor Hamm, a prominent gynecologist. He lived in a house in the Old City, not far from the church of St. Thomas on Salzmanngasse. He was a busy man, but he called for me at the Conservatory office, which had assigned me to him, and walked me to Salzmanngasse. On the way he entertained me with interesting facts about the Old City. I was overwhelmed when we stopped outside the handsome, imposing house. I sensed that the Cathedral was nearby—I wouldn't have dared imagine that I would be living so close to the goal of my desires, for it was mostly because of the Cathedral that I had accepted the invitation to Strasbourg. We entered the vestibule, it was larger than one might have expected in this narrow street. Professor Hamm led me up a broad stairway to the second floor and opened the door to the guest room: a large, comfortable room, furnished in the taste of the eighteenth century. In the doorway I was overtaken by a feeling that it was unseemly for me to sleep in this room, a feeling so intense that I fell silent. Professor Hamm, a lively man, who seemed very French, had expected a cry of delight, for who could have wished for a finer room? He felt the need of explaining where I was, pointed to the Cathedral spire, which seemed within

Late at night I came home to the room which I am certain no one but me looked upon as Herder's room at the Auberge du Louvre. I couldn't get rid of the feeling that I was a usurper. Night after night I experienced the same agitation, a kind of terror, I felt guilty of a profanation, for which I was being punished by insomnia. But when it came time to get up in the morning, I wasn't tired, I was glad to hurl myself into the bustle of the festival, and during the day I gave no thought to what awaited me at night. For my anguish over the past into which I had drifted by mistake as it were, and to which I would gladly have belonged, there was only one compensation. But this was something so wonderful that each day I took time for it. I am speaking of the Cathedral.

I had been in Strasbourg only once, on my way back from Paris to Vienna in the spring of 1927. I had stopped over in Alsace to see the Strasbourg Cathedral and the Isenheim altar in Colmar. After spending an hour or two in Strasbourg I had gone looking for the Cathedral. And then suddenly—late in the afternoon—I was on Krämergasse, and there it loomed in front of me. I hadn't expected the red glow of the stone of the immense west façade; all the photographs I had seen had been black and white.

And now, six years later, I was back in this town, not for a few hours, but for several weeks, for a whole month. It had all come about by accident, or seemingly so. In his restless search for new men, H. had invited me; if I wasn't a musician, I was at least a playwright, and he had picked me from among a hundred others to lend spice to his festival. In accepting his invitation, I had involuntarily cut short my violent passion for Anna, for which H., by using me as a messenger, had also been responsible. Despite outward difficulties, I did not seriously hesitate. I had started *The Comedy of Vanity* and was still working on the first part. Thus I had two things to hold me in Vienna, both very serious, my first passion since my meeting with

Veza and—after the novel and *The Wedding*—a third literary work, begun under the impact of the events in Germany. Since the burning of the books my mind had been aflame with the *Comedy*. My relationship with Anna began to go bad only when my departure for Strasbourg, though decided on, was delayed by passport problems. The *Comedy* became increasingly urgent while I was sitting about in consulates waiting. I wrote the sermon of Crumb at the French Consulate, while waiting for my visa.

When I ask myself today what turned the balance in favor of attendance at the festival—apart from Scherchen's overpowering will—I believe it was the name of Strasbourg, that short glimpse of the Cathedral in the late afternoon, and all I knew about Herder, Goethe and Lenz in Strasbourg. I do not think I was clearly aware of all this; my recollection of the Cathedral cannot have been all that irresistible, but my feeling for the Storm and Stress period in German literature was strong, and it was bound up with Strasbourg. And this literature was now in danger. What had chiefly distinguished it at that time, its drive for freedom, was threatened, and that was the essential content of the play I was then full of. But Strasbourg, the breeding ground of that movement, was still free. Small wonder that it attracted me along with my *Comedy*, only a small but powerful part of which was written. And what of Büchner, who had introduced me to Lenz? Hadn't I for the last two years regarded Büchner as the fountainhead of *all* drama?

The Old City was not large and I always ended up in front of the Cathedral. Not deliberately, yet that was what I really wanted. I was drawn to the figures on the portals, the Prophets and especially the Foolish Virgins. The Wise Virgins didn't move me, I think it was the smiles on the faces of the Foolish ones that won me over. I fell in love with one, who struck me as the most beautiful. I met her later in the Old City and took her to see her likeness, which no one had ever shown her before. She was amazed at the sight of herself hewn in stone; a stranger had the good fortune to discover her in her native town and convince her that she had been there long before she was born, smiling on the church portal, a Foolish Virgin, who in reality, as it turned out, was not so foolish at all, for it was her smile that had charmed the artist into putting her among the seven figures on the left portal. And among the Prophets I found a local burgher, whose acquaintance I also made in the course of those weeks. He was a specialist in Alsatian history, a hesitant, skeptical man, who spoke little and wrote less. God knows how he had come to be one of the Prophets, but there he was, and if I didn't lead the man himself to the portal, I told him and his clever wife where he was to be found. While he, the skeptic, found nothing to say about my discovery, his wife agreed with me.

But my great experience during those weeks so full of people, smells and sounds was climbing to the top of the Cathedral. This I did every day, omitting none. I did not climb slowly and patiently, I was in a hurry to reach the platform and was out of breath when I got there. A day that didn't begin with this climb was for me no day at all, and I counted the days according to my visits to the Cathedral tower. Accordingly, I spent more days in Strasbourg than there were in the month, for sometimes I succeeded, in spite of all there was to hear, in visiting the tower in the afternoon as well. I envied the man who lived up there, for he had a head start on the long way up the winding stairs. I had fallen in love with the view of the mysterious city rooftops and with every stone that I grazed in climbing. I saw the Vosges and the Black Forest together, and made no mistake about what divided them in this year. The war that had ended fifteen years before still weighed on my mind, and I felt that before many years there would be another.

I crossed over to the finished spire, and there I stood

a few steps from the tablet on which Goethe, Lenz and their friends had written their names. I thought of Goethe, how he had waited up here for Lenz, who in a blissful letter had spoken to Caroline Herder of the imminent meeting. "I can write no more. Goethe is with me, he has been waiting for me atop the Cathedral spire for the last half hour."

Nothing was more alien to the spirit of this town than Scherchen's festival. I had nothing against modernism, not against modern art at least, that would have been unthinkable. But at night, after the concert, when I sat at the Broglie, the most fashionable café in town, among the visiting musicians, few of whom could afford expensive dishes, and watched H. devouring his caviar—he always, he and no one else, ordered caviar on toast—I wondered if he had even noticed the presence of a cathedral in this town. He liked people to watch him eating his caviar, and if they watched him hungrily enough, he would order a third portion, for himself of course, concentrated food for the man who worked so hard. Gustel, his wife, was busy until late with Scherchen's paperwork and seldom attended the caviar eating; she would be waiting at the hotel. He couldn't bear for anyone in his entourage to be idle; like a true orchestra conductor, he kept everyone busy.

He never felt guilty about the constant strain he imposed on others, for he himself was under the worst pressure. He would sit at the Broglie until midnight over caviar and champagne, though he had summoned a singer to the hotel at six in the morning for a tryout. No hour was too early for him, he would regularly tack a few minutes on to the beginning of the day, and since he took the lead with his terrifying industry, no one would have dared complain of the early hours. No fees were paid for any of the work done at this festival. The musicians had come for love of the new music. The Conservatory and the concert halls were made available free of charge. After all, number one, the man who was contributing the most, far more as he thought than anyone else, was also lending his services for nothing. Innumerable concerts were given; despite the difficult, unfamiliar music, they all "came off"; the captain worked like a dog, kept his eye on everything, made sure that nothing went wrong. An impressive achievement; the conductor after all was much more important than the composers, it was he who had taken the initiative of presenting a wide variety of music, much of it for the first time; nothing could have been done without him. A few handpicked, culture-loving locals, who had opened their homes to visiting musicians or given sumptuous receptions, were privileged to sit at Scherchen's table at the Broglie and watch him eat his caviar. All felt that he had richly deserved it and his champagne as well. One of them, a doctor whom I knew to be an unbeliever, turned to me one evening and said: "There's something Christlike about him."

But the day was not yet over. A much smaller group would carry on at the Maison Rouge, the hotel where H. was staying. These were the initiates, as it were, no townspeople or common musicians, but only the upper crust, who, by the nature of things, lived at the Maison Rouge. The younger Jessner with his wife, he too an impresario (he had been engaged to direct Milhaud's *Le Pauvre Matelot* at the Stadtheater); Gundolf's widow, who had left Heidelberg; Gundolf had died only recently, but she enjoyed the lively, often boisterous conversations. When H. was not being silent or giving orders, he made cynical remarks; the select guests felt honored and chimed in.

It seems worthwhile to take a look at the time when this modern-music festival took place—a few weeks after the burning of the books in Germany. For six months the man with the unpronounceable name had been in power. Ten years earlier, Germany had been shaken by uncontrollable inflation. Ten years later his troops were deep inside Russia and had planted their banner on the highest peak of the Caucasus. Strasbourg, the city that played host to our festival, was a French-administered city where a German dialect was spoken.

Its streets and buildings had preserved a "medieval character" which, thanks to a garbage collectors' strike that had been going on for weeks, lost no time in assaulting the visitors' noses. But the Cathedral spire rose high above the stench, and we were all free to seek relief on the platform. Though as a conductor he had taught himself dictatorial habits, H. refused to perform in the new Germany, where, thanks to his spotless lineage and Teutonic energy, he would have achieved high honor. In this he was one among not very many, a point decidedly in his favor. In that month in Strasbourg he managed to assemble a kind of Europe consisting entirely of musicians engaged in new experiments, a courageous, confident Europe, for what would have been the point of experiments if they didn't reckon with a future?

At that time I lived in very different worlds. One focus was the Conservatory, where I spent most of my time during the day. On entering the building, I was engulfed by a deafening din. Practicing was going on in every room, which, I suppose, is only natural in a conservatory, and much of the music being practiced was most unusual. In other conservatories you think you can identify the compositions you hear, and most often you get a jumble of familiar dribs and drabs. Here, on the contrary, everything was strange and new, the details as well as the overall sound. This may have been just what fascinated me and made me go back time and again. I was amazed at the endurance of those musicians, who in addition to mastering difficult new scores managed to practice in this hell and somehow, in the midst of such pandemonium, judge whether they were improving or not.

Maybe I left the Conservatory so often for the pleasure of going back often. For on leaving the noise, I would plunge into the stench of the streets. I never got used to it, I was always aware of it, I had never experienced such a smell. It got worse from day to day and the only thing that could assail the senses with comparable force was the acoustic chaos of the Conservatory.

It was then and in those streets that I began to think about the Plague. Suddenly, without transition or preparation, I was in the fourteenth century, a period that had always interested me because of its mass movements, the flagellants, the plague, the burnings of Jews. I had first read about all this in the Limburg Chronicle, and since then I had read many other accounts. Now I myself was living in the midst of it. One step from Dr. Hamm's elegantly furnished house took me into the streets, where garbage and its smell reigned supreme. Instead of avoiding them, I invested them with images of my horror. Everywhere I saw the dead, and the despair of those who were still alive. It seemed to me that in the narrow streets people avoided contact with one another, as though fearing infection. I never took the shortest route from the Old City to the pretentious new quarter where the Conservatory was located. I zigzagged through the streets; it's amazing how many itineraries one can devise in so limited an area. I breathed in the danger and was determined to stay with it at all costs. Every door I passed was closed. I never saw any of them open; in my mind's eye I saw interiors full of the dead and dying. What in Germany, beyond the Rhine, was felt to be a fresh start struck me here as the consequence of a war that had not yet begun. I did not foresee—how could I foresee?—what lay ten years ahead. No, I looked six hundred years back, and what I saw was the Plague with its masses of dead, which had spread irresistibly and was once again threatening from across the Rhine. The processions of suppliants all ended at the Cathedral, and against the Plague they were useless. For in reality the Cathedral existed for its own sake; you could stand in front of it, you had been inside it, that was the help it provided: it was still there, it hadn't collapsed in any of the plagues. The movement of the old processions communicated itself to me; we had assembled in every street and made our way together to the Cathedral. And there we stood, perhaps not to entreat but to give thanks, thanks that we could still stand here, for nothing had fallen on us, and the glory of glories, the spire, was still pointing heavenward. Last but not least, I had the privilege of climbing it, of looking down on everything that was still intact, and when, looking down, I breathed deeply, it seemed to me that the Plague, which was once again trying to spread, had been thrust back into its old century.

Anna

H.'s power over women was amazing. He seemed to *conduct* them into loving him, and dropped them before they had even settled into their new position. They accepted their fate, because in their musical activity they remained in contact with him. In their work together, he would be as precise and conscientious as before. Some of the old atmosphere was saved, and there was always hope that one day his desire would be rekindled. There was little jealousy among them; at every possible opportunity each felt distinguished by him, but did her best to keep the secret of his favor to herself. It was more important to protect her good fortune from the public eye than to nurture the jealousy and hatred of her rivals. Jealous scenes would have had no effect on him. He saw himself as an autocrat who did just as he pleased, and he saw right.

But there was one exception: a woman who, for historical reasons as it were, was in duty bound to be jealous and did her duty to the full. Gustel, who was his official companion during the days in Strasbourg, was his fourth wife. She hadn't been his wife for long, she had taken the plunge only a few weeks before. She had hesitated for quite some time before becoming his fourth wife, and with good reason, as she had also been his first. In his early Berlin period, she had stood by him when he was still a nobody trying to get ahead by sheer hard work. She was his Indian slave and the reddish hue of her skin even made her look like an Indian. She had a weather-beaten look induced by her long-suffering loyalty. She spoke little, but when she did, the tone was tart and crisp. She made the impression of a martyr at the stake, resolved to concede nothing and gritting her teeth to the end. From the first she helped with his clerical work; all his correspondence, contracts, etc., went through her, and she helped him to track down prospects. Even when the prospects became reality and she saw that every success brought her incalculable torment, she stood firm at her stake and invited new torment. For he too was taciturn, and it was impossible to get any more out of him than out of her. She kept her unhappiness to herself, he never breathed a word about his good fortune. Both had thin, tightly closed lips.

When, still quite a young man, he came to Frankfurt as Furtwängler's successor and took over the management

of the Saalbau Concerts, he made the acquaintance of
Gerda Müller, the Penthesilea of my youth, one of the
most fascinating actresses of her day. He soon left Gustel
for her. Gerda Müller was utterly different from Gustel.
In her he found intense, outspoken passion, a vitality that
was a law unto itself and subservient to no one; to her,
martyrdom was not a virtue but would have signified
ineptitude. Scherchen's interest in the theater may have
dated from this time. It was a turbulent, though not the
most turbulent, period in his private life. Thus thrust
aside, Gustel was forced to attempt a regular, untortured
life. She found a lover and lived happily with him for
seven years.

H. didn't tell me much about Gerda Müller, but he had
more to say of the next woman to play a major part in
his life, the only one who left him against his will. She
too was an actress, but while Gerda Müller took refuge
in drink, Carola Neher lived for adventures, and of the
wildest sort.

A year or two after Strasbourg I spent some time in
Winterthur, where H. was conducting Werner Reinhardt's
orchestra. Late at night, after attending one of his concerts, I sat with him in his room. I sensed the man's
nervous tension, but it was not of the usual kind, springing
from an urge to dominate, to crush someone. He himself
seemed crushed. Yet the concert had gone off well,
certainly no worse than usual. It was very late, but he
asked me not to leave just yet. He looked around the
room in a strange way, as though seeing ghosts; his eyes
never came to rest for long but roamed restlessly back
and forth. All he wanted was for me to listen to him. I
kept calm, though I was rather troubled by his darting
eyes; I had never seen him like that. Suddenly it burst
out; with a passion I wouldn't have expected of him, he
said: "It was here, right here in this room, that we had
our last talk. We talked all night." And then by fits and

starts, almost panting, he told me about his all-night talk with Carola Neher.

She announced her intention of leaving him and he begged her to stay. She wanted to do something big, this life was too small for her. She had decided to drop everything, her acting, her fame, and him, H., whom she ridiculed as a puppet. She despised him, she said, because he catered to a concert audience. The sweat dripped off him when he conducted; whom was he sweating for, what kind of sweat was that? It was phony sweat, it meant nothing, what had meaning for her was a Bessarabian student she had recently met, who was ready to stake his life, who feared nothing, neither prison nor the firing squad. H. realized that she was serious, but he was sure he could hold her. Thus far he had always dominated, women as well as men; if anyone left, it was he. When he felt like it, he walked out. He tried every argument. He threatened to lock her up to save her from herself. This would be her death, he told her. Her student was a nobody, a young whippersnapper with no experience of life. He reviled him, paid her back for all she had said about his conducting. When he attacked the student as an *individual*, she seemed to waver. But then she countered that what she took seriously was the cause, not the man. If he were someone else, but as deeply committed to a similar cause, he would mean just as much to her. The battle went on all night. He had thought he could wear her down with fatigue; she was incredibly tough, she cursed as she yielded to his physical assault. Finally, it was already dawn; she fell asleep and he thought he had defeated her. He gave her one last look of satisfaction before falling asleep in his turn. When he awoke, she was gone and she hadn't come back.

For weeks and weeks he waited for her to return. He waited for news but none came. He had no idea where she was. Nor had anyone else. He made inquiries and found out that the student had vanished too. So she had run away with him, just as she had threatened. Every theater where she was known sent the same answer. She had vanished without a trace. He felt as if she had been snatched away from him. He couldn't bear it, he was unable to work.

His condition was so hopeless that he asked Gustel to come back to him. He said he needed her; he swore he would never leave her again; she could impose any condition she wished; he would never again be unfaithful. But she must come at once, or it was all up with him. Gustel broke off her seven years' friendship with a man who had never given her anything but kindness, and returned to H., who had always treated her like dirt. She set hard conditions and he accepted them. He would always tell her the truth, she would always know what he was up to.

My perception of H. during the weeks in Strasbourg was sharpened by certain circumstances, the full bearing of which escaped both of us. In Vienna he had used me as a messenger, sending me to Anna with a letter. That was how I met her. The content of the letter was unknown to me, but he had made it plain that I must put it into her own hands. I called her on the phone and she asked me to come to her studio in Hietzing.

I saw her before she saw me. I saw her fingers. They were pressing the clay of a larger-than-life figure. Her back was turned, and I couldn't see her face. The crunching of the gravel sounded loud to me, but she didn't seem to hear it. She was so deeply immersed in her still-unformed figure that perhaps she didn't want to hear it. Possibly this visit was unwelcome to her. Still, I had undertaken to deliver this letter. When I entered the greenhouse that served her as a studio, she turned abruptly and looked me in the face. By then I was fairly close to her and I felt enveloped by her eyes. From that moment on, they held me fast. It was not a surprise attack, for I had had time to come close, but a surprise it was, I hadn't been prepared for such superabundance. She was all eyes; anything else one might have seen in her was illusory. This I sensed at once, but where would I have found the strength or insight to own it to myself? How was I to acknowledge a reality so prodigious: that eyes can be more spacious than the person they belong to? In their depth there is room for everything one has ever thought, and since there is room for it, it all demands to be said.

There are eyes that you fear because they are out for blood; they are on the lookout for prey which, once sighted, can only be prey; even if it manages to escape, it will still be marked as prey. The rigidity of this merciless gaze is terrible. It never changes; no victim can influence it, it is foreordained for all time. Anyone who enters its field becomes its victim, he can offer no defense, and his only hope of saving himself would be total metamorphosis. Since such metamorphosis is impossible in the real world, it demanded the creation of myths and mythical figures.

Another myth is the eye that is not out for blood, though it never releases what it has once caught sight of. This myth can come true, and anyone who has experienced it must think back with fear and trembling to the eye that has forced him to drown himself in it. What spaciousness, what depth! Plunge into me with everything you can think and say; say it and drown.

The depth of such eyes is infinite. Nothing that falls into them reaches the bottom. Nothing is washed up again. What then becomes of it? Such an eye is a lake without memory. What it demands it obtains. You give it everything you have; everything that matters, your innermost substance. You cannot withhold anything from this eye, though no force is used, nothing is snatched away. What is given is given happily, as though it had become aware of itself for no other reason, come into being for no other reason.

When I gave Anna the letter, I ceased to be a messenger. She did not take it, she only wagged her head in the direction of the corner table, which I had not noticed before. I went over to it in three steps and reluctantly put the letter down, reluctantly perhaps because I then had a hand free for her and couldn't give it to her. I extended it halfway, she looked at *her* right hand, which was smeared with clay, and said: "I can't give you a hand like this."

I don't know what was said after that. I've tried to recall our first words, hers as well as mine. They have gone under. Anna was all in her eyes, otherwise she was almost mute; her voice, though deep, never meant anything to me. Perhaps she didn't like to talk; she used her voice as little as possible, she always borrowed other people's voices, in music and among people. She preferred *action* to words, and since she had no gift for her father's kind of action, she tried to create *form* with her fingers. I have preserved my first meeting with her by stripping it of all words, hers because they may have contained nothing worth preserving, mine because my amazement over her had not yet found audible words.

Still, I know that something had been said before she asked me over to the table and we both sat down. She wanted to read some of my writing, and I said there was no published book; I had only the manuscript of a long novel. Could I bring her the manuscript someday soon? Yes, she liked long novels, she didn't care for short stories. She told me the name of her teacher, Fritz Wotruba, who taught her sculpture. I had heard of him, he was known for his independence and feared for his violence. But he was not in Vienna just then. Previously she had painted and had studied with Chirico in Rome.

She ignored H.'s letter. It lay unopened on the table,

she couldn't fail to see it. I remembered my mission, the orders, as it were, that H. had given me, and said hesitantly: "Aren't you going to read the letter?" She picked it up with distaste and glanced through it as one would a three-line note. Though it was quite a long letter and though, as I knew, H.'s handwriting was hard to read, she seemed to have taken it all in at a glance. She put the letter down with a gesture of disparagement and said: "It's without interest." I looked at her with surprise. I had supposed there was some sort of friendship between them, that he had something important to communicate, something too important to be entrusted to the mails. "You may read it," she said. "But it's hardly worthwhile." I did not read it.

Why would I bother with a message that she thought so little of? I was aware of her rudeness, of the contempt she was showing for the man who had sent me. But I wasn't a messenger anymore. I was now a free agent, for she had relieved me of my mission. The ease with which she thrust his letter aside, showing no sign of anger or displeasure, communicated itself to me. It didn't even occur to me to ask if she wished to send H. an answer.

When I left, I had a new mission: to come back soon with my manuscript. I came three days later, it was hard for me to wait that long. She read my novel at once, I don't believe anyone else read it so quickly. From then on, she regarded me as an individual in my own right, and treated me as if I had all the necessary attributes, even eyes. She told me she expected many such books from me and spoke of my book to others. She urged me to come and see her and sent letters and telegrams. I had never known that love could begin with telegrams, I was amazed. At first I found it hard to believe that a message from her could reach me so quickly.

She asked me to write to her and gave me a mailing address. I was to put my letter in a carefully sealed

envelope, which I was to insert in another envelope
addressed to Fräulein Hedy Lehner, Porzellangasse. Fräulein Lehner, a young model who came to Anna's studio
every day, was a beautiful redhead with a face like a fox;
I'd get a glimpse of her when I came to the studio, an
almost imperceptible smile would cross her face, then she
would disappear without a word. Sometimes when I got
there, she had just brought a letter from me, which Anna
had not yet opened, let alone read. Anna was careful,
because someone could come into the studio any minute.
She owned that she found it hard to talk to me before
reading my letter, and that at such moments she would
rather I hadn't come. True, I told her lots of stories, and
she loved stories, but she was still fonder of the letters in
which I glorified her.

"Drums and Trumpets" was her name for what I wrote
her. Transposing my sentences into her own medium.
She had never before received such letters; many came,
sometimes three in one day, Fräulein Hedy Lehner couldn't
always bring each one separately; it would have attracted
attention if she had come several times a day, and Anna
was under strict supervision (to which she had consented).
Permission to have a model was a special privilege, which
she had no desire to forfeit. Anna always replied to my
high-flown eloquence by means of telegrams (which Hedy
would take to the post office on her way home from the
studio). Words did not come easy to her, but she was
determined to thank me for the inventive glorification of
my letters, and telegrams were just the thing.

Anna had many secrets, which made her mysterious to
me; I did not realize how much she had to keep secret
and how vitally important it was for her to keep it secret.
Luckily for her, she forgot easily, but others were capable
of reminding her of the past. Most secret of all was her
sculpture, on which she worked hard. She regarded hard

work as honorable; she had inherited that from her father, but she was also influenced in that direction by her young teacher, Fritz Wotruba, who worked in hard stone. She also modeled, chiefly heads; that was not hard work but played an entirely different role, it was her only access to people that was not blocked by her mother's loving, domineering ways.

She did not expend herself in letters, but tried to *react*, and as long as her letters served that purpose, she was content. But when she did not want to react—in times of disillusionment that were frequent because she was blind to people she did not happen to be modeling and especially to those she had taken it into her head to love—in such times of disillusionment, she gave herself wholly to music. She played a number of instruments, but in the end she had gone back to the piano. I rarely heard her play, I avoided opportunities to do so, so I never found out what those solitary sessions meant to her. I distrusted music that left room for sculpture.

The aura of fame surrounding Anna was so great that I could think no harm of her. Someone could have shown me a confession, written in her hand, of the most hideous thoughts and deeds, I wouldn't have believed him or the testimony of her handwriting. What made it all the easier to preserve an untainted image of her was that I soon had a very different image of her mother to contrast it with. On one side I saw a silent light feeding on sculpture and glorification, on the other an insatiable, tipsy old woman. I was not deceived by their close family ties, I saw the daughter as a victim, and if it is true that one is the victim of what one has seen around one from early childhood, I saw correctly.

H. would not have employed me as a messenger if he had thought me very dangerous. He took himself too dead seriously to doubt that a handwritten letter from him would divert all possible attention from a mere messenger. Besides, he may have felt that the author of *The Wedding* was bound to be harmless, since only an unfeeling monster could have written so glacial a play. He may even have thought it clever to entrust a love letter to such a creature. But he never got an answer, not even a rebuff. Soon after arriving in Strasbourg I saw him briefly between rehearsals. He squeezed out three sentences, one of which was "Did you give 'Anni' my letter?" "Of course," I replied, and added in a tone of astonishment: "Hasn't she answered you?" From this he inferred that I had seen her more than once and that we might have become intimate. For the present a mere suspicion; as a dictator he was always inclined to suspicion. "Hasn't she answered you?" suggested to him that I knew her well enough to know that she habitually answered letters. Reasonable enough. But at the same time, his contempt for an unimportant young man was so great that he felt the need of dispelling his suspicion. So he did his best to find out that there was nothing to find out.

During the first days of the festival he tried to provoke me with contemptuous remarks about Anna. Her yellow hair was dyed, it had formerly been mouse gray; he put the emphasis on "formerly," implying that when H. had first met her as a young woman of twenty, married to Ernst Krenek, she had had gray hair. Hadn't I noticed her walk? No real woman would walk like that. Every one of his remarks infuriated me. I defended her with such passion and rage that he soon knew the whole truth. "You really are in love," he said. "I wouldn't have thought you capable of it." I admitted nothing, less out of discretion than because I hated him for his remarks. But I spoke of her in such glowing terms that only a simpleton would have failed to conclude that I loved her. Thus he forced me to step forward as her paladin. A strange irony, for soon after my arrival in Strasbourg I received a letter and a telegram from her, giving me my walking papers. In two months, no more, she had got over what was to haunt me for years. She offered no explanation, not a word of reproach. Her letter began with the words "I don't believe, M., that I love you." This Irish name (M.) she had given me was as unreal as the letters in which she had protested her love. And now H. collided unsuspecting with this misfortune which had laid me low and which—so I thought—he had been the cause of, for I assumed that she had been disillusioned by my going to Strasbourg. And here he was trying to demolish my image of her and taking obvious pleasure in this beastly pursuit. Every time he opened his mouth he said something horrible about her.

We saw each other briefly, between his rehearsals and concerts, while he was stuffing himself on toast and caviar at the Broglie, or longer late at night in his hotel, when the inner circle met to exchange catty observations. But he preferred to tell me unpleasant things about her when we were alone. It wasn't long before he issued his strange warning: "Steer clear of her. You're too inexperienced, too naïve." Every word was an insult to me, but I was hurt a lot more by what he said about her. He soon caught on to this, and once he had worked himself up to a certain pitch, he would come out with something so unspeakable that I still can't bring myself to write it down. I stared at him in horror, while at the same time wondering if I hadn't heard wrong. And then with visible relish he would repeat his words. "But why, why are you saying this?" I cried out, too horror-stricken to hit him. His accusations were so monstrous that they reflected on him more than on her. He saw he had gone too far. "But don't let it get you down. There are more things in heaven and earth than you let yourself dream of."

I didn't ask how he had discovered these horrors. I knew he was lying, and I also knew why. I remembered how Anna had put his letter aside, saying: "It's not important." He meant nothing to her. She had always thrust him aside like his letter. He didn't interest her, not even as a musician, let alone as a man. There *were* conductors who interested her, with whom she associated, and as her father's daughter she had every right to decide whom she regarded as a good conductor. She looked upon H. as a kind of military band leader; in that respect, his looks and his manner were no help to him. To this innovator, who took the trouble to discover new and difficult music, she preferred men who wouldn't so much as look at a modern, unfamiliar work. Her rejection came as a hard blow to him. He was trying to get a foothold in Vienna. He had got nowhere with Anna's mother, who had great influence, and that made it all the more important for him to get somewhere with Mahler's daughter. Since she would have nothing to do with him, his only recourse was to slander her.

Suddenly I found myself in an intolerable situation, and if I had not been so taken up with Strasbourg itself, its literary history and the many outstanding musicians I soon met there, I doubt if I would have had the strength to stay. I had been exalted to high heaven and now I was flung down. A woman whom I greatly admired, whom I thought beautiful and regarded as the living creation of a great man, had received me into her world, read my novel and found me worthy of her love. The novel had not yet been published and few people knew of its existence. And few knew of the play I had read to the conductor and because of which he had invited me to a conclave of modern musicians. I owed this invitation to *The Wedding* and I owed Anna's love to *Kant Catches Fire*. Immediately after my arrival in Strasbourg I climbed to the platform where Goethe had waited for Lenz. There I stood, face to face with the tablet on which they had inscribed their names. I was made welcome into one of the beautiful houses at the foot of the Cathedral, and lodged in a room where Herder was believed to have lain sick and received Goethe's visit. The strange coincidence between my happiness and my veneration for the men who had lived here might have produced a dangerous hubris. In my illustrious bedchamber I might have given myself over to wishful fantasies, "temple dreams," as it were, and abandoned the arduous and essential tasks I had set myself. But as my luck would have it, misfortune struck me at that very time. I had been there only three days when a letter and a telegram from Anna were handed me in the office of the Conservatory. In the midst of that musical pandemonium, under a hundred eyes, I tore them open and read their ice-cold message. Not a word of reproach, she simply let me know that her feeling for me was gone. She made no attempt to spare my feelings but told me quite plainly that it was my letters and not me she had loved. She added that she was seeing no one, that she had shut herself up with her piano and played for herself alone. Yet, in this cold letter, devoid of overtones, I sensed a faint sorrow over her disappointment. She hoped, she said, for more letters from me, but held out no prospect of answers. I had ceased to be of interest, I had been sent back to earth, but I was free to penetrate her atmosphere with letters, only with letters. There was something almost sublime in the way she had treated me, as if she had a natural right to exalt and depose without explanation or forbearance, as though the victim should be grateful for the hardest of blows, because it came from her.

The sense of annihilation that invaded me was held in check by the battle my sense of chivalry obliged me to fight for her. Every time he spoke to me, H. tried to drag her lower, and the worst of it was that his slanders were shot through with a strange sort of lubricity, calculated to arouse my jealousy. He himself was motivated by jealousy, thinking me in possession of the happiness I had lost. I threw every one of his ignominies back in his teeth, I was as obstinate as he was, though I was far from being as sure of my poison as he was of his. At first I exercised some restraint for fear of exposing her and myself—as though we were still a couple—to his attacks. But then, as his insults grew worse and worse, I threw caution to the winds and spoke of Anna as I had in the letters I had written her and could write her no longer. In my battle against H.'s vileness, everything that had supposedly existed between her and me remained intact. I couldn't lament, I couldn't tell him the new truth. Instead, I proclaimed the old truth with such force of conviction that he was dumbstruck at my unswerving faith.

Since H. tended to say everything in public, his large entourage must have found it strange that he sometimes asked explicitly to be alone with me. "I must speak to C.," he would say in a tone suggesting that there was something of importance to be discussed. But these few minutes wrested from the furious activity of his day were devoted entirely to our battles over Anna. He savored my violent counterattacks, because I never attacked him personally, but only defended Anna. They contrasted so sharply with his obscene denunciations that he *needed* them. He couldn't do without them, he needed both, and maybe I too—though I certainly didn't think so at the time—needed both to get me over the pain and humiliation inflicted on me by Anna.

To the others, though, to those who had no idea what these conversations were about, it looked as if H. were asking my *advice*, as though I were his trusted collaborator during those difficult weeks.

Gustel, who kept watch over him in her way, thought so too. Because he needed her, he had called her back; to show her how much he needed her and allay her misgivings, he had promised to tell her the truth about

everything and enjoined her to guard him against new
entanglements. His collapse after the flight of Carola
Neher, who had abandoned him so shamefully, was not
yet far behind him. Never before had a love affair, or
more accurately a rebuff at the hands of a woman,
impaired his capacity for work. In mortal fear, this
otherwise dauntless man had run for protection to Gustel,
his first wife and love. He was not deceiving her when he
begged her to watch over him and make sure that no
other woman ensnared him.

Thus Gustel had good reason to try to find out about
those confidential discussions of ours. Though ordinarily
rather crisp and tight-lipped, she approached me and
talked to me of herself in an attempt to win my friendship
and possibly my help as well. She suffered cruelly from
all his associations with women, and there were numerous
female musicians at the festival: several singers, including
one who was exceedingly seductive, exuberant and ready
for everything, as well as a magnificent violinist, whom
he had known in Vienna, a childlike, delightfully original
creature, combining perfect naturalness with rigorous
intelligence. She came of a highly musical family and one
of her Christian names had been given to her in honor
of Mozart. It suited her, she was musical in every fiber of
her being, what a man like H. had acquired by superhuman industry was hers by nature. The rhythms she had
to play were to her a form of obedience. To her, scores
were in the strictest sense of the word instructions. Conductor and score were one and the same thing, and
whatever a conductor ordered was a prolongation, an
extension of the score. She would have given her life for
the sake of a score and, it goes without saying, for the
author of a score. Amadea, to call her by the middle
name given her after Mozart—actually it was used only
in an abbreviated form—made no distinction between the
reigning sovereigns of music. When it came to composi-

tions, however, her tastes were most decided, not to say capricious. Her abilities were not merely technical—she had a thorough knowledge of Bach, who was perhaps the foremost among her gods, and of Mozart, but she also understood new compositions, which the general musical public of Vienna shunned like the Devil. She was one of the first to play the works of Alban Berg and Anton von Webern and was even called to London to perform them. But she was a slave to the instructions of the true beneficiaries of all musical compositions, the conductors, not to their persons, for about them she knew nothing, but to their tyrannical orders. In Strasbourg, H., who had already worked with her in Vienna, would summon her to rehearsals at six in the morning, and since she was by nature ingenuous and outgoing, she was unable to conceal his mastery over her. She was the principal object of Gustel's jealousy.

I didn't know much about music. I had never studied musical theory. I was an enthusiastic listener but would never have set myself up as a judge. My taste was catholic, ranging from Satie to Stravinsky, from Bartók to Alban Berg. I enjoyed them all in an uninformed way that I would have scorned in literary matters.

My attention was therefore concentrated on the people at the festival and the complex relationships among them. My impressions of these people were indelible; I never saw most of them again, yet now, fifty years later, I can call them clearly to mind, and there's nothing I would enjoy more than telling each of them the impression he then made on me. The main object of my scrutiny was the man who had organized the festival, its working heart. I studied him closely and mercilessly just as he was; not a word, not a silence, not a movement of his escaped me; at last I had before my eyes a perfect specimen of something I was determined to understand and portray: a dictator.

A banquet was held in Schirmeck, a small town in the Vosges mountains, to celebrate the end of the festival. Some of the participants would have preferred to leave sooner, but feeling that they owed H. a debt of thanks for the enormous amount of work he had done, most of them stayed on.

There we sat at long tables in the garden of an inn. A good many speeches were made. H. asked me to say a few words about my impressions of the festival. Precisely because I was a writer and not a musician, he felt it was important. I found myself in a difficult situation. How was I to tell the truth without touching on the darker aspects of H., which moreover I had not yet clearly formulated in my own mind? As it was, I praised him for his gift of bringing people together and getting them to work together. My speech may have struck him as lukewarm, he probably wanted a paean of praise, such as he got from most of the orators. Late that evening, with the official proceedings disposed of, he took his revenge.

He had been praised as a master conductor, and indeed he had done wonders with his musicians in those few weeks. He had been drinking heavily and now he wanted to relax in his own way. Apart from conducting, he had another talent that none of those present suspected: palm reading. All of a sudden he shouted that he wanted to read our palms. "Not one of you, not a few, the whole lot of you." One look at a person's hands, he said, and he knew that person's fate. "But don't shove, you'll all get your turns. Just form a line." And so we did, hesitantly at first, but once he had started on his first palm half the company rose from the long tables and formed a line. The people who had been sitting near him were taken first. He was quick, as in everything he did; he never kept a hand for long, a brief glance was enough; and his verdicts were delivered with his usual assurance. He was interested only in one thing—longevity; he had no time for character, adventures or anything else. He simply told each victim how long he would live without explaining how he arrived at his figure. He spoke no louder than usual; only those closest to him could hear what he said.

After the reading I saw satisfaction on some faces, consternation on others. All went back to their places and sat quietly down. Conversation, there was none. No one asked a returning neighbor: "What did he say?" The atmosphere had changed perceptibly. There was no more joking. Those with long lives to look forward to kept the good news to themselves. And no word of protest or lamentation was heard from those who had come off badly. H., who appeared to be deep in the study of hands, kept close track of who reported and who didn't. Most of his clients were people who meant little to him, and he dealt with them only for form's sake. Others he was obviously awaiting with eagerness. I held back for quite some time, and I could feel him glowering at me. Sitting across the table from him, I showed no sign of standing up and taking my place in line. Several times, between hands, he shot me quick glances. Finally, he looked me straight in the eye and said so loudly that the whole table could hear: "What's the matter, C., are you afraid?" I couldn't have it thought that I was afraid of his palmistry. I stood up and went to the end of the line. "No, no," he said. "Step right up. I don't want you running away on me." Reluctantly I moved up and, making an exception for me, he took me out of turn. He grabbed my hand and, before he'd even looked at it, decreed: "You won't live to be thirty." For once, he added an explanation: "This is where the life line breaks off." Dropping my hand like something he no longer had any use for, he beamed at me and hissed: "I'll live to be eighty-four. Only half my life is behind me. I'm just forty-two." "And I'm twenty-eight." "You won't live to be thirty." He said it again and shrugged his shoulders. "And you can't do one thing about it. Call that a life? What can you do with a life like that?" Even the two years allowed me were worthless. What can you do in two years?

I stepped aside. He thought he had crushed me, but the game wasn't over yet. All had to take their turns, he had to pronounce sentence on each one. With most his tone was one of bored routine, they might just as well have been flies. Others he really had it in for. I didn't always know why. My place on the other side of the table was not far away, I sat down again and listened. A few evaded his clutches, pretending to be drunk and ignoring his orders. Most came and were treated to varying fates. For those who had never thwarted him his mood was benign and they came off with a promise of middle age. None got to be eighty-four. A few harmless, compliant souls made it to their sixties. But these were not his favored targets, at whom he took closer aim. He was obviously determined to dispose of everybody. There were several women and he treated them no better than the men. All would die younger than their husbands. He wasn't interested in widows. Women who didn't have to be taken from anyone depressed his libido. I alone was doomed to die before my thirtieth birthday.

PART TWO

Dr. Sonne

A Twin Is Bestowed on Me

My *Comedy of Vanity* was written in 1933 under the impact of the events in Germany. Hitler had come to power at the end of January. Everything that happened from then on seemed sinister and of evil omen. Everything affected me deeply, I felt involved in everything, it was as though I were present at every incident I heard about. Nothing had been foreseen; measured against the reality, all explanations and calculations, even the most daring prophecies, were empty words. What had happened was in every way unexpected and new, out of all proportion to the paltry ideas that had sparked it off. These events defied understanding, yet one thing I knew: they could culminate only in war, not a shamefaced, hesitant war, but one that would come forward with the proud and gluttonous appetite of a biblical Assyrian war.

I knew this, yet cherished the hope that war could be prevented. But how could it be prevented unless the process was understood?

Since 1925 I had been trying to determine the nature of crowds, since 1931 to discover how power springs from crowds, from the masses. In all those years there was seldom a day when my thoughts did not turn to the phenomenon of crowds. I made no attempt to simplify, to make things easy for myself; I saw no point in singling out one or two aspects and neglecting all the rest. Thus it is not to be wondered at that I had not got very far. I was on the track of certain phenomena such as the connection between crowds and fire or the tendency of crowds to expand—a characteristic they share with fire—but the more I worked, the clearer it became to me that

I had taken on a task which would demand the better part of my life.

I was prepared to have patience, but events were not so patient. In 1933, the year of the great speedup which was to carry everything with it, I had as yet no theoretical answer to it and felt a strong inner need to describe something I did not understand.

A year or two before, and not at first in connection with current events, it had occurred to me that mirrors should be prohibited. When I sat in the barber chair having my hair cut, it got on my nerves to have always the same image in front of me, it seemed to hem me in. My eyes would stray to the right and left; the men to the right and left of me were fascinated by what they saw. They studied themselves, they scrutinized themselves, they made faces to broaden their knowledge of their features, they never wearied, they never seemed to get enough of themselves, and what surprised me most was that in their exclusive self-immersion they didn't seem to notice that I was watching them. These men were young and old, dignified and less dignified, totally different from one another and yet alike in one thing: all were sunk in self-worship, in adoration of their own image.

Once, while observing two especially grotesque specimens, I asked myself: What would happen if men were forbidden this most precious of moments? Could any law be stringent enough to divert men from their image and likeness? And what detours would vanity take if such a barrier were placed in its path? Imagining the consequences was an amusing game, without serious implications. But when the books were burned in Germany, when I saw what interdictions could be promulgated and enforced and how readily, taking on an imperturbable will of their own, they lent themselves to the formation of enthusiastic crowds, I was thunderstruck and came to regard my playful prohibition of mirrors as something more than a game.

I forgot everything I had read about crowds, I forgot what little insight I had gained, I cast all that behind me and started from scratch, as though confronted for the first time with so universal a phenomenon. It was then that I wrote the first part of my *Comedy of Vanity,* the great temptation. Some thirty characters, speaking in very different ways but all Viennese to the last syllable, live in a place that suggests the Prater amusement park. But it's a very special sort of Prater; its main attraction is a fire stoked by the characers, which gets bigger from scene to scene. Sound effects are provided by the crashing of mirrors that are hit by balls in galleries set up for that very purpose. The characters bring their own mirrors and pictures, the former to smash, the latter to burn. A barker accompanies this plebeian entertainment with his spiel, in which the word heard most frequently is "We!" The scenes are arranged in a kind of spiral, first long ones, in which characters and events explain one another, then shorter and shorter ones. More and more, everything relates to the fire; at first it is far away, then it comes closer and closer, until in the end one of the characters *becomes* fire by throwing himself into it.

I can still feel the passion of those weeks in my bones. There was a heat in me, as though I myself were the character who becomes fire. But despite the rage that drove me on, I had to avoid every imprecise word and I champed at the bit. The crowd formed before my eyes, in my ears, but in my thinking I was far from having mastered it. Like the old porter Franzl Nada, I collapsed under the weight of mirrors. Like Franzi, his sister, I was arrested and imprisoned because of my lost brother. Like Wondrak the barker, I lashed the masses on; like Emilie Fant, I screamed heartlessly, hypocritically, for my heartless child. I myself became the most monstrous characters and sought my justification in the downtrodden whom I loved.

I have forgotten none of these characters. Every one

of them is more alive for me than the people I knew at that time. Every fire that had made an impression on me since my childhood went into the fire in which those pictures were burned.

The heat in which I wrote those scenes was still with me when I went to Strasbourg. I was still in the middle of the first part when I started out and, strange to say, my hectic weeks in that city did not blur my vision of the *Comedy*. It was more firmly performed in my mind than anything else I have written. I spent the September after the festival in Paris, and there I took up just where I had left off in Vienna. When I finished the first part, I was intoxicated with it. I had done something new, I thought, presented the story of a crowd in dramatic form, shown how it formed, increased in density and released its charge. A good deal of the second part was also written in Paris. I knew how it would continue; even the third part was clear in my mind.

I did not feel defeated on my return to Vienna. Anna's cold rebuff had hit me hard, but it did not destroy me as it might have at another time. Under the protection of my *Comedy*, I felt so safe that I called Anna as if nothing had happened, and arranged to see her at her studio. On the phone I made myself sound as cool and indifferent as she actually was, and that pleased her. She was relieved that I made no reference to what there had been between us; she detested scenes, reproaches, bitterness, lamentation. She was pleased with herself for having acted on her strongest impulse, which was to preserve her freedom, yet when I spoke of my *Comedy*, which I had mentioned before leaving, she expressed interest, though she cared little for plays. I hadn't expected real sympathy.

Ever since she had known me, she had wanted me to meet Fritz Wotruba, her young teacher; before I went to Strasbourg he had been away from Vienna; now he was back. She said she would ask him to come on the day of my visit and we could have lunch together in her studio. This was a good idea on her part. It would be our first meeting since the break. Crossing the garden; the crunching of the gravel, which seemed much louder than I remembered; the greenhouse that served her as a studio; Anna in the same blue smock, but a little to one side of the figure that was standing in the center of the studio; her fingers not in the clay; her arms at her sides; her eyes resting on a young man who, kneeling beside the figure, was working on the lower part of it with his fingers. He had his back turned to me and didn't stand up when I came in. He didn't remove his fingers from the clay but kept kneading it. Still kneeling, he turned his head toward me and said in a deep, full voice: "Do you kneel at your work too?" It was a joke, a kind of excuse for not getting up and giving me his hand. But with him even a joke had weight and meaning. With the word "too" he bade me welcome, put his work and mine on the same level; with "kneel" he expressed the hope that I took my work as seriously as he took his.

It was a good beginning. Of this first conversation I remember only the sentence with which it began. But I see him clearly before me as soon afterward he sat across the table from me, busy with his schnitzel. Anna had had lunch served for us, she herself did not sit with us. She stood there, took a few steps around the studio from time to time, then came back to the table and listened. She participated only in part. Food meant nothing to her. She could work for days without bothering to eat. But this time it was out of kindness that she did not sit down; she wanted to do something for me, but she was thinking also of Wotruba, whom she respected for his work in hard stone and his unswerving determination. That was why she tried to help him and had become his first pupil. She felt she was doing a good deed in bringing us together and left us to our first conversation without taking part or attracting attention to herself. She showed great tact on that occasion, for if she had left the room entirely we should have felt like domestics, having their meals served in some far corner. She busied herself around the studio but kept coming back to us, stood listening to our conversation as though standing there to wait on us, but didn't stay long for fear that her presence would distract us. A few months before, she wouldn't have let a single word of such a conversation escape her. She had decided then that she cared for me and acted accordingly. Now that she had decided the opposite, she was able to be tactful and leave us to our conversation.

But eating interfered with our talk. My attention was held by Wotruba's hands, long, sinewy, powerful, but wonderfully sensitive hands that seemed to be creatures in their own right with a language of their own. I began to look at them instead of listening to his words, they were the most beautiful hands I had ever seen. His voice, which had appealed to me with that one sentence, left me for the moment, it meant nothing to me compared with my first impression of those hands. That may be why I've forgotten our conversation. He cut meat, almost perfectly square chunks of meat, which he raised with quick decision to his mouth. The impression was more of determination than of greed, the cutting appeared to be more important than the swallowing, but it seemed unthinkable that the fork would stop halfway, that he would ask a question or fail to open his mouth because his companion had said something. The morsel vanished inexorably, followed in quick time by the next.

The schnitzels were shot through with gristle, which I did my best to remove from mine before eating. I found more and more of it, I kept cutting it out, and what I removed remained on my plate. All this twisting and turning and doubting, this poking and excising, this obvious reluctance to eat what had been set before me, contrasted so strongly with his way of eating that for all his concentration on his plate he noticed it. His movements slowed down a little, he looked at the battlefield on my plate, it was as though we had been served two entirely different dishes or belonged to two different species. Our conversation, which had been interrupted by the earnestness of his eating process, took on a different character: he expressed amazement.

He was amazed at this creature across the table from him, who treated meat so disrespectfully. At length he asked me if I was going to *leave* all that. I said something about the gristle; gristle meant nothing to him, he ate every speck of his square chunks. You couldn't fuss over so perfect a shape. Poking around in meat repelled him. This first meeting left him with an impression of fuzziness, and as I later found out, he passed his impression on to his wife when he got home.

In those days, while Fritz Wotruba was becoming my close friend—we soon regarded each other as twin brothers—my self-confidence as a writer attained a high point. To the aggressiveness I had known and admired in Karl Kraus was now added that of the sculptor, whose work consisted of daily blows on hardest stone. Wotruba was the most uncompromising man I have ever known; whatever we discussed or did together had a dramatic character. He felt infinite contempt for people who made things easy for themselves, accepted compromises or perhaps didn't even know what they wanted. Like two superior beings, we rushed through the streets of Vienna. Wotruba always rushed; suddenly, forcefully he arrived, demanded or took what he wanted and rushed away before one could even tell if he was pleased with it. I liked this kind of motion, which was known to all and feared by some.

I felt closest to Wotruba in his studio. Two vaulted

enclosures under the Stadtbahn tracks had been assigned
to him by the city. In one—or outside it in good weather—
he hacked away at his stone. When I went to see him
there for the first time, he was busy with a recumbent
female figure. He struck powerful blows and I could see
how much the hardness of the stone meant to him.
Suddenly he would jump from one part of the figure to
another and apply his chisel with renewed fury. It was
clear that his hands were all-important to him, that he
was utterly dependent on them; and yet he seemed to be
biting into the stone. He was a black panther, a panther
that fed on stone, that clawed at it and bit into it. You
never knew at what point he would attack it next. It was
these leaps that reminded me most of the great cats, but
they didn't start from a distance, he leapt from one point
on the figure to another. He attacked each point with
concentrated energy, with the force of a leap from some
distance.

During my first visit—he was working on a funerary
statue of the singer Selma Kurz—the leaps came from
above; that may be why I couldn't help thinking of a
panther, leaping on its victim from a tree. He seemed to
be tearing his victim to pieces. But how can one tear
granite to pieces? Despite his somber concentration I
didn't forget for a moment what he was contending with.
I watched him a long time. Not *once* did he smile. He
knew I was watching him, but there was nothing amiable
about his look. This was deadly serious work with granite.
I realized he was showing himself as he really was. He
was so strong by nature that he had sought out the most
difficult of occupations. To him *hardness* and difficulty
were one. When he suddenly leapt away, it was as though
he expected the stone to strike back, and was dodging in
anticipation. He was enacting a murder. It took me a long
time to realize that to him murder was a necessity. This
was no hidden murder that left only obscure traces; he

kept at it until a monument remained behind. Usually he committed his murder alone; sometimes, however, he felt the need to commit it in the presence of others, though without changing in any way, entirely himself, not as an actor but as a murderer. He needed someone who understood how very serious he was about it. It has been said that art is play; his was not. He might have populated the city and the whole world with his deeds. I had gone there with the prevailing opinion that what mattered to the sculptor was the *permanence* of the stone, which secured his work against decay. When I saw him at work, engaged in his inexplicable action, I realized that what mattered to him in the stone was its *hardness* and nothing else. He had to do battle with it. He needed stone as others need bread. But it had to be the hardest stone and he enacted its hardness.

From the first I took Wotruba seriously; he was usually serious. Words always had meaning for him; he spoke when he *wanted* something, then his words *demanded*. And when he spoke to me of something that weighed on him, he meant what he said—how few people there are whose words count. It was probably my hatred of business that led me to look for such words. The way people dither with words, trot them out only to take them back, the way their contours are blurred, the way they are made to merge and melt though still present, to refract like prisms, to take on opalescent colors, to come forward before they themselves want to; the cowardice, the slavishness that is imposed on them—how sick I was of seeing words thus debased, for I took them so seriously that I even disliked distorting them for playful purposes, I wanted them *intact*, and I wanted them to carry their full force. I recognized that everyone uses them in his own way, distorts them in a way that does not clash with his better knowledge, that is not playful, that corresponds to the speaker's innermost being—such a distortion I respected and left it untouched,

I would not have dared lay hands on it, to *explain* it would have repelled me most of all. I had been captivated by the terrible seriousness of words; it prevailed in every language, and through it every language became inviolable.

Wotruba had this terrible seriousness of words. I met him after suffering the opposite for a year and a half in F., another friend. For him words had no inviolable meaning; their purpose was seduction and they could be twisted this way and that. A word could mean one thing, it could mean another, it could change its meaning in a matter of hours, even though it referred to such apparently stubborn realities as convictions. I saw F. take in my statements, I saw my words become his, so much so that I myself might not have recognized where they came from. At times he could use my words in arguing against me or, what was even more striking, against himself. He would smile ecstatically while surprising me with a sentence he had heard from me the day before; he would expect applause and he may even have thought he was being original. But as he was careless, something was always different, with the result that in the new formulation my own idea repelled me. Then I would argue against it and he seemed to think we were debating, that opinion was fighting opinion, while in reality an opinion was fighting its distortion, and he had distinguished himself only by the ease with which he had distorted it.

Wotruba, on the other hand, knew what he had said and did not forget it. Nor did he forget what others had said. Our conversation was a sort of wrestling match. Both bodies were always present, they didn't slip away; they remained impermeable. It may sound incredible when I say it was my passionate conversations with him that first taught me what *stone* is. In him I did not expect to find pity for others. Kindness in him would have seemed absurd. He was interested in two things and in them alone: the power of stone and the power of words, in both cases power, but in so unusual a combination of its elements that one took it as a force of nature, no more open to criticism than a storm.

The "Black Statue"

In the first months of our friendship I had never seen Marian without Fritz Wotruba. Together they came plunging toward me, together they stopped close to me. Since there was always some undertaking to talk about, something that had to be done, a stubborn enemy who stood in the way of a commission, a creature of the official Vienna art world, against whom it would be necessary to pit another more favorably inclined, since Marian was the battering ram that resolutely assaulted every wall, and since it was her nature to report on every detail of her battle, Wotruba let her do the talking, merely punctuating the flow now and then with a grunt of confirmation. But even the little he said on such occasions sounded Viennese to the last syllable, whereas Marian's rushing torrent, which nothing and no one could interrupt, rolled on in High German with a barely noticeable Rhenish tinge. She was from Düsseldorf, but to judge by her manner of speaking she could have been from anywhere in Germany—except the south. She spoke urgently and monotonously, without rise or fall, without punctuation or articulation, above all without pauses. Once she got started, she chattered on mercilessly, not a chance of getting away before she had said it *all*, and her reports were always interminable, she was never heard to deliver a short one.

There was no escape. Everyone turned to stone in her presence. You couldn't just *pretend* to listen. She spoke with such emphasis that you were doomed to take in every sentence; it was—as I realize only now—a hammering to which one could only submit. Yet she was never trying to force *my* hand, I was merely a friend to whom she was reporting. How the actual victims of her assaults must have felt I hardly dare imagine. For them there was only one way to get rid of her: to grant what she wanted for Fritz. If she was interrupted, either because an office closed at a certain hour or because her victim was called to the phone or summoned by a superior, she would come again and again. No wonder she won out in the end.

She came to Vienna as a young girl and studied under Anton Hanak; it was in Hanak's studio that she met Fritz Wotruba. She had lived in Vienna ever since, but had acquired no trace of a Viennese accent, though for many years exposed day after day to Wotruba's thick Viennese. He remained fanatically true to the language he had absorbed as a child on the streets of Vienna. He never learned a foreign tongue. When in later years he attempted a few words of English or French, he sounded ridiculous—like a stammering petitioner or a crippled beggar. Like all Viennese, he could produce some sort of bureaucratic High German when necessary, and then, as he was intelligent and *wrote* good German, he did not sound ridiculous. But he did this so unwillingly, it made him feel so cramped, that one suffered with him and sighed with relief when he reverted to himself and his native intonations. Of these, Marian, who lived entirely for him and his interests, who had long ago given up her own sculpture for his sake, who never had a child, who spoke incessantly and spoke *his* thoughts, never acquired the slightest trace. What she heard from him was immediately converted into action. When she sallied forth on her expeditions, she heard nothing and thought of nothing but what she wanted to get for Fritz. She talked and talked, nothing else could get to her. When he was present, her talk didn't bother him—not then at least. When I was alone with him, he told me, I believe, everything that passed through his head or that weighed on him. But not once did he complain about Marian's chatter. Occasionally he would disappear for a few days; Marian was wild with worry, she went looking for him everywhere, and sometimes I went with her. But I don't think it was her flow of words he ran away from, it was his early fame, the art business in which he felt caught; or perhaps it was something deeper, the *stone* he wrestled with may have been a kind of prison to him, and he feared nothing so much as imprisonment. I never saw him so moved to pity as by caged lions and tigers.

They invited me to lunch at 31 Florianigasse, where he had always lived. He was the youngest of eight children. Now only he and Marian lived there with his mother and his youngest sister. His mother would cook, that way the three of us would be able to sit quietly and eat. They had told his mother about me. She was full of curiosity and choleric by nature. If you vexed her, she would throw a dish at your head, and you'd better duck quickly. You had to pass through the kitchen to reach the living room. But the room, he assured me, was beautiful because Marian had decorated it to her own taste, it was a good place to sit and talk. He would call for me, because if I had to go through the kitchen by myself, I might get a dish thrown at me. I asked him if his mother objected to my visit. Not at all, she was looking forward to it, she herself was making the schnitzels, she was a good cook. Then why should she throw a dish at me? You never can tell, he said, sometimes for no reason at all; she likes to get mad. When he was late for meals, for instance. When he was working, out under the Stadtbahn tracks, he'd

forget everything else and be two hours late for dinner.
Then the dishes would fly, but none had ever hit him.
He was used to it; she was temperamental, a Hungarian
from the country, she had walked all the way to Vienna
as a young girl and found employment in good house-
holds. Then she had to hold her temperament down, she
had saved it up for her eight children. They had given
her a rough time, she had let it out on them. "If we're
late she'll give us hell, she doesn't always throw dishes."

The appointment was made. He insisted on escorting
me. The subject made him more talkative than usual.
Ordinarily so carefree and self-assured, he seemed worried and nervous. He respected his mother, he admired
her for the very things that he warned me about. He
seemed to be giving her a buildup for my benefit. She
looked emaciated, but that was deceptive, she was tough
and wiry and no one could get the better of her. When
she gave you a clout, you didn't forget it. She always wore
a headscarf, the same as in her Hungarian village. She
had never changed, after all these years in Vienna she
was still her same old self. Wasn't she proud of him? I
asked. You could never be sure, she never showed it, but
maybe to a visitor. Writers impressed her. She liked to
read books, but you had to watch your step.

He was almost an hour late in picking me up. I was
nervous after all he had told me. He seemed to be looking
forward to a clash with his mother. "Today you'll see
something," he said when he finally arrived. "We'd better
hurry." He never apologized for being late, though this
time he might have offered an explanation. I was on edge,
I could feel a dish hitting me in the face long before we
turned into Florianigasse. As we entered the kitchen, he
raised his forefinger in warning. His mother was standing
at the stove, I first saw her headscarf, then the small,
slightly bent form. She didn't say a word, she didn't even
turn around. Her son shook his head in alarm and

whispered to me: "Oh-oh! Take care." We had to cross the whole kitchen. He ducked and pulled me down with him. We had just reached the open doorway of the living room when the dish came, well aimed but too high. Then she wiped her hands on her apron and came over to us. "I ain't talking to him," she said to me in a high-pitched Hungarian singsong, and gave me a hearty welcome. "He does it on purpose," she said. "He likes his friends to see his mother angry." She'd known he'd be late so as to make her do her number. So she had waited before starting her schnitzels. "That way they won't be dry and I hope you like them."

In the living room the glass tabletop and the steel-pipe chairs gleamed, an extreme modernism, which fitted in with Marian's intentions if not with her personality. On the white walls hung pictures by Merkel and Dobrowsky, gifts from the painters to the young sculptor, who embodied the avant-garde of the Sezession, its most controversial member. The absence of any superfluous object in the room made the pictures especially striking. I was attracted most by Merkel's Arcadian landscapes, with which I was already familiar. There was no door between kitchen and living room, only the open doorway. My friend's mother did not come into the living room, but she heard every word and, at least with her ears, participated intensely in the conversation. The dishes were handed in through a serving hatch. Marian took them from there and put them on the glass table. There lay the giant schnitzels; they were the meal. Wotruba assured me there would be no gristle in them, I'd better not pick at them as I had done at Anna's, his mother would be offended. Then he bent over his meat and ate it without a word, in big square chunks. Not once did he take his eyes off his meat and as long as there was anything on the plate he didn't join in the conversation with so much as a syllable or a gesture.

Marian monopolized the conversation. First she went on about my sin at Anna's studio, when I had cut the gristle out of my meat and left half of it standing; my plate had been strewn with spurned bits and pieces, in all his life Fritz had never seen anything like it. "There was a nervous character at Anna Mahler's," he had said the moment he got home, and he'd given her a demonstration of what I'd done to my meat, he'd brought it up every day at table; that had aroused her curiosity, they'd come to the conclusion that I was an enemy not only of gristle but of meat in general, and now we'd see if that was the case. She soon saw that in their house it was not, and when I had finished, a second, equally gigantic schnitzel appeared on my plate without my being consulted. Marian apologized, they didn't eat much else, there was never any dessert, Fritz hated cheese, from childhood on he'd never touched it, or compote for that matter, he couldn't bear to see fruit cut into little pieces. On hearing such statements I turned to him with a questioning look, and he grunted confirmation; he was incapable of saying a word as long as he had meat on his plate. I took an interest in everything concerning him, especially in practical matters, otherwise I'd have run away; as it was, I listened as raptly as if she had been talking about his sculptures. His mother called in from the kitchen: "Is he eating it, or is he messing it up again?" So she too had been told of our first meeting. Marian carried out my empty plate, to prove that I had left nothing. Whereupon I was offered a third schnitzel, which I declined amid words of praise for the first two.

When Fritz had finished eating, he found his tongue again and I heard some interesting things. I asked him if he had started right in with his *stones*, for his hands didn't look as if he had always worked in stone. I have already said how very sensitive they were; when we shook hands, I was never indifferent to their touch, in all the many years of our friendship I never ceased to feel it, but at first they awakened in me the memory of two different hands that were close together in a picture, each so vivid that neither was dominant. I thought of God's finger in *The Creation of Adam* on the ceiling of the Sistine Chapel. I can't explain it, for life passes into Adam's hand from a single finger and here I was shaking a whole hand, but evidently I felt the life-giving force that passed from God's finger into the future man. And I also thought of Adam himself, of his whole hand.

Stones, he said, had come early, but he hadn't begun with stone. When still a small boy, no more than five years old, he had scratched the putty out of the windows to model with it. The panes came loose, one fell out and smashed. He was found out and beaten. He did it again, he had to model and he had nothing else to do it with. Bread was harder to get, there were eight children, and putty was easier to handle; he was beaten again, but by his mother, which was nothing compared to what his father dished out.

His father beat his elder brothers so hard that they became criminals. But I didn't hear that until later; he seldom spoke of his father, whom all the children hated, never within earshot of his mother. He was a Czech tailor and had long been dead. Fritz's eldest brother had been sent to jail for murder and armed robbery, he had died miserably in Stein on the Danube. This Fritz confided to me only after we had become twins. The stigma of violence weighed heavily on him, and when I heard the story of this brother, I began to understand his strange way of fighting stone. The police had always kept an eye on the Wotruba brothers. Fritz, the youngest, much younger than his recalcitrant brothers, couldn't show himself on Florianigasse without being stopped by a policeman. Still a small boy, he had seen his father whipping his brothers with a leather belt and heard their desperate screams. His father's cruelty repelled him more than his brothers' crimes. He felt sure that those beatings had made criminals of his brothers. But when he thought of his father's brutality, it also occurred to him that the sons may have *inherited* these qualities.

Fear of this heredity had never left him; his dread of imprisonment entered into his daily battle with stone. Stone of the hardest, densest kind held him captive; he dug into it, he dug deeper and deeper. For hours each day he battled with it, stone became so important to him that he could not live without it, as important, not as bread, but as meat. It is hard to believe, but his work owes its existence to the conflict between his father and his brothers, and to the fate of his brothers. No sign of this is noticeable in the finished work; the connection is so deep that it entered into the stone itself. One must know his history, his recurrent escapes, his passionate love for caged animals—he felt more sympathy for a captive tiger than he could for any human—his fear of having children, because the killing instinct might be hereditary. Instead of a son he kept a tomcat. One had to know all this (and a lot more) to understand why he had to get so far away from the flesh quality of stone, which is present in such early works as the famous torso.

When I saw him in this room, furnished along Bauhaus lines, but with Arcadian pictures by Georg Merkel and elegant Dobrowskys on the walls, while the rest of the apartment, especially the kitchen, remained as it had been in the days of the battering father, in whose place the mother now ruled—but what were a few hurled and smashed dishes compared with the father's never-ending hard blows?—when her choleric campaign against unpunctuality and his dish-dodging act were staged for my benefit, how could I have suspected that all this added up to an achievement, to a step on the road to civilization? For the father was gone, the brother was in jail or already dead—and in their stead this foolery with his mother, the privileged position of this woman who had survived so much and now, thanks to her youngest son, had come to a new life, a life worthy of her, but relinquishing no part of the old locale—the apartment, the kitchen, the cobblestones of Florianigasse.

On my first visit to the studio under the Stadtbahn tracks, I saw a large black basalt figure of a standing man. No work by a living sculptor had ever moved me so. I stood facing it, I heard the rumbling of the Stadtbahn trains overhead. I stood there so long that I heard several trains. In my memory I can't separate the figure from the sound. A difficult work, it had taken him a long time and had come into being amid this noise. There were other figures to look at, though not too many. The studio didn't seem overcrowded; it consisted of two big vaults supporting the Stadtbahn trestle; in one stood figures that would have got in his way while he was working in the other. When the weather wasn't too bad, he liked best to work in the open. At first I was put off by the plainness of the studio and the noise of the trains, but since nothing here was superfluous, since everything appealed to me and had a function, I soon got used to the place and sensed that it was right and couldn't have been more appropriate.

But much as I wished to show respect for the artist, I didn't look closely enough at most of the things, because the "Black Statue," as we called it from then on, held me fast. It was as though I had come for its sake. I tried to tear myself away from it, I felt called upon to say something, but it struck me dumb. Wherever I stood, whatever I tried to look at, it was always to the "Black Statue" that my eyes returned. I viewed it from every possible angle and showed it the greatest honor by the silence it instilled in me.

This figure has disappeared. According to Wotruba, it was buried during the war and never found again. It had been much criticized and he may have wanted to disown it. When events parted us—he took refuge in Switzerland, I in England—he may have been put off by my passion for this figure, and since in our havens we had gone entirely different ways he may not, on returning to Vienna, have wished to be associated with work he had done at the age of twenty-five. It is true that my constant talk about this figure barred his way to new things. I was as persistent as he was and my persistence got on his nerves. When he first visited me in London after the war, I measured everything he had done since by the "Black Statue" and made no secret of my disappointment. His really new period, with which, as I alone perceived, he continued and greatly surpassed the work of his early days, began only in 1950. Thus the work that formed a link between us disappeared; it dominated my view of him from autumn 1933 when I first saw it up to the day in 1954, twenty-one years later, when I wrote an essay about him, no word of which I ever want to change.

Today I am well aware of the weaknesses that can be found in the "Black Statue." Accordingly, I shall confine my remarks to what the figure meant to me that first day.

Black and larger than life, it held one hand, the left, hidden behind its back. The upper arm protruded strikingly from the body and formed a right angle with the forearm. Thus the elbow stood out aggressively, as though preparing to repulse anyone who came too close. The empty triangle, bounded by the chest and the two parts of the arm, the only empty space in the figure, had a menacing quality; this was related to the missing hand, which could not be seen and which I felt the need of locating. It seemed to be hidden, not cut off. I didn't dare look for it, the spell I was under forbade me to change my position. Before embarking on the inevitable search,

I satisfied myself that the other hand was visible. The right side of the figure was at rest. The right arm lay extended along the body, the open hand reaching almost to the knee; it seemed quiet, charged with no hostile intent. It was so still that I gave it no thought, because the other hand was so conspicuously hidden.

The egg-shaped head sat on a powerful neck that tapered slightly at the top; it would otherwise have been wider than the head. The narrow face, flattened toward the front, stern and silent, despite its simplification more face than mask; the slitlike mouth firmly and painfully closed to any confession. Chest and belly divided circumscribed areas, as flat as the face, overshadowed by strong cylindrical shoulders, the knees stylized and almost semispherical, the big feet pointing clearly forward, side by side, enlarged, indispensable for the weight of the basalt; the sexual parts not hidden and not obtrusive, less explicitly formed than the rest.

But the moment came when I tore myself loose in search of the withdrawn hand. And unexpectedly I found it, enormous, stretched across the lower part of the back; palm outward, larger than life even measured by the rest of the figure. I was stunned at the power of this hand. It betrayed no evil intent, but it was capable of anything. To this day I am convinced that the figure was created for the sake of this hand, and that the man who hewed it from basalt *had* to hide it, because it was too powerful, that this was the secret the mouth which refused to speak was keeping, and that the elbow thrust menacingly outward was barring access to it.

I went to that studio innumerable times. My passion for that figure became the heart of our friendship. For hours I watched Wotruba's hands at work and wearied no more than he did. But excited as I might be by whatever new piece he was working on, I never turned to it without first paying homage to the "Black Statue."

Sometimes I found it in the open; expecting my visit, Fritz had rolled it out for me. Sometimes he put it behind the open door of one of the vaults; there I could see it all by itself and no other figure got in the way. I never spoke of the *hand*; we talked about innumerable things, but he was much too perceptive to fail to see that I had fathomed something that he could only say in basalt, because he was much too proud to say it in words. One of his brothers was Cain, who had killed, and all his life he was tormented by fear that he would have to kill. He owed it to stone that he never did, and in the "Black Statue" he divulged, to me at least, the threat that he lived with.

This figure may have embodied his most immutable essence. His language also partook of it. His words were charged with the strength that enabled him to hold them back. He was not a silent man and he expressed opinions on many matters. But he knew what he was saying, I have never heard idle chatter from his lips. Even when he was not talking about his main interest, his words always had *direction*. When he was trying to win someone over, he could say things that sounded like crass calculation. But then he would trot out some gross exaggeration in an attempt to pass it off as a joke, though he never wavered in his purpose. Or he could also set all purpose aside and speak so clearly and forcefully that his interlocutor was moved to speak clearly and forcefully in his turn. At such times, he never borrowed an alien language, he always expressed himself in the idiom of the Viennese district with whose cobblestones he had played as a child, and one was amazed to find that everything, literally everything, could be said in that language. It was *not* the language of Nestroy, which had shown me long ago that there was a Viennese idiom full of startling possibilities, an idiom that fostered delightful bursts of inspiration, an idiom both comical and profound, inexhaustible, varied, sublime in its acuteness, which no man of this hapless century can completely master. Perhaps Wotruba's language had only one thing in common with Nestroy's: its hardness, the exact opposite of the sweetness for which Vienna is famed and ill-famed throughout the world.

I speak of him as he was *then*, at the age of twenty-six, when I first met him, obsessed by stone and by purposes inseparable from stone, unrecognized, full of an ambition in which he did not doubt for one moment, as sure of his plans as I was of mine, so that we immediately, without diffidence, without hesitation, shame or presumption, felt ourselves to be brothers. To each other we could say things that no one else would have understood, because in talking to each other we found it quite natural to reveal things that had to be guarded against others. His cruelty put me off and my "morality" put him off. But magnanimously each found excuses for the other. I explained his cruelty by the hardness of his work processes. He interpreted my "morality" as my need to safeguard the purity of my artistic purpose, and put it on a plane with his own exalted ambition. When he proclaimed his hatred of kitsch, I was with him heart and soul. As I heard it, he was talking about corruption. To me kitsch was what you did for money alone, to him it was something soft and easy to model. In childhood I had felt threatened by money, he by his brother's imprisonment.

I gave him the manuscript of *Kant Catches Fire* to read. He was no less overwhelmed by it than I by the "Black Statue." He fell in love with Fischerle. He knew the surroundings in which Fischerle lived, and he knew the obsessiveness of such ambition. He thought the unscrupulousness of the chess dwarf perfectly plausible; he himself would have stopped at nothing to lay hands on a block of stone. He did not find Therese "overdone," he had seen harder people. He liked the sharp delineation of the characters; naturally Benedikt Pfaff, the pensioned policeman, struck him as right, and so—to my great surprise—did the sexless sinologist; it was only the sinologist's psychiatrist brother that he couldn't stomach. Hadn't I, he asked me, gone wrong out of love for my youngest brother, whom I had told him about? No one, he insisted, could have so many skins; I had constructed an ideal character; what a writer does in his books Georges Kien did in his life. He liked the "gorilla," and by comparison hated the doctor. Essentially he saw the "gorilla" as Georges Kien himself saw him, but he found fault with Georges for submitting to conversion; Wotruba distrusted conversions at the time and told me that he even preferred Jean the blacksmith, that narrow-minded old man, to the successful psychiatrist. He gave me credit for making him come to grief at the end of the book and having him bring about the sinologist's fiery death by an ill-advised speech. Georges's abysmal failure, Wotruba once told me, had reconciled him to the character.

Silence at the Café Museum

At the Café Museum, where I went every day after moving back to town, there was a man whom I noticed because he was always sitting alone and never spoke to anyone. That in itself was not so unusual, lots of people went to cafés to be alone among many. What struck me about this man was that he was invariably hiding behind his newspaper and that on the rare occasions when he did show his face it was the well-known face of Karl Kraus. I knew he couldn't be Karl Kraus, he wouldn't have had a moment's peace in the midst of all those artists, writers and musicians. But even without being Karl Kraus, he seemed determined to hide. His face was grave and unlike Karl Kraus's impassive mien. Sometimes I thought I detected a vaguely sorrowful look, which I attributed to his constant newspaper reading. I caught myself waiting for the rare moments when his face became visible. Often I put my own newspaper aside to make sure that he was still immersed in his. Every time I entered the Café Museum, I looked around for him. Since his face was not to be seen, I recognized him by the rigidity of the arm that held his newspaper—a dangerous object that he clung to, that he would have liked to put aside but went on reading with rapt attention. I tried to choose a seat from which I could keep my eye on him, if possible obliquely across from him. I began to attach great importance to his silence; it intimidated me, and I would never have sat down at an empty table in his immediate vicinity. I too was usually alone, I knew few of the habitués of the Museum, and I had no more desire than he did to be disturbed. I would sit across from him for an hour or more, waiting for the moments when he might show his face. I kept my distance; without knowing who he was I had great respect for him. I felt his concentration as if he *had* been Karl Kraus, but a silent Karl Kraus such as I had never encountered.

He was there every day; usually he was there when I arrived, I couldn't have dared suppose that he was waiting for me. But when he chanced not to be there, I was impatient, as though I had been waiting for him. I only pretended to steep myself in my paper, I kept looking toward the entrance and I couldn't have said what I was reading. In the end he always turned up, a tall, thin figure with the stiff, dismissive, almost arrogant gait of a man who didn't wish to be importuned and was wary of windbags. I remember my surprise when I first saw him walking; he seemed to be riding toward me, and he could not have held himself more erect if he had been in a saddle. I had expected a smaller man with a bent back. It was the head which showed that amazing resemblance. As soon as he was seated, he was Karl Kraus again, hidden behind the newspapers he was gunning for.

For a year and a half I saw him in this way, he became a silent element in my life. I mentioned him to no one and made no inquiries. If he had stopped coming, I would probably have ended by asking the waiter about him.

At that time I sensed that a change was taking place in my attitude toward Karl Kraus. I was none too eager to see him and I did not attend all his readings. But I did not impugn him in my thoughts and I doubt if I would have dared to contradict him. I could not bear to hear him utter an inconsistency, and even when it was something I couldn't quite put my finger on, I wanted him to stop talking. Thus his likeness at the Café Museum, which I saw day after day, became a necessity for me. It was a likeness and not a double, for when he was standing or walking he had nothing in common with Karl Kraus; but when he sat reading the paper, the resemblance was unmistakable. He never wrote anything down, he took no notes. He just read and hid. He was never reading a book, and though I had a feeling that he must be a big reader, he read only newspapers.

I myself was in the habit of jotting down one thing and another at the café and I did not like to think of his watching me. To write in his presence struck me as insulting. When he peered out for a moment, I quietly lowered my pencil. I was always on the qui vive, eager for a look at his face, which would quickly vanish. The air of innocence I put on at such times must have fooled him. I don't think he ever caught me writing. I was sure, though, that he saw not only me but everything around him, that he disapproved of what he saw, and that that was why he went back into concealment so quickly. I felt sure he was a genius at seeing through people, possibly because I knew Karl Kraus to be one. It didn't take him long, he didn't persist, and perhaps, or so I hoped, it didn't greatly matter to him because he was concerned with important things; obviously the newspapers sickened him. Printer's errors had become a matter of indifference to him. He sang no Offenbach, he didn't sing at all, he had realized that his voice was not for singing. He read foreign newspapers, not just Viennese or German. An English paper lay at the top of the pile the waiter brought him.

I was glad he had no name. For once I knew his name, he wouldn't be Karl Kraus anymore, and the great man would cease to undergo the transformation that I so fervently desired. Only later did I realize that this silent relationship brought about a cleavage. Little by little, my veneration detached itself from Karl Kraus and turned to his silent likeness. My psychological economy, in which veneration has always played a prominent part, was undergoing a profound change, all the more profound because it took place in silence.

Comedy in Hietzing

Three months after my return from Strasbourg and Paris, I finished my *Comedy of Vanity*. The sureness with which I wrote the second and third parts gave me great satisfaction. This work was not born in pain. It was not written against myself; it was not a judgment on myself; it was not written in self-mockery. On the surface I was writing about vanity, taking a candid view of the world, about

which I had misgivings. In my handling of the basic idea,
the interdiction of mirrors and images, I had submitted
in the second part to the influence of the man whom I
regarded and still regard as the richest and most stimulating writer of comedies, Aristophanes, and my frank
admission of this, despite the enormous distance between
him and me or anyone else, may have helped me to write
more freely than usual. For it is not enough to admire a
predecessor and to recognize that he cannot be equaled.
One must venture a leap in his direction and run the risk
that it will fail and bury one in ridicule. One must take
care not to *use* the unattainable as though it were just
right for one's own purposes, but to let oneself be stim-
ulated and inspired by it.

It may have been because of my confidence in this
model that I hoped my *Comedy* could be an immediate
success. I felt a keen sense of urgency, things were moving
faster and faster in Germany, but I did not yet regard
the situation as irreversible. What had been set in motion
by words could be stopped by words. Once my *Comedy*
was finished, I thought it an appropriate answer to the
burning of the books. I wanted it to be played immediately,
everywhere. But I had no connections in the theatrical
world. Still inhibited by Karl Kraus's condemnation of
the modern theater, I had despised and neglected it.
True, in 1932 I had sent *The Wedding* to the S. Fischer
Verlag in Berlin, which accepted it for its theatrical agency,
but it was already too late in the day and a production
was out of the question. The reader responsible for
accepting *The Wedding* had left Berlin and was now head
of the drama department at the Zsolnay Verlag in Vienna.

To appreciate the *Comedy*, one had to *hear* it; it was
based on what I have called acoustic masks; each character
was clearly demarcated from all the others by choice of
words, intonation and rhythm, and there was no way of
showing this in writing. My intentions could be made clear

only by a complete reading. At this point Anna suggested that I should read the play at the Zsolnays' to a small audience of persons with theatrical taste and experience. It would of course be attended by the reader who knew *The Wedding* and who in Berlin had spontaneously, knowing nothing about me, come out for it. The suggestion appealed to me, my only misgiving was the *length* of the play.

"It takes four hours," I said. "I refuse to omit a single scene. Or a single sentence. Who can stand that?"

"You can do it in two two-hour sessions," Anna suggested. "If possible on two successive days."

She hadn't read the play, but after reading my novel, which she praised wherever she went, she was sure that the play I had told her so much about would go over. True, she had little enthusiasm for the theater, in fact she seemed to have an innate distaste for it. I had aroused an interest in this play by telling her about it, and my storytelling was the one thing about me she liked.

Paul Zsolnay's mother, whom Anna called "Aunt Andy," was the dominant figure in the family; she had great influence on her son. She had been largely instrumental in founding the publishing house as a "home" for Werfel. A number of then reputed authors and a few of undoubted excellence, such as Heinrich Mann, had been recruited. Anna had given her mother-in-law the manuscript of *Kant Catches Fire* to read, and she, who was not unacquainted with women's capacity for evil, had been taken with it. The house on Maxingstrasse was hers and she was the actual hostess, though the invitations to the reading were sent out by Anna. I had expressed the urgent wish that her mother, Alma, should *not* be present. Anna assured me there was no danger, I was much too unknown, her mother wouldn't dream of coming. But Werfel would come in her stead; he was curious; formerly, when working with Kurt Wolff, he had spent much of his time discovering new writers. "I doubt if he is interested in such discoveries these days," I said, with no suspicion of how greatly I was understating the truth. I looked forward with curiosity to his coming and wasn't the least bit afraid of him, though I didn't care for his books and had disliked him when we met at the concert.

Hermann Broch had been invited, and to him I attached importance. For over a year I had looked upon him as a friend. I felt that he valued me most as a dramatist. On my return from Paris in the late autumn, I had taken him to meet Anna at her studio. We had also called on her mother together. "Annerl, look," she had said in Broch's presence, "Broch has meestical eyes." The three of us, Anna, Broch and I, had been thoroughly embarrassed at this expression of supreme approval. I knew that Broch took a real interest in this play. I had often spoken to him about it and in view of his enthusiasm over *The Wedding*, I felt sure the *Comedy* would appeal to him. In short, I had high hopes of him. I meant nothing to this particular circle. If anything, I suspected, they regarded me as a troublemaker. Consequently, I saw Broch and Anna as my only real allies. Most of the others would be connected with the publishing house; Paul Zsolnay himself, whom I did not take very seriously, his managing editor, Costa, a bon vivant with an everlasting smile, and the head of the drama department, whom I've already mentioned.

The reading took place in the afternoon. I don't believe there were a dozen people present. This wasn't my first visit to the house. Old Frau Zsolnay had invited me several times and given me a warm welcome. She had a weakness for writers, it was to help them that she had set up the publishing house in her son's name, but this had taken a long time. On the day of my reading, I was keenly aware of the incongruity between the fashionable drawing room and my play, the first part of which takes place in a sort of amusement park, among crude characters with a vocabulary that stops at nothing. I was afraid that in spite of myself, under the influence of this drawing room, I might read more softly and suavely than befitted the characters. I was determined that this should not happen. So before starting I said to the lady of the house: "It's a kind of a folk play, and it's not very refined." This remark was received graciously, though with some incredulity. Zuckmayer, another of Zsolnay's authors, was a writer of "folk plays," so when the genre was mentioned these people inevitably thought of him. I could hardly have said anything more inept.

I felt alien in this circle. I was too inexperienced to realize why I was being granted a hearing. If I had known, I would certainly not have come. I put my reliance on two people, whom I regarded as friends, Broch and Anna. I felt sure they would help me. Him I esteemed, her I loved; though she had made short shrift of me and sent me packing, my feeling for her remained unchanged. Though they were sitting rather far apart, they had a good view of each other. As their approval meant everything to me, I kept an eye on them. Werfel sat spread out in front of me, not a stirring of his facial muscles escaped me; he was as close to me as to the door of the drawing room, through which he had entered last, as befitted the most important member of the audience. I couldn't help seeing how eagerly all the others, especially the executives of the publishing house, watched for his reactions. He had a familiar way of saying "*Grüss Gott*" on entering the room, as though he were still a child, open, guileless, incapable of any ugly thought, on intimate terms with God and man, a pious pilgrim with room in his heart for all living creatures, and though I had little use for his books and for him none at all, *I* was childlike enough to put faith in his "*Grüss Gott*" and to apprehend no hostility from him in this, for me, critical situation.

I began with the barker. "And we and we and we, ladies and gentlemen!" From that point on, the action in my amusement park proceeded with such gusto and violence that I forgot Aunt Andy's drawing room and the whole Paul Zsolnay Verlag, which I couldn't stomach anyway. I read for Anna and Broch. I also imagined that I was reading for Fritz Wotruba, who wasn't there of course, he wouldn't have taken to these people. As I was thinking of him, I took on something of his tone for the barker, which wasn't quite right, but it gave me a kind of protection, which I needed in that drawing room.

To Werfel I paid no attention at all until he made himself noticed and his gestures could no longer be ignored, but by then I was far along in the first part with Preacher Brosam. The violence of his sermon, its baroque tone, which, like so much blustering in German literature, derives from Abraham a Sancta Clara, must have irritated him particularly: he slapped his fat face, kept his hand pressed flat against his cheek and looked around the room as though pleading for help. I heard the slap and that attracted my attention. And there he was, sitting directly in front of me, looking unhappy, pressing his hand against his convulsed face, determined to preserve his tortured look. But refusing to be put out of countenance, I went right on reading.

I averted my eyes and looked for Anna, in the hope of finding approval and support. But she wasn't looking at me, she wasn't paying attention to me; her eyes had plunged into Broch's and his into hers. I knew that look; those eyes had once looked at me like that, and, as I thought, created me anew. But I had no eyes to answer with, and what I now saw was new. For Broch *had* eyes, and when I saw how immersed in each other the two of them were, I knew they didn't hear me, that outside of themselves nothing existed, that the meaningless clatter of the world which my vociferous characters embodied for me did not exist for them, and that as far as they were concerned there was no need to combat this emptiness. They didn't feel tormented by it, they were as out of place in this drawing room as I with my characters, nor would they get back to my characters later; they were released from everything into each other.

The play of Anna's eyes was so effective that I paid no further attention to Werfel. I forgot him and went on reading. When I read the terrible ending of the first part—a woman flings herself into the fire but is saved at the last moment—the play of Anna's eyes was rekindled within me, I was not yet free of it. I had given her an opportunity to turn it on someone else, and this someone was an esteemed writer, whom I had courted with a kind of passion and, I believed, in vain. She had the best means of winning him, I myself had brought him to her, and was now a witness to the inevitable. The incidental music to this principal event of the immediate future was my play, on which I had placed so much hope.

After the first part I announced an intermission. Werfel stood up and said without enthusiasm, but still with his "*Grüss Gott*" voice, as if he had forgotten his erstwhile sufferings: "You read it well." His emphasis on *read* did not escape me; about the play itself he said nothing. Perhaps he sensed that those among the audience to whom I attached no particular importance had been moved by the crescendo of shorter and shorter scenes leading up to the fire, and he wished to reserve judgment. Anna was silent, she hadn't heard a word, she was busy, she would have been repelled by the vulgarity of my scenes in any case, but as it was, with Broch to look at, she had no need to waste a thought on them. Broch too was silent. I sensed that this was no interested or benevolent silence. I was shocked, though in view of what I had seen, I expected nothing from him and certainly no help, his obvious state of bemusement came as a hard blow to me. I would have given up in that intermission if the others, who were not my friends, had not urged me to go on. Someone said: "But let him get his breath, he must be exhausted. It's fatiguing to read like that." That was "Aunt Andy," who wasn't afraid of showing pity for the unhappy reader. And it was from her that I had expected the worst resistance, the most decided revulsion for these "folk characters," as I had called them in speaking to her. But when the baby screamed at the sight of the fire she had laughed aloud. Her son, who was connected with her laughter as by an umbilical cord, who derived what little vitality he had from her, had laughed too, and that may have accounted for Werfel's momentary restraint.

I started the second part and soon sensed a radical change of mood. When the three friends, the widow Weihrauch, Sister Luise and Fräulein Mai, met at the lodgings of the longshoreman Barloch, the contrast between those sordid surroundings and the drawing room where we were all sitting—reader and listeners alike— became intolerable. What was shown in this scene was not only indigent but also ugly and immoral in a way unusual for Vienna. Wife and concubine in the same apartment, if you could call it an apartment, and mention was also made of two girls who lived there, though they did not appear on the stage. And then the friends visit the widow Weihrauch and the unbelievable living conditions in those cramped quarters are not only described but loudly heralded by the widow in her inimitable way; the peddler appears with his shard and his sales talk, which, precisely because it was accurate and familiar, provoked especial outrage.

Werfel soon opened his campaign; instead of slapping himself on the face again, he ran first one hand, then the other over his cheeks, buried his eyes in one hand, as though the sight of the reader was more than he could bear, looked up again, sought other eyes, especially those of his subordinates at the publishing house, to whom he wished to communicate his displeasure, shook his head solemnly at every gross phrase, wriggled massively in his chair, and suddenly, in the middle of the peddler's speech, cried out: "You're an imitator of animal voices, that's what you are," meaning me. This he regarded as an annihilatingly cruel insult that would make it impossible for me to go on reading, but he accomplished the exact opposite, because I had been aiming at just that: every character was meant to be as clearly differentiated from the others as a specific animal, and I wanted them all to be recognizable by their voices. Suddenly it dawned on me that he had hit the nail on the head with his insults, though of course he could not suspect what I was driving at with my imitation of animal voices.

In defiance of his open hostility, with which he was trying to infect the others, I went on reading. The scene drew to an end amid the bellowing of the longshoreman Barloch, who lets the peddler go. Werfel said: "It sounds like Breitner with his idiotic luxury tax." But he kept his seat, for he was planning a more effective demonstration. In the next scene, the aged porter, Franzl Nada, is heard; standing on a street corner, he is treating the passersby to flattering remarks, and they reward him with a few coins. The mood of the audience shifted, I felt a sudden wave of warmth. But before the scene had ended, Werfel jumped up and shouted: "This is unbearable." Turning his back on me, he headed for the door. I stopped reading. In the doorway he turned around and shouted: "Give it up! Give it up!" This last insult, designed to demolish both me and my play, aroused old Frau Zsolnay to pity, and she called after him in a loud voice: "You should read his novel, Franzl!" He shrugged his shoulders, said: "Sure, sure," and left.

With that my *Comedy*'s goose was cooked. He may have come just for this killing. Or perhaps while listening to me he had recognized a disciple of Karl Kraus, who was his bitter enemy, and that was what infuriated him. I was well aware of the disaster but went on reading, unwilling to admit my defeat. I paid no attention to anyone, I don't know whether or not Anna was put off by Werfel's behavior and suspended her eye-work. I tend to think that she ignored Werfel's outburst and kept on doing what seemed most important to her at the moment. I broke off my reading in the middle as planned, after the scene in Therese Kreiss's shop. Her last frantic words were: "The Devil! The Devil!"

When I stopped, Broch spoke up for the first time. He too, like old Frau Zsolnay, felt sorry for me, and said something that restored my right to exist. "It wouldn't surprise me," he said, "if that turned out to be the drama of the future." If he wasn't exactly standing up for me, at least he was raising a question and granting that I had attempted something new. Old Frau Zsolnay thought he was going too far. "Not necessarily," she said. "And tell me, do you call that a folk play?" Nothing that could be said after that would have counted. The real power in this house was Werfel, who couldn't have stated his opinion more plainly. But decorum was maintained. It was arranged that I should complete my reading in a week's time.

Apart from the protagonist, the same people came. I read for the sake of the characters, whose voices I had seldom heard as yet. Hope, I had none; nothing would be done with my play. And yet my faith in it—I find this hard to explain—was enormously increased by this reading that served no purpose and brought no hope. It is defeats of such catastrophic proportions that keep a writer alive.

I Discover a Good Man

There were quite a few people in Vienna at that time with whom I associated, whom I saw fairly often, whom I did not avoid. They can be broken down into two contrasting groups. The one, numbering perhaps six or seven, I admired for their work and the seriousness with which they took it. They went their own ways and let no one deter them, they hated all convention, and shrank back from success in the common sense of the word. They had roots, though not always their first roots, in Vienna; it was hard to conceive of them living anywhere else, but they did not let Vienna corrupt them. I admired these people, they taught me that it is possible to carry a project through even if the world shows no interest in it whatsoever. True, they all hoped to find recognition in their lifetime, yet, though intelligent enough to realize that their hopes might be vain and that contempt and derision might dog them to the end of their days, they went right on with the tasks they had set themselves. It may sound bombastic to speak of them as heroes, and I am sure they themselves thought nothing of the kind, but courage they undoubtedly had, and their patience was almost super-human.

And then there were the others, those who would go to any lengths for money, fame or power. They too fascinated me, though in a very different way. I wanted to know them inside and out, to fathom every fiber of their being; it was as though the salvation of my soul depended on understanding them and seeing them as complete characters. I saw them no less frequently than the others, I may have been even more eager to see them, because I could never quite believe my perception of them and felt the need of confirming it over and over again. But it should not be thought that I demeaned myself in their company, I did not adapt to them, I did not try to please, but often enough they were slow to find out what I really thought of them. Here too there were six or seven main characters, the most rewarding being Alma Mahler.

What I found hardest to bear were the relations between the two groups. Alban Berg, whom I loved, was a close friend of Alma Mahler; he came and went freely in her house and attended every reception of any importance; I was always relieved to find him in the corner with his wife, Helene, and join him. True, he held aloof from the others, he took no part in Alma's feverish activity when there were new or "special" guests to be introduced. True, he made remarks about certain of those present which might have come from *Die Fackel* and which relieved me as much as they did him, but the fact remained that he was always there, and I never heard him say a word against the lady of the house.

Broch, too, called on undesirable people. When we were alone, he told me frankly what he thought of them, but it would never have occurred to him to avoid them. The others whom I respected and took seriously behaved the same way. They all had a second, class-B world in which they moved without sullying themselves; indeed, it often looked as if they *needed* this second world to keep their own world pure. The most standoffish was Musil. He was very careful in choosing the people he wished to associate with, and when by chance he found himself in a café or elsewhere among people he disapproved of, he fell silent and nothing could move him to open his mouth.

In my conversations with Broch one of us raised a question that may seem strange: Was there such a thing as a *good* man? And if so, what would he be like? Would he lack certain drives that motivate others? Would he be reclusive or would it be possible for him to associate with people, react to their challenges and nevertheless be "good"? The question fascinated us both. We did not try to evade it by hairsplitting. We both doubted that a good man could exist in the life around us. But if he did exist, we felt sure that we knew what he was like, that if we met him, we would recognize him at once. There was a strange urgency in this discussion of ours, and we wasted no time in sterile argument about the meaning of goodness. This was most unusual, if only because of the many matters on which we agreed to differ. We both harbored a pristine image of the good person. Was he a mere image? Or was there such an individual? And if so, where?

We passed all the people we knew in review. At first we discussed people we had only heard about, but soon realized that we didn't know enough about them. What was the point in forming opinions for or against if we couldn't check them against direct observation? We then decided to consider only persons we knew and knew *well*. As one or another came to mind, we studied him closely.

This sounds pedantic, but in practical terms it meant only that we reported aspects of his life that one or both of us had observed, that we could vouch for, as it were. Obviously we were not looking for a naïve person, the person we had in mind must *know* what he was doing. He must have within him a number of drives and motives to choose among. He must not be feebleminded or diminished, he must not be innocent about the world or blind about people. He must not let them deceive him or lull him, he must be vigilant, sensitive and alert, and only if he had all these qualities, could one put the question: Is he nevertheless good? Both Broch and I knew, or had known, plenty of people. But one after another they fell like tenpins, and after a while we began to feel ashamed of ourselves, for who were we to set ourselves up as judges? I felt ashamed for not giving anyone a passing mark, and Broch, though less impetuous than I, may have felt the same way, for suddenly he cried out: "I know one! I know one! My friend Sonne! He's our good man!" I had never heard the name. "Is that really his name?" I asked. "Yes, or call him Dr. Sonne if you prefer. That sounds less mythical. He's just the man we're looking for. That may be why I didn't think of him sooner." I learned that Dr. Sonne lived in retirement, met with only a few friends and rarely, very rarely, called on them. "You just spoke of Georg Merkel, the painter." He had been one of our "candidates." "He goes to see Merkel now and then, out in Penzing. You can meet him there. That's the simplest, most natural way."

Georg Merkel, a painter whose works had attracted me at exhibitions, was a man of about Broch's age. I had seen him at the Café Museum, though less frequently than some other painters. He had attracted my notice by the deep hole in his forehead, just above the left eye. I had admired some of his pictures in Wotruba's living room; they had a French quality, they had clearly been influenced by the neoclassical movement and their palette was unusual for Vienna. I had asked about him at the time. Later at the Café Museum, Wotruba had introduced me to him as to most of the leading painters of the day. The elegance of his German had delighted me from the start. He spoke slowly, with a Polish intonation; every sentence carried deep conviction, his diction had a lofty, biblical ring, as though he were courting Rachel. Actually he spoke of things that had nothing to do with the Bible, but in such a way that he seemed to be paying homage to his interlocutor, who invariably felt honored and respected when Merkel addressed him. At the same time it was clear that, though not overbearing, he took himself very seriously. Once he pronounced a name, it rang in one's ears just as he had spoken it; one sometimes felt tempted to say it in his way, but that would have been ridiculous, for what in anyone else sounded theatrical made an impression of natural dignity coming from him. His opinions were charged with emotion, no one would have dreamed of getting into an argument with him. To question anything he said would have been to call the whole man into question. He was incapable of a vulgar action or word. In the case of so vehement, so passionate a man this seems unbelievable. One had to see the force and firmness with which he countered an insult without ever demeaning himself, looking around to make sure everyone had heard him. At such times the deep wound in his forehead would look like a third, cyclopean eye. I was sometimes tempted to make him angry, because what he said in anger sounded so magnificent, but I loved him and respected him enough to resist the temptation.

Georg Merkel seemed a striking example of the proud Slav one met with so frequently in the Vienna of those days. He had studied in Cracow, under Wyspianski, which may have accounted for the persistence of his Polish accent. It remained with him after decades in Vienna and in France. He lived to a ripe old age, and neither his French nor his German ever lost its Polish tinge. There were certain vowels that he never mastered. He never managed in my presence to say a proper "ö" and he never learned to pronounce two of the most important words in his life: "*schön*" and "Österreich." He said "Esterreich" and when carried away by a woman's beauty, he would say: "*Ist sie nicht schén? Schén ist sie.*" Veza was treated to that, enunciated with captivating vehemence. Never, regardless of whether he came to see us or we went to see him, or whether we met at the Café Museum, could he refrain at the sight of Veza from saying: "*Schén ist sie!*"— which was all the more striking because everything else he said was couched in choice and elegant German.

I had met Georg Merkel only a short while before the

previously mentioned conversation with Broch, and his name came up quite naturally in the course of our search for a "good" man. He had much in his favor, but we did not vote for him, because he saw himself too exclusively as a painter. This set him apart, so to speak, from the section of mankind that took no interest in art and made him somewhat less of a "good" man as we defined one.

Merkel had gone to Paris as a young man, some years before the First World War, and had never lost the imprint of those Paris years. It seems likely that such a wide variety of talented painters had never before, or since, been concentrated in one place. They came from everywhere and were buoyed by great hopes. They did not try to make things easy for themselves, to achieve fame and recognition by trickery. Painting meant so much to them that they did nothing else. With so many painters at work there was no lack of inspiration, Oriental and African influences made themselves felt, but the treasures of medieval and classical art served as a counterweight. It took fortitude to live in poverty, but another kind of strength may have been even more important: the strength of character needed to steer a course amid all the many possible influences and stimuli, to take only what one needed and disregard the rest. In the Paris of those years a new nation came into being: the nation of painters. When we pass in review the names with which those years will no doubt be identified for all time, we are amazed at the diversity of their origins. It was as though the young people of every imaginable country had been summoned to Paris for painting duty. But they had not been summoned, they had come of their own free will. For the privations they took upon themselves without hesitation, they were rewarded by the companionship of fellow painters, who were having just as hard a time but like themselves were confident of winning fame in this world capital of painting.

The outbreak of the First World War caught Merkel in Paris, living happily with his wife, Luise, who was also a painter. It would have been hard to find an atmosphere more congenial to him; he returned to Paris time and again; all in all, he must have spent a good third of his life there. Yet at the end of July 1914 he had only one thought, to get back to Austria with his wife and join the army. In those days a kind of Austrian patriotism was common among educated Galician Jews. They never lost sight of the Russian pogroms and they thought of the Emperor Francis Joseph as a protector. So strong was Merkel's Austrian feeling that he would not have been satisfied to sit in a government press office whipping up martial spirit in others. Surmounting all difficulties, he made his way from Paris to Vienna, where he lost no time in enlisting.

The price he paid for his Austrian patriotism was a severe head wound. A shell fragment struck him just above the eyes and blinded him. For several months he lived in total darkness, a painter deprived of his eyesight. That was the worst time in his life. He never mentioned it to me or, as far as I know, to anyone else. The deep scar remained, I couldn't look at it without being reminded of his blindness. He recovered his eyesight, a miracle which influenced all his painting from then on. His eyesight was his paradise that he had lost and regained. One cannot find fault with him for painting "beauty"— his pictures became a hymn of thanks for the light of his eyes.

Soon after that half-playful, half-serious conversation with Broch, I was invited for the first time to visit Georg Merkel in Penzing, where he lived. He had his studio there too, and sometimes on Sunday afternoons he would invite friends and show his pictures. I didn't know him very well at the time, but I had heard his story, especially the story of his wound and the terrible dent in his forehead. I liked his lilting speech, and though those of his paintings I had seen, despite the charm of his palette, were a far cry from what ordinarily fascinated me in modern art, I was curious to see more of his work. I had always delighted in watching painters show their work. They do it in a manner compounded of pride, lavish generosity and diffidence, in proportions varying with the individual.

I was a little late, the guests were still drinking tea. With some I was personally acquainted, others were known to me by name or through their works. Off to one side, half in darkness, sat a man whose face I had known for a year and a half. He sat in the Café Museum every afternoon, hidden behind a newspaper. As I've already related, he looked like Karl Kraus. I knew he couldn't be Karl Kraus, but I was so keen on seeing a *silent* Karl Kraus who wasn't accusing or crushing anyone that I tried to imagine it *was* Karl Kraus. I used my silent daily meetings with *this* face to free myself from the overwhelming power of *that* face when it was speaking.

And now the face was here; I was struck with amazement. Merkel saw that something had happened. He took me gently by the arm, led me to the face and said: "This is my dear friend Dr. Sonne." There was feeling in his way of introducing people, he had no interest in cold acquaintance; when he brought two people together it was for life. He had no way of knowing that I had been scrutinizing this man's movements for a year and a half. Or that just a week ago Broch had mentioned Dr. Sonne to me for the first time. Our game of "find a good man," which we had played so doggedly and taken quite seriously, had become reality, and it was significant that the name and the face, which had existed separately in my mind, should have become one in the house of this painter with the lilting voice.

Sonne

What was it about Sonne that made me want to see him every day, that made me look for him every day, that inspired an addiction such as I had not experienced for any other intellectual?

For one thing, he was so utterly impersonal. He never talked about himself. He never made use of the first person. And he seldom addressed me directly. By speaking in the third person, he distanced himself from his surroundings. You have to imagine this city with its coffeehouses and their floods of I-talk, protestation, confession and self-assertion. All these people were bursting with self-pity and self-importance. They all lamented, bellowed and trumpeted. But all banded together in small groups, because they needed and tolerated each other for their talk. Everything was discussed, the newspapers provided the main topic of conversation. This was a time when a great deal was happening and when people sensed that much more was *in the offing*. They were unhappy about events in Austria, but well aware that the events in neighboring Germany weighed far more heavily in the balance. Catastrophe was in the air. Contrary to the general expectation, it was delayed from year to year. In Austria itself things were going badly, how badly could be seen from the unemployment figures. When snow fell, people said: "The unemployed will be glad." The municipal government hired unemployed to shovel snow; they made a little money. You saw them shoveling and hoped for more snow for their sake.

It was only seeing Dr. Sonne that made this period bearable for me. He was an authority to which I had daily

access. We discovered innumerable things that were happening on all sides and more that were *threatening* to
happen. I would have been ashamed to speak of them in
personal terms. No one had a right to regard himself as
singled out by the events that were threatening. This was
no private menace, it confronted everyone without exception. Perceiving it and talking about it were not enough;
what mattered was *insight* and nothing else, but that was
so hard to come by. I never decided in advance what I
was going to ask Dr. Sonne. I made no plans. Topics
came up as spontaneously as his explanations. Everything
he said had the freshness of new thought. It never struck
me as falsified by emotion, yet it was never cold and
unfeeling. Nor was it ever biased. I never had the feeling
that he was talking in support of one party or another.
Even then the world was saturated with slogans, it was
hard to find a place that was free of them, where the air
was fit to breathe. The best thing about his talk was that
it was concise without being schematic. He said what was
to be said clearly and sharply, but omitted nothing. He
was thorough, and if what he said had not been so
fascinating, one might have called his statements expert
opinions. But they were much more than that, for, though
he never said so, they contained the seeds of rich new
developments.

We talked about everything imaginable. I mentioned
something that had struck me; sometimes he wanted to
know more about it, but his requests for information
never sounded like questions, for he always seemed to
address them to the subject matter, rather than to the
person questioned. One could get the impression that the
person he was sitting with was in no way involved, only
the question under discussion. But this was not the case,
for when a third party was present, he spoke in a different
way. Evidently he drew distinctions, but they were imperceptible to the person concerned; it was inconceivable that

anyone in his presence should feel belittled. Stupidity made him very unhappy, and he avoided stupid people, but if through circumstances beyond Dr. Sonne's control, he found himself in the company of a stupid person, no one could possibly notice how stupid that person was.

After a few preluding chords, the moment always came when he took up a topic and began to speak of it exhaustively and aptly. It would never have occurred to me to interrupt him, not even with questions, as I often did with others. I cast off all outward reaction like an ill-fitting carnival costume and listened with the closest attention. I have never listened to anyone else so intently. I forgot that the speaker was a human being, disregarded his peculiarities of speech, never regarded him as a character; he was the opposite of a character. If anyone had asked me to imitate him, I would have refused, and not only out of respect, I would have been quite incapable of *playing* him, the very thought strikes me even today not only as sacrilege but as an utter impossibility.

What he had to say on a subject was always thorough and exhaustive; one also knew that he had never said it before. It was always new, it had just come into being. It was not an opinion concerning realities; it was their law. The amazing part of it, though, was that he would not be speaking of some specialty in which he was well versed. He was not a specialist, or rather, he was not a specialist in any particular subject, he was a specialist in all the matters I ever heard him talk about. From him I learned that it is possible to concern oneself with a wide range of subjects without becoming a windbag. This is a bold statement, and it will not seem more credible when I add that for that very reason I cannot reproduce any of his observations, for each one was a serious, yet animated, dissertation, so complete that I can remember none of them in full. And to cite fragments of his discourse would be a grave falsification. He was not an aphorist; in connection with him, the word, which I otherwise hold in high regard, seems almost frivolous. He was too thorough to be an aphorist, he lacked the onesidedness and the desire to startle. When he had made a complete statement, one felt enlightened and satisfied; something had been settled and nothing more would be said about it; what more was there to say?

But though I would not presume to reproduce his statements, there is a literary creation to which I believe he can be likened. In those years I read Musil. I could not get enough of *The Man without Qualities*, the first two volumes of which, some thousand pages, had been published. It seemed to me that there was nothing comparable in all literature. And yet, wherever I chanced to open these books, the text seemed surprisingly familiar. This was a language I knew, a rhythm of thought that I had met with, and yet I knew for sure that there were no similar books in existence. It was some time before I saw the connection. Dr. Sonne *spoke* as Musil *wrote*. But it should not be supposed that Dr. Sonne sat at home writing things which for some reason he did not wish to publish and subsequently drew on them in his conversations. He did not sit at home and write; what he said came into being while he was speaking. But it was said with the perfect clarity that Musil achieved in writing. Day after day I was privileged to hear chapters from a second *Man without Qualities* that no one else ever heard of. For what he said to others—and he did speak to others, though not every day—was a *different* chapter.

For amorphous eclecticism, the tendency to reach out in all directions, to drop what one has barely touched on, for this sort of curiosity, which is undoubtedly more than curiosity since it has no purpose and ends nowhere, for such thrashing about in all directions there is only one remedy: to associate with someone who has the gift of exploring a subject, of not dropping it before the whole ground has been covered and not analyzing it to pieces. Sonne never reduced a subject, never *disposed* of it. His talking about it made it more interesting than before, articulated and illuminated it. He founded whole countries in the mind of his listener, where previously there had only been question marks. He could describe an important public figure as accurately as a field of knowledge. He had no use for anything that could turn conversation into gossip, and avoided speaking of persons known to both of us. But with that reservation he had the same methods in dealing with persons and things. It may have been this that most reminded me of Musil—his conception of individuals as distinct fields of knowledge. The sterile notion that any single theory might be applicable to all people was utterly alien to him. Each individual was distinct and different. He detested every instrumentality directed by men against men; never has anyone been farther from barbarism. Even when he had to name the things he hated, there was no hatred in his tone; he was merely laying bare an absurdity, nothing more.

It seems almost unbelievable how strictly he avoided all personal observations. You could spend two hours with him and learn an incredible lot, so much that you always left with a sense of wonderment. How, in view of this unquestionable superiority, could I look down on others? Humility was certainly not a word he would have used; yet I left him in a state of mind that no other word can describe; but it was a *vigilant* humility, not the humility of a sheep.

I was in the habit of listening to people, total strangers with whom I had never exchanged a word. I listened with genuine fury to people who did not concern me in any way, and I was best able to capture a person's tone of voice once it seemed certain that I would never see him again. I had no compunction about encouraging such a person to speak by asking questions or by playing a role.

I had never asked myself whether I had a right to store up everything a person would tell me about himself. Today I find the naïveté with which I claimed this right almost beyond belief. Undoubtedly there are *basic* qualities that cannot be analyzed, and any attempt to explain them *ought* to fail. My passion for people is just such a basic quality. It can be described, it can be characterized, but its origin must remain forever obscure. Fortunately, I can say that thanks to my four-year apprenticeship with Dr. Sonne I became aware of its dubious character.

I soon realized that, though he disregarded what was near at hand, it did not escape him. If he never wasted a word about the people who sat near us day after day, it was out of tact; he never impugned anyone, not even people who could never have found out. He was never lacking in respect for the dividing lines between individuals. I called this his *ahimsa*, the Indian word for the inviolability of all life. But I see today that there was something more English about it. He had spent an important year of his life in England, that was one of the two or three autobiographical facts I was able to infer from his conversation. For at bottom I knew nothing about him, and even when I spoke of him with other people who knew him, there was little concrete information to be gleaned. Maybe we were reluctant to talk about him as we did about anyone else, for his essential qualities were hard to formulate, and even persons who were themselves devoid of moderation admired his moderation. Thus we were exceedingly careful, in talking of him, to avoid distortions.

I asked him no questions, just as he asked none. I made suggestions, that is, I brought up a topic as though it had been going through my head for some time, hesitantly rather than urgently. And hesitantly he took it up. While continuing to talk about something else, he pondered my suggestion. Then with a sudden knife thrust he would cut into the topic and treat it with brilliant clarity and stunning thoroughness. He spoke with the ice-cold clarity of one who grinds perfect lenses, who will have nothing to do with anything murky until it is clarified. He examined an object by taking it apart, yet preserved it in its wholeness. He did not dissect; he irradiated. But he selected specific parts to irradiate, removed them with care, and his operation once completed, carefully rejoined them into a whole. What to me was marvelously new was that so penetrating a mind neglected no detail. Every detail had to be treated with care and for this reason alone became important.

He was not a collector, for with all his vast knowledge he kept nothing for himself. He had read everything, yet I never saw him with a book. He himself was the library he did not own. Whatever book we talked about, he seemed to have read it long ago. He never tried to conceal his knowledge of it. He didn't boast, he never trotted it out inopportunely but there it was without fail when the need arose, and most amazing of all, no part of it was ever missing. Some people were irritated by his precision. He did not change his manner when speaking to women; he never spoke *lightly*, never belied his intellect or his seriousness, never flirted; he did not overlook beauty or hide his admiration for it, but it never led him to change his ways. Even in its presence he remained the same. The presence of beauty might inspire other men to eloquence; he on the contrary fell silent and only found his tongue again when it had gone away. He was capable of no greater homage, but this was something few women understood. Some women may not have been prepared for him in the best possible way. I would begin by putting him on a pedestal, high above myself, and this was bound to put a woman off if her love for me contained an element of veneration in which she lived and breathed.

That's how it was with Veza, and she was steadfast in

her refusal to appreciate Sonne. When she saw him for the first time at the house of the painter Georg Merkel, she said to me: "He does *not* look like Karl Kraus. How can you say such a thing? A mummy of Karl Kraus, that's what he looks like." She was referring to his sunken, ascetic look and she was referring also to his silence. For in company, among many people, he never said a word. I sensed that he was impressed by Veza's beauty, but how was she to read that in those rigid features? And even when she heard from others and of course from me what surprising things he said of her beauty, she didn't change her mind.

Once when I came home after a marvelous conversation with him at the Café Museum, she received me with hostility: "You've been with your seven-month baby, I can tell by looking at you, don't tell me about it. It only makes me miserable to see you wasting yourself on a mummy." By my seven-month baby she meant that he was not a normal, complete person, that something was missing. I was used to her extreme reactions, we had bitter arguments about people; she would see something that was really there and exaggerate it in her passionately intransigent way. As my reactions were just as extreme, there were violent clashes, but we both loved them, for they were lasting proof that we told each other the whole truth. It was in connection with Dr. Sonne that she showed a deep resentment, resentment against me, for here was I, who had never submitted to anyone, who, as she recognized, had guarded whole areas of myself even from Karl Kraus, submitting wholly and without hesitation to Dr. Sonne, for she had never heard me express doubt about anything he said.

I knew nothing about Sonne; he consisted entirely of his statements, so much so that the prospect of discovering anything else about him would have frightened me. No particulars of his life were bandied about, no illness, no complaint. He was *ideas*, so much so that one noticed nothing else. We didn't make appointments, and when occasionally he failed to appear, he never felt obliged to explain his absence. Then of course I thought he might be ill, he was pale and did not seem to be in good health, but for over a year I didn't even know where he lived. I could have asked Broch or Merkel for his address. I didn't, it seemed right that he should have none.

I was not surprised when a busybody whom I had always avoided sat down at my table and asked me at once whether I knew Dr. Sonne. I quickly replied in the negative, but he refused to be silenced, for he had something on his mind that puzzled him and left him no peace: a fortune had been *given* away. This Dr. Sonne, he told me, was the grandson of an immensely wealthy man in Przemysl, and he had donated the whole of the fortune inherited from his grandfather to charitable causes. But he was not the only lunatic in the world. Another was Ludwig Wittgenstein, a philosopher, the brother of the one-armed pianist Paul Wittgenstein; he had done the same, except that he had inherited from his father rather than his grandfather. And my busybody knew of other cases, which he listed, along with the testator's name and net worth. He was a collector of refused or donated inheritances, I've forgotten the names, which meant nothing to me; it may be that I wasn't interested in the others because the information about Sonne meant so much to me. I accepted it without further inquiry, I believed it because it appealed to me and because I knew the story about Wittgenstein to be true. I had gathered from a number of conversations with Sonne that he had had firsthand experience of war but had not been a soldier. He knew what it meant to be a refugee as well as if he himself had been one, or rather, as if he had borne responsibility for refugees, organized whole shipments of refugees and taken them to a place where their lives were no longer in danger. Accordingly, I inferred from what the busybody had told me that he had spent his inherited fortune on refugees.

Sonne was a Jew. That was the only fact concerning him that was known to me from the start. We often talked about religions, those of India and China and those based on the Bible; in his concise way, he showed a sovereign knowledge of every religion we came across in our conversation. But what impressed me most was his mastery of the Hebrew Bible. He could quote any passage from any book verbatim, and translate it without hesitation into a supremely beautiful German that struck me as the language of a poet. Such conversations developed from his objections to Martin Buber's translation, which was then coming out. I liked to bring the conversation around to it, it gave me a chance to get acquainted with the Hebrew text. This was something I had hitherto avoided, it would have narrowed me down to learn more about things that were so close to my origins, though I had preserved a keen interest in every other religion.

It was the clarity and firmness of Sonne's diction that reminded me of Musil's way of writing. Once he started on any path, he did not deviate from it until he reached a point where it branched out quite naturally into others. Arbitrary steps were avoided. In the course of the two hours or so that we spent together every day, we spoke of many things, and a list of the topics that came up would look—contrary to what I have just said—like an aimless hodgepodge. But that would be an optical illusion, for if the exact wording of such conversations were available, if a single one had been recorded, it would be evident that each and every topic under discussion was exhausted before we went on to something else. But it is not possible to show how that was done; it would be necessary—and quite impossible!—to write Sonne's *Man without Qualities.* Such a book would have to be as clear-headed and transparent as Musil; it would command one's full attention from the first to the last word; far removed from sleep or twilight, it would be equally engrossing regardless of where you opened it. Musil could never have come to the end of his book; once a writer starts refining such a precision process, he will never be free of it; if it were given him to live forever, he would have to go on writing forever. That is the true, the essential eternity of such a work; and inevitably it is passed on to the reader, who can content himself with no stopping place and reads again and again what would otherwise come to an end.

Of this I had a twofold experience: in Musil's thousand pages and in a hundred conversations with Sonne. The convergence of the two was a stroke of good fortune probably granted to no one else. For though they were comparable in intellectual content and quality of language, they were contrary in innermost intention. Musil was chained to his undertaking. True, he had total freedom of thought, but he felt subordinated to his purpose, regardless of what might befall him; he never *forwent* an experience, he had a body, which he acknowledged, and through his body retained his attachment to the world. Though himself a writer, he observed the goings-on of others who called themselves writers; he saw through their futility, and condemned it. He respected discipline, especially that of the sciences, but did not deny himself other forms of discipline. The work he undertook can be regarded as a war of *conquest*; he was reconquering a lost empire, not its glory, not the shelter it had offered, not its antiquity; no, he was reconquering the ramifications of all its greater and lesser spiritual itineraries, reconquering a *map* composed of human beings. The fascination of his work is comparable, I believe, to that of a *map*.

Sonne, on the other hand, wanted nothing. His posture,

so tall and erect, was misleading. The days when he had thought of reconquering his country were past. That he had also undertaken to reconquer its language was long unknown to me. He had access to all religions but seemed committed to none. He was free from purpose of any kind and was in competition with no one. But he took an interest in other people's purposes, thought about them and criticized them. Though he applied the highest standards and there was much that he could not approve, it was never the project that he judged but solely the outcome.

He seemed the most down-to-earth of men, not because earthly possessions were important to him but because he wanted nothing for himself. A lot of people know what selflessness is, and some are so sickened by the self-seeking they see around them that they try to eradicate it from themselves. But in those years in Vienna I knew only one man who was totally free from self-seeking and that was Dr. Sonne. Nor have I met anyone like him since. For in the period when Eastern wisdoms were finding countless adepts, when large numbers of people were renouncing earthly aims, this attitude was invariably accompanied by hostility to European thought. Everything was thrown overboard, and what was condemned most of all was *clear thinking*; in eschewing participation in the environing world, our adepts also relinquished responsibility for it. In other words, they declined responsibility for phenomena they rejected. A widespread attitude was summed up in the words: "It serves you right." Sonne had given up his activity in the world, why I did not know. But he *remained* in the world, he clung to the world with every one of his thoughts. He withdrew from action, but he did not turn his back; even in the unbiased justice of his conversation one sensed a passion for this world, and my impression was that his only reason for *doing* nothing was that he wished to do no one an injustice.

Through Sonne I learned for the first time what a man's integrity means; it means that he will not be swayed by questions, even by problems, that he will go his own way without revealing his motives or past history. Even to myself I did not put questions about his person; even in my thoughts he remained inviolable. He spoke of many things and was not sparing of his judgment when something displeased him. But I never looked for motives for his words, they stood for themselves, clearly demarcated even from their source. Quite apart from their quality, this had become most unusual at that time. The psychoanalytic plague had spread, how much so I saw in Broch. It troubled me less in Broch than in more commonplace natures, for, as I've said before, his senses were so uniquely fashioned that even the cheapest explanations then in circulation could not detract from his originality. But in general, it was impossible in those days to say anything which would not be invalidated by the motives that would immediately be adduced. Everything was attributed to the same infinitely boring and sterile motives, but that didn't seem to bother many people. The most astonishing things were happening in the world, but they were always seen against the same background; talk about the background was thought to explain them and once explained they ceased to be astonishing. Much-needed thought was replaced by a chorus of impertinent frogs.

In his work Musil was free from this infection, as was Dr. Sonne in his conversation. He never asked me a question remotely connected with my private life. I told him nothing about myself and made no confessions. I let myself be guided by the example of his dignity and, passionate as our discussions became, they never touched on his person. He often accused, but took no pleasure in accusing. He foresaw the worst and said so, but found no satisfaction in seeing his predictions confirmed. To him evil was still evil, even though he had been right. No one

saw what was coming as clearly as he did. I hardly dare
list all the calamities he foresaw. He did his best not to
show how his foreboding tormented him. It would never
have occurred to him to threaten or torment anyone with
them. He was keenly aware of his interlocutor's sensibilities
and took care not to offend them. He offered no magic
formulas, though he knew many. He spoke with the
authority of one passing judgment, but managed, with a
simple wave of the hand, to exclude his interlocutor from
that judgment. In this there was something more than
kindness, there was delicacy, and I am amazed to this day
by this combination of delicacy and extreme rigor.

It has only recently come to me that without my daily
meetings with Sonne I could never have torn myself away
from Karl Kraus. It was the same face. How I wish I had
pictures with which to demonstrate the similarity between
those faces; unfortunately there are none. But—incredible
as it may seem—there was yet another face, which I saw
three years later in the death mask of Karl Kraus. This
was the face of Pascal. Here anger had become suffering,
and a man is marked by the suffering he inflicts on
himself. The amalgamation of these two faces: that of the
prophetic zealot and that of the sufferer, who was able
without presumption to discourse on everything accessible
to the human mind—this amalgamation released me from
the rule of the zealot without depriving me of what he
had given me, and filled me with respect for something
that was for me unattainable. Pascal had given me an
intimation of it, in Sonne I had it before me.

Sonne knew a great deal by heart. As I've said, he had
memorized the whole Bible and could quote any passage
in Hebrew without hesitation. But he performed these
mnemonic feats with restraint and never made a show of
them. I had known him for over a year before I raised
an objection to the German of Buber's Bible translation

and he not only agreed with me but supported my criticism with a considerable number of references to the Hebrew original. His way of reciting and interpreting certain short chapters came as a revelation to me; I realized that he must be a poet, and in the Hebrew language.

I didn't dare ask him about it, for when he himself avoided a subject I was careful not to bring it up. But in this case my tact did not go so far as to stop me from inquiring of others who had known him for years. I learned—and it sounded as if this had been a secret for some time—that he was one of the founders of modern Hebrew poetry.

It seems that when only fifteen he had written, under the name of Abraham ben Yitzhak, some poems which had been compared to Hölderlin by persons versed in both languages—only a very few hymnlike poems, perhaps less than a dozen, of such perfection that he had been numbered among the masters of the newly revived language. But then he had stopped writing poetry and after that no one had ever seen a poem by him. He was thought to have forbidden himself to write poetry. He never talked about it, and preserved an unbroken silence as he did about so many things.

I felt guilty at having made this discovery against his wishes and for a whole week I stayed away from the Café Museum. I had come to regard him as a perfect sage, and what I had learned about the poems of his youth, honorable as it sounded, seemed in a way to detract from that image. He was diminished, because he had *done* something. But he had done more things and this too I found out gradually and by chance. He had turned away from everything; though he became a master at everything he attempted, none of his efforts had allayed his misgivings and he had abandoned them all on strictly conscientious grounds. And yet, to speak only of his first activity, he had undoubtedly remained a poet. Wherein consisted the magic of his conversation, the precision and charm with which he steered a course among the most difficult subjects, omitted nothing that was worth considering (with the exception of his person); what was it that enabled him to scrutinize the things of the world closely but without identifying with them, how did he hold the horror he felt in check; what was the source of his delicacy, his secret insight into every impulse of the person he was talking to? But now I knew that he had won *recognition* as a poet and turned his back on it, whereas I was busy fighting for the recognition I had not yet won. I was ashamed of not wanting to forgo it and ashamed of having found out that he had once been something great, which he no longer regarded as great. How could I face him without asking myself the reason for this disparagement of fame? Did he disapprove of me for attaching so much importance to writing? He had read nothing of mine, no book by me had been published. He could know me only from our conversation, and I provided only a minimal part of that.

Not seeing him was almost unbearable, for I knew he was sitting there at that hour, possibly looking at the revolving door to see if I was coming in. Each day I felt more keenly that I couldn't survive without him. I would just have to summon up the courage to appear before him and not to speak of what I now knew, to take up where we had last left off and dispense with knowing what he thought of me until the book, which I wanted to submit to his judgment and to his judgment alone, should be available.

I knew the intensity of obsessions, the incisiveness of constant repetition; it was to this that Karl Kraus owed his power over his audience. And here I was sitting with a man who wore *his* face, who though no less rigorous was serene, for there was no fanaticism in him and he wasn't interested in taking people by storm. His was a mind that despised nothing, that addressed itself with the same concentrated power to every branch of knowledge. He saw a world divided into good and evil; there could never be any doubt as to what things were good and what things were evil, but the decision is up to every individual. He neither attenuated nor embellished, but painted a picture of stunning clarity which I was almost ashamed to accept as a gift in return for which nothing was asked of me but an open ear.

He accused no one. That was spared me. The reader must bear in mind the profound effect Karl Kraus's perpetual accusations had had on me. They took possession of one and never let one go (to this day I detect wounds they left me with, not all of which have healed), they had the full force of *commands*. Since I accepted them in advance and never tried to evade them, I might have been better off if they had had the stringency of commands; then it would have been possible to carry them out and they would not have become thorns in my flesh. But as it was, Karl Kraus's periods, as solidly built as fortresses, lay heavy and unwieldy on my chest, a crippling burden that I carried around with me, and though I had thrown off a good part of it while slaving over my novel and later while my play was erupting, there was still a danger that my rebellion would fail and end in serious psychic enslavement.

My liberation came from the face that so much resembled the oppressor's, but that said everything *differently*, in a richer, more complex, more highly ramified way. Instead of Shakespeare and Nestroy, it gave me the Bible, not as *the* gospel, but as one among many. And always he knew the exact wording. When the conversation turned to it apropos of something or other, he would recite a passage of some length, which I did not understand, followed quickly, sentence after sentence, by the luminous but thoroughly sound translation of a poet, a privilege for which anybody would have envied me. I alone received it, I received it without asking, just as it flowed from his mouth. Of course I received other quotations as well, but many of these were known to me, and they did not give me the feeling that they represented the authentic essence of the speaker's childhood wisdom. Then for the first time I began to appreciate the *language* of the Prophets, whom I had encountered fifteen years before in the paintings of Michelangelo, which had made so powerful an impression on me that they had kept me away from the written words. Now I heard these words from the mouth of a *unique* man, it was as though he were all the Prophets in one. He resembled them, and yet he did not; he resembled them, not as a zealot, but as one who was filled with the torment of things to come, about which he spoke to me without apparent emotion. In any case, he lacked the one most terrible passion of the Prophets, who insisted on being right even when they proclaimed the worst. Sonne would have given his last breath *not* to be right. He saw the war he detested coming, he saw the course it would take. He saw how it could have been prevented, and he would have given anything to invalidate his dire prophecy. When we parted after a friendship of four years, I going to England, he to Jerusalem, neither of us wrote any letters. Step by step, in every detail, everything he had predicted came to pass. The events affected me doubly, for I was to live through what I had already heard from him. All those years I carried them within me and then, mercilessly, they came true.

Long after Sonne's death I learned the reason for his rather stiff gait. As a young man, in Jerusalem I believe, he had hurt his spine in a fall from a horse. How well it mended, whether he had to wear a brace, I do not know. But this was the reason for what some friends, in poetic exaggeration, called his "royal bearing."

When he translated the Psalms or Proverbs to me, I saw him as the royal poet. Yet this same man, prophet and poet in one, could disappear completely; hidden behind his newspaper, he was quite invisible, while he himself was aware of everything around him. This absence of color, as it were, and his lack of ambition—these were what truly amazed me about him.

I have singled out just one of the subjects touched on in our conversations at the Café Museum, the Bible. My not naming the others might arouse the impression that Sonne was one of those who make a display of their Jewishness. The exact opposite is true. Neither in reference to himself nor to me did he ever use the word "Jew." It was a word he didn't use. As a point of pride or as the target of vicious mobs, it was unworthy of him. He was imbued with the tradition but did not pride himself on it. He took no credit for the glories that were so well known to him. I had the impression that he was not a believer. The esteem in which he held all men forbade him to exclude any, even the basest, from the full claim to humanity.

In many ways he was a model. Once I had known him no one else could become a model for me. He was a model in the only way that can make a model effective. Then, fifty years ago, he seemed unequalable, and unequalable he has remained for me.

Operngasse

Anna received many visitors in her ground-floor studio at Operngasse 4. It was in the center of the city. The true center of Vienna was, after all, the Opera, and it seemed right that Gustav Mahler's daughter, after definitively casting off the fetters of marriage, should live where her father, the superior emperor, the music emperor of Vienna, had wielded his power. Those who knew her mother and were received in the villa on Hohe Warte without wanting anything for themselves, those who were famous enough to need a rest from their careers, were glad to call on Anna when their occupations left them time.

But there was something else that attracted them, the heads she sculptured of her guests. The lions whom Alma liked to attach to her person, one or another of whom she occasionally singled out for pleasure or for marriage, were reduced, or I should say ennobled by Anna, to a portrait gallery. Anyone who was sufficiently famous was asked for his head, and few were those who were not glad to give it. Consequently, I often found people engaged in lively conversation while Anna was working on a head. My visit on such occasions was not unwelcome, because I drew her visitors into conversations that helped Anna in her work. She seemed to listen while modeling. Some people thought her real talent lay in this direction.

I should like to name a few of the people who called on her and build up a kind of gallery of my own. Some I had already met either on Maxingstrasse or on Hohe Warte. One of these was Zuckmayer, whose head she did. He had just come back from France and was talking about

his impressions. He was a great storyteller, dramatic,
bubbling with enthusiasm. It seems that wherever you
went in France you ran into Monsieur Laval. He was the
universal face. You went into a restaurant, you were still
in the doorway: who stepped up to welcome you? Monsieur Laval. In a café that was full to bursting, you were
looking for a place to sit down: who stood up to go,
leaving you his seat? Monsieur Laval. At the hotel, one
desk clerk after another: all were Monsieur Laval. You
took your wife shopping on the rue de la Paix: who waited
on you? Monsieur Laval. He was the public figure, the
image and likeness of the average Frenchman. This
sounds ominous in light of the subsequent events; at the
time it was just funny. What held your attention was not
the theatrical aspect, but the narrator's hearty crudeness.
The spice was in the repetition; you kept bumping into
the same man in a hundred forms; all were him and he
was all, but you never felt that this was a real Monsieur
Laval, it was always Zuckmayer, a stage Zuckmayer disguised as Monsieur Laval. He did all the talking, he didn't
care who was listening. Apart from Anna, no one was
there but me, I felt as if I were many listeners; just as
Zuckmayer played the part of many Lavals, I played the
part of many listeners. I was the lot of them, and all were
amazed at the incredible innocence he emanated, a carnival atmosphere in which nothing really evil happened;
all evil was metamorphosed by comedy. When today I call
to mind that Laval episode, what strikes me most is how
Zuckmayer made situation comedy out of this sinister
character.

There were those who captivated me with their beauty,
in some a beauty of the purest sort, such as I saw in death
masks. De Sabata, the conductor, was one of these. He
was conducting at the Opera and dropped in on Anna
between rehearsals. It was only a few steps along Operngasse, Anna's studio was virtually an annex of the opera

house. That was how he must have felt, he had just come from Mahler's music desk. A few steps took him to Mahler's daughter, and it not only made sense, I thought, but was the high point in his life that she should immortalize his countenance. I was sometimes there when he appeared, tall, with quick, self-assured movements. Despite his haste there was something somnambulistic about him; his face was very pale, with the beauty of a corpse, but of a corpse that resembled no one, though the features were regular; he seemed to walk with his eyes closed, and yet they saw, and there was happiness in them when they rested on Anna. It was no accident, I thought, that de Sabata's was one of her best heads.

She also did Werfel's head at that time. He undoubtedly found it pleasant to be having his portrait done so near the house of music. He enjoyed sitting here: it was a very simple studio, a far cry from the sumptuous villa on Hohe Warte or from his publisher's palace on Maxingstrasse. I stayed away when I knew he would be there. But one day, as I often came unannounced, I saw Werfel sitting in the little glassed-in courtyard. He responded to my greeting as if nothing had happened and showed no sign of resentment for the way he had treated me. He even carried charity so far as to ask me how I was getting along. Then he brought the conversation around to Veza, whose beauty he admired. Once at a soirée on Hohe Warte he had knelt at her feet and, the whole time on one knee, had sung a love aria. He had sung it to the end and stood up only when he felt certain of his success. He had a good voice and sang as well as a professional tenor. He likened Veza to Rowena, the famous actress of the Habima, who had played the lead in *The Dybbuk* in Vienna to great acclaim. Nothing could have pleased Veza more, she was sick of Andalusian metaphors. He meant it when he said it, it wasn't flattery, it seems likely that he always meant what he said, which may be one reason for the distrust he aroused in critical minds. Those who tried to defend him despite the repugnance he inspired called him "a wonderful instrument."

It was interesting to see Werfel just sitting and not doing anything in particular. One was accustomed to hear him holding forth or singing, the one readily merging with the other. He always perorated standing. He had plenty of ideas but spoiled them with verbiage. One might have liked to stop and think, one hoped for a pause, for a moment, no more, of silence, but the verbal torrent rolled on, washing everything away. He attached importance to everything that issued from his mouth, the stupidest remarks were made in the same tone of urgency as unaccustomed, surprising aperçus. Not only his nature but his deepest conviction as well made him incapable of saying anything without putting feeling into it. His propensity for singing distinguished him from a preacher, but like a preacher he was most himself when standing. He wrote his books standing at a lectern. He thought his hymns of praise had their source in love of mankind. He abominated both knowledge and reflection. To avoid reflecting, he would blurt out everything at once. Since he took any number of important ideas from others, he often held forth as if he were a font of infinite wisdom. He overflowed with sentiment, his fat belly gurgled with love and feeling, one expected to find little puddles on the floor around him and was almost disappointed to find it dry. Sitting did not come easy to him except when he was listening to music, which he did avidly, for that was when he charged his batteries with feeling. I often wondered what would have become of him if for three whole years there had been no opera available anywhere on earth. I think he would have wasted away, singing dirges to the bitter end. Others feed on knowledge after wearing themselves out getting it; he fed on music, which he absorbed with feeling.

Anna did something splendid with his ugly head. She, who execrated the grotesque unless it was cloaked in fairy-tale colors, exaggerated the size of his head, which consisted largely of fat, and making it larger than life gave it a force it did not have. Among the great men's heads lying about in her studio his didn't even cut a bad figure. It couldn't hope to resemble de Sabata's—which was as beautiful as Baudelaire's death mask. But it could hold its own with Zuckmayer's.

Some of Anna's visitors were quite surprising. One day—I had already sat down and was talking to Anna—Frank Thiess drifted in with his wife, a well-dressed couple in fluffy woolen coats, with variously shaped parcels suspended from every finger, nothing heavy, nothing large, samples, as it were, of precious commodities. When they gave you their hands, they seemed to be offering you your choice of a present. They didn't put their parcels down because, as they explained apologetically, they could only stay a moment. Thiess spoke very rapidly—a northern-sounding German in a rather high voice; though dreadfully short of time, they couldn't think of passing without rushing in and saying hello to Anna. They would look at her work another time. And then, in spite of their hurry, a flood of chitchat about the Kärntnerstrasse shops, in none of which I had ever set foot. It sounded like a report on an exotic expedition, delivered in breathless haste, standing, because there wasn't time enough to put down their coats and presents. Now and then he would start one of his parcels swinging, to show he was talking about the shop where it came from. Soon all the parcels were bobbing up and down on his fingers like marionettes. They were all perfumed; in a few minutes the room was filled with the finest scents, which emanated not from the parcels but from the shopping report. He talked of nothing else; only Anna's mother—in a passing word of homage—was briefly mentioned. When they had gone—

in leaving they had cautiously refrained from holding out their parcels—I asked myself: Has someone been here? Anna, who wasn't in the habit of making disparaging remarks, went over to her figure and gave it a slap. The shopping world that had just drifted in and out of her studio was not as strange to her as it was to me, she knew it through her mother, whom she had often accompanied to Kärntnerstrasse and the Graben, but it was a world she hated, and in leaving the husband her mother had forced on her for reasons of family politics, she had left it too.

She was no longer under obligation to give receptions on Maxingstrasse. She no longer had to worry about giving offense to any social faction. She no longer had to waste her time, for she was no longer under her mother's control. If something infuriated her, she picked up her chisel. She was determined to make her work as hard as possible for herself. What she had learned from Wotruba, with whom she had no deep friendship, was to strive for the monumental, because it demanded the hardest work. In the determination that showed itself in the lower half of her face, she resembled her father.

Thiess's call was purely a matter of form. He may not even have known that he had nothing to say to her. He could have served up his quick chatter to anyone. But Paul Zsolnay, Anna's last husband, was his publisher. Forsaking the delights of Kärntnerstrasse for this rather fleeting homage to Anna was a friendly gesture, a declaration of neutrality, as it were. He was satisfied just to show his face; perhaps he knew that everything she had lost by her flight from Zsolnay was dangling from his fingers.

Only really "free" writers, who were well known and widely read enough not to be dependent on the publishing house (because any other publisher would have taken them on), could afford to honor Anna with a visit. People came and went at her place, and it would get around that one had been there. Writers who were felt to be lackeys of the publishing house would have been ill advised to come. Some who had previously flattered Anna, who would have given their eyeteeth to be invited to her receptions, avoided her and kept away from Operngasse. There were some who suddenly began to speak ill of her. Her mother, who had a great influence on the musical life of the city, was spared, though calculation and power politics oozed from her every pore.

Anna stood up to the world's gossip, she was a brave woman. In her little studio on Operngasse she built up a kind of museum of famous heads. It was her own achievement insofar as her heads were successful, which was often enough the case. She did not suspect to what extent her museum was a reflection of her mother's life.

Her mother was out for power in every form, for fame, for money and for the power that confers pleasure. Anna's driving force was something weightier, her father's enormous ambition. She wanted to work and to make work as hard as possible for herself. Wotruba, her teacher, gave her just the long, hard work she needed. She made no excuses for herself as a woman, she was determined to work as hard as the powerful young man who was her teacher. It would never have occurred to her that his kind of work called for a different kind of life. She made no class distinctions, whereas her mother pronounced the word "proletarian" with the contempt she felt for slaves, as if it denoted a being with no claim to humanity, an indispensable commodity which could be bought, which at the most, in the case of an unusually beautiful specimen, might be used for love. While her mother liked to raise up people who had already been raised, Anna drew no such distinctions; class and social status meant nothing to her, she was interested only in people themselves. But it turned out that this noble sentiment was not enough: to estimate people at their proper worth, experience is not enough, one must also register and remember one's experience.

Her love of freedom meant a great deal to her; it was the main reason why no relationship could hold her for long. It was so strong that when she formed a new relationship one always had the impression that she didn't take it seriously but conceived it from the start on a short-term basis. On the other hand, she wrote "absolute" letters and expected "absolute" declarations. The letters written for her may have meant more to her than love itself, and what captivated her most were the stories one told her.

I often went to see her, especially after she acquired the studio on Operngasse, and spoke to her of everything that interested me. I told her what was going on in the world and what I was writing. Sometimes, when I was full of Sonne, I spoke to her of very serious matters; she always listened, apparently with deep interest. Then after long hesitation I took Sonne to her studio—he had expressed interest in Gustav Mahler's daughter—and presented her with what was for me the best thing in the world, the quietest of men. I introduced him with the respect that I owed him and had never concealed from her, and she reacted with the generosity that was the best thing about her; she took him for what he was, admired him despite his ascetic appearance, listened to him as she always listened to me, but with the degree of earnestness that I expected in his presence, and asked him to come again. The next time I saw her alone, she praised him, said she found him more interesting than most people, and often asked when he would repeat his visit.

Yet he had made some discerning comments about her heads, and I had passed them on to her; even in her large figures he recognized an unrealized romantic yearning. The tragic, he said, was still beyond her reach, and she had nothing whatever in common with Wotruba, for she had been inspired by music, which played no part in his work. Her figures were related to aspects of her father's music and owed more to her will than to her inspiration. There was no way of knowing what would come of her work; possibly, thanks to some *break* in her life, something very important. He spoke benevolently, he knew how much she meant to me and wouldn't have hurt my feelings for anything in the world, but I could tell by the way he relegated hope in her work to the future that for the present he found little originality in it. Still, he spoke well of her heads. He especially liked the one of Alban Berg; Werfel's, he thought, was as bloated as Werfel's sentimental novels, which he detested. Werfel, he observed, had infected her with himself; she had exaggerated his hollow sentimentality in such a way that some people who were quite familiar with his ugly real-life head would find it significant as portrayed.

She listened to Sonne as I listened to him. She never interrupted, never asked him a question, he couldn't ever talk long enough for her. He never stayed more than an hour. Seeing her surrounded by stone, dust and chisels, he assumed she wanted to work. Her tools told him how resolutely she worked, he needed none of her figures for that. He was struck by the resemblance to her father in the lower part of her face, where the will is localized. There alone did he recognize her as Gustav Mahler's daughter, for her other features, her eyes, forehead and nose, were not the least bit like his. She was most beautiful when she was listening in her impassive way, her wide-open eyes full of what she was listening to, a child for whom a serious, sometimes dry, but above all exhaustive report became a fairy tale. She was like that when I told her a story, and now he was there, he whose words meant as much to me as those of the Bible when he recited them to me. I listened to the very different things he said for her, and I was able without embarrassment to watch her as she listened. Here, I felt, she was no longer in her mother's world, she had passed beyond success and utility. I knew that she was finer and nobler than her mother, neither greedy nor bigoted, but that the massive old woman's power play repeatedly drove her into situations that had nothing to do with her nature, that concerned her not at all, situations in which she was obliged to follow instructions, a marionette moved by malignant wires.

Only in her studio was she free from all this and that may have been why she was so attached to her work. Her work was the last thing her mother would have urged on her, for considering the effort it required, it was unprofitable. But I don't believe she was at her freest when I was alone with her, for though she wanted me to come, everything depended on incessant exertion, on my invention, and of this I was so well aware that I would not have felt justified in staying if no ideas occurred to me. She seemed freest when I brought Sonne to see her. Because then, without hesitation or affectation, she submitted to a lesson the depth and purity of which she perceived, which was of no use to her, which she could not apply, which would have made no impression on any of her mother's retinue, for the name of Sonne meant nothing in those quarters; as he wished to have no name and consequently had none, he would not even have been invited.

When after an hour he stood up and left, I stayed behind. I am sure he thought I would want to stay longer, but it was only a kind of delicacy that held me. I thought it unseemly to leave the studio at his side. I had brought this extraordinary man to the studio; I was a kind of retainer, who showed him the way. Now he knew the way and wished to leave. In this no one should interfere with him. On his way he went on thinking, he continued the conversation with himself. If he had asked me to, I'd have gone with him. But he was too considerate to express such a wish. He thought me privileged because I often went to the studio. But that was all he knew. It would never have occurred to me to tell him any more about so intimate a matter. He may have suspected how downcast I was. But I don't believe so, because he never tried to comfort me in his inimitable way, by describing an ostensibly very different situation, which was simply a transposition of my own. So I stayed on, and when we met next day at the Café Museum, he made no mention of our visit. I hadn't stayed long after his departure. I waited only long enough for him to be out of reach, then I made up a pretext for taking my leave of Anna.

We didn't discuss him. He remained inviolable.

PART THREE
Chance

Musil

Musil was always—though one wouldn't have noticed it—prepared for defense and offense. In this posture he found safety. One thinks of armor plate, but it was more like a shell. He hadn't built the barrier he put between himself and the world, it was an integral part of him. He eschewed interjections and all words charged with feeling. He looked with suspicion on mere affability. He drew boundaries between objects as he did around himself. He distrusted amalgamations and alliances, superfluities and excesses. He was a man of solids and avoided liquids and gases. He was well versed in physics; not only had he studied it, it had become part and parcel of his mind. It seems doubtful that any other writer has been so much a physicist and remained so in all his lifework. He took no part in vague conversation; when he found himself surrounded by the windbags it was impossible to avoid in Vienna, he withdrew into his shell. He felt at home and seemed natural among scientists. A discussion, he felt, should start from something precise and aim at something precise. For devious ways he felt contempt and hatred. But he did not aim at *simplicity*; he had an unerring instinct for the inadequacy of the simple and was capable of shattering it with a detailed portrait. His mind was too richly endowed, too active and acute to content itself with simplicity.

No company made him feel inferior; although in company he seldom went out of his way to pick a quarrel, he did interpret every controversy as a fight. The fighting started later, when he was alone, sometimes years later. He forgot nothing. He remembered every confrontation in all its details, and since it was an innermost need with him to triumph in all of them, this in itself made it impossible for him to complete a work intended to encompass them all.

He avoided unwanted contacts. He was determined to remain master of his body. I believe he disliked shaking hands. In his avoidance of handshaking, he was at one with the English. He kept his body supple and strong and took good care of it. He paid more attention to it than was usual among the intellectuals of his day. To him sports and hygiene were one, they governed his daily schedule, and he lived in accordance with their requirements. Into every character he conceived he injected a healthy man, himself. In him extreme eccentricity contrasted with awareness of health and vitality. Musil, who understood a great deal because he saw with precision and was capable of thinking with even greater precision, never lost himself in a character. He knew the way out, but liked to postpone it because he felt so sure of himself.

To stress his competitiveness is not to diminish his stature. His attitude toward men was one of combat. He did not feel out of place in war, in war he sought to prove himself. He was an officer, and tried by taking good care of his men to make up for what he regarded as the brutalization of their life. He had a natural or, one might call it, a traditional attitude toward survival and was not ashamed of it. After the war, competition took its place; in that he resembled the Greeks.

A man who put his arm around him as around all he wished to appease or win over became the most long-lived of his characters and was not saved by being murdered. The unwanted touch of this man's arm kept him alive for another twenty years.

Listening to Musil speak was a particular pleasure. He had no affectations. He was too much himself to put one in mind of an actor. As far as I know, no one ever surprised him playing a role. He spoke rather rapidly but never in a rush. One could never tell from his way of speaking that several ideas were pressing in on him at once. Before expounding them, he took them apart. There was a winning orderliness in everything he said. He expressed contempt for the frenzied inspiration that was the principal boast of the expressionists. To his mind inspiration was too precious to use for exhibitionistic purposes. Nothing so sickened him as Werfel's foaming at the mouth. Musil had delicacy, he made no display of inspiration. In unexpected, astonishing images he suddenly gave rein to it, but checked it at once by the clear progression of his sentences. He was hostile to torrents of language, and when to the general surprise he submitted to someone else's, it was with the intention of swimming resolutely through the flood and demonstrating that the muddiest waters have a far shore. He was glad when there was an obstacle to overcome, but he never showed his determination to take up a fight. Suddenly he was standing self-reliant in the midst of the subject, and one lost sight of the battle, one was captivated by the subject matter, and even when the victor stood supple but firm before one, the argument itself had become so important that one forgot how eminently victorious *he* had been.

But this was only one aspect of Musil's public behavior. His self-assurance went hand in hand with a sensibility I have never seen outdone. To come out of himself, he had to be in company that recognized his rank. He did not function everywhere, he needed certain ritual circumstances. There were people against whom his only defense was silence. He had something of the turtle about him, there were many people who knew only his shell. When his surroundings didn't suit him, he didn't say a word. He could go into a café and leave it again without having uttered a single sentence. I don't think that was easy for him; though you couldn't tell it by his face, he felt offended throughout this silent time. He was right not to recognize anyone's superiority; among those who passed as writers in Vienna, or perhaps in the whole German-speaking world, there was none of his rank.

He knew his worth, in this one decisive point he was untroubled by doubt. A few others knew it too, but not well enough for his liking, for to give their support of him greater force, they would mention one or more other names in the same breath. In the last four or five years of Austrian independence, during which Musil returned from Berlin to Vienna, the avant-garde trumpeted three names: Musil, Joyce and Broch, or Joyce, Musil and Broch. Today, fifty years later, it is not hard to understand why Musil was not particularly pleased at that odd triad. He categorically rejected *Ulysses*, which by then had appeared in German. The atomization of language went against his grain; if he said anything about it, which he did reluctantly, he called it old-fashioned, on the ground that it derived from association psychology, which according to him was obsolete. In his Berlin period he had frequented the leaders of Gestalt psychology, which meant a good deal to him; he probably identified his book with it. The name of Joyce was distasteful to him; what that man did had nothing to do with him. When I told him how I had met Joyce in Zurich at the beginning of 1935, he grew irritable. "You think that's important?" I counted myself lucky that he changed the subject instead of leaving me flat.

But he found it absolutely insufferable to hear Broch's name mentioned in connection with literature. He had known Broch a long time, as industrialist, as patron of the arts, as late student of mathematics, and he refused to take him seriously as a writer. Broch's trilogy struck him as a copy of his own undertaking, which he had been working on for decades, and it made him very suspicious that Broch, having scarcely begun, had already finished.

Musil didn't mince matters in this connection and I never heard him say a kind word about Broch. I can't remember the details of what he said about Broch, possibly because I was in the difficult situation of thinking highly of them both. Tensions between them, let alone a quarrel, would have been more than I could bear. I had no doubt that they belonged to the small group of men who made writing hard for themselves, who did not write for the sake of popularity or vulgar success. At the time that may have meant even more to me than their works.

It must have given Musil a strange feeling to hear about this triad. How was he to believe that somebody recognized the importance of his work if that somebody mentioned him in the same breath with Joyce, who to his mind represented the antithesis of what he was trying to do? And even when Musil, who had no existence for the readers of the then popular literature, from Zweig to Werfel, was glorified, he found himself in what he regarded as unfit company. When friends told him that someone had praised *The Man without Qualities* to the skies and would be overjoyed to meet him, Musil's first question was "Whom else does he praise?"

His touchiness has often been held against him. Though I was to be its victim, I would like to defend it on the strength of my profound conviction. He was in the midst of his great undertaking, which he was determined to complete. He could not know that it was destined to be endless in two senses, immortal as well as unfinished. There has been no comparable undertaking in all German literature. Who would have ventured to resurrect the Austrian Empire in a novel? Who could have presumed to understand this empire, not through its peoples, but through its center? Here I cannot even begin to say how much else this work contains. But the awareness that he himself, he alone more than anyone else, was this defunct Austrian Empire gave him a very special right to his touchiness, which no one seems to have appreciated. Was he to let this incomparable material that he was be buffeted this way and that? Was he to let it suffer any admixture that would sully it and mar its transparence? Touchiness concerning one's person, which seems ridiculous in Malvolio, is not ridiculous when it relates to a special, highly complex, richly developed world which a man bears within himself and which, until he succeeds in bringing it forth, he can protect only by being touchy.

His touchiness was merely a defense against murkiness and adulteration. Clarity in writing is not a mechanical aptitude that can be acquired once and for all; it has to be acquired over and over again. The writer must have the strength to say to himself: This is how I want it and not otherwise. And to keep it as he wants it, he must be firm enough to bar all harmful influences. The tension between the vast wealth of a world already acquired and the innumerable things that demand to enter into it is enormous. Only the man who carries this world within himself can decide what is to be rejected, and the late judgments of others, especially of those who bear no world whatever within themselves, are paltry and presumptuous.

This touchiness made him react against the wrong kind of food. And here it should be said that a reputation, too, must be constantly fed if it is to steer the project of the man who bears it in the right direction. A growing reputation requires its own sort of food, which it alone can know and decide on. As long as a work of such richness is in progress, a reputation for touchiness is best.

Later on, when the man who has preserved himself by being touchy is dead and his name is displayed in every marketplace, as ugly and bloated as stinking fish, then let the snoopers and know-it-alls come and draw up rules for proper behavior, then let them diagnose touchiness as monumental vanity. No matter, the work is there, they can impede its progress no longer, and they themselves with all their impertinence will seep away without trace.

Some people ridiculed Musil's helplessness in practical matters. The first time I mentioned Musil to Broch, who was well aware of his worth and not inclined to malice, he said to me: "He's king of a paper empire." He meant that Musil was lord of people and things only when at his writing desk, and that otherwise, in practical life, he was defenseless against things and circumstances, bewildered, dependent on other people's help. Everyone knew that Musil couldn't handle money, that he even hated to touch it. He was reluctant to go anywhere alone; his wife was almost always with him, it was she who bought the tickets on the streetcar and who paid at the café. He carried no money on him, I never saw a coin or bank note in his hand. It may be that money was incompatible with his notions of hygiene. He refused to think of money, it bored and upset him. He was quite satisfied to let his wife shoo money away from him like flies. He had lost what he had through inflation, and his financial situation was very difficult. His means were hardly equal to the long-drawn-out undertaking he had let himself in for.

When he returned to Vienna, some friends founded a Musil Society, the purpose of which was to enable him to work on *The Man without Qualities*. Its members obligated themselves to monthly contributions. He had a list of contributors and reports were given him about the regularity with which they paid up. I don't think the existence of this Society shamed him. He believed, quite correctly, that these people knew what they were doing. They felt honored at being permitted to contribute to his work. It would have been even better if more people had felt the urge to join. I always suspected that he regarded this Musil Society as a kind of secret society, membership in which was a high honor. I often wondered if he would have barred persons he regarded as inferior. It took a sublime contempt for money to keep up his work on *The Man without Qualities* under such circumstances. When Hitler occupied Austria, the jig was up; most members of the Musil Society were Jews.

In the last years of his life, when he was living in utter poverty in Switzerland, Musil paid dearly for his contempt for money. Painful as it is for me to think of his humiliating situation, I wouldn't have wanted him any different. His sovereign contempt for money, which was not combined with any ascetic tendencies, his lack of any talent for moneymaking, which is so commonplace that one hesitates to call it a talent, partook, it seems to me, of his innermost essence. He made no fuss about it, did not affect to rebel against it and never spoke of it. He took a serene pride in ignoring its implications for his own life, while keeping well in mind what it meant to others.

Broch was a member of the Musil Society and paid his dues regularly. I found this out from others, he himself never mentioned it. Musil's harsh rejection of him as a writer—in a letter Musil accused him of having in his *Sleepwalkers* trilogy copied the plan of *The Man without Qualities*—must have irked him, and one is inclined to forgive him for calling Musil "king of a paper empire." This ironic characterization is without value in my mind. Even now—long after their deaths—I feel the need of rejecting it. Broch, who had suffered sorely under his father's commercial heritage, died in exile in just such poverty as Musil. He had no wish to be a king and he was not one. In *The Man without Qualities*, Musil *was* a king.

Joyce without a Mirror

The year 1935 began for me amid ice and granite. In Comologno, high above the beautifully ice-clad Val Onsernone, I tried for several weeks to collaborate on a new opera with Wladimir Vogel. It was foolish of me, no doubt, to attempt anything of the kind. The idea of subordinating myself to a composer, of adjusting to his needs, didn't appeal to me at all. Vogel had told me that this would be an entirely new kind of opera, in which composer and writer would function as equals. This proved to be impossible: I read Vogel what I had written, he listened patiently, but I felt humiliated by his supercilious way of expressing approval with a nod of the head and the one word "Good," followed by words of encouragement: "Just keep it up." It would have been easier on me if we had quarreled. His approbation and his words of encouragement soured my enthusiasm for that opera.

I've kept some of my notes; nothing could have come of our collaboration. As I was leaving Comologno, he honored me with one more "Just keep it up," sensing, I'm sure, that he would never receive another word from me. I would have been ashamed to tell him so—what reason could I have given for my lack of enthusiasm? It was one of those puzzling situations that have occurred time and again in my life; I was offended in my pride, though the "offender" couldn't possibly have guessed what had happened. Perhaps he had given me an almost imperceptible impression that he felt superior to me. But if I was to subordinate myself to anyone, it had to be of my own free will. And it was for me to decide to whom. I chose my own gods and steered clear of anyone who set himself up as a god, even if he really was one; I regarded such a person as a threat.

Yet my weeks in Comologno were not fruitless. One sunny winter's day I read my *Comedy of Vanity* to Vogel and my hosts in the open air, and found a better audience than at the Zsolnays'. From then on my hosts were well disposed toward me; they suggested that on my way home I should give a reading at their home in Zurich. They had a fine auditorium suitable for such purposes, and all the intellectuals would be sure to come. The outcome, in January, was my first reading of *The Comedy of Vanity* to a large but select audience. It was there that I met James Joyce.

I read the first part of the play in unadulterated Viennese dialect. As it never occurred to me that many of those present would not understand this language, I provided no explanatory introduction. I was so pleased with the rigorous consistency of my Viennese characters that I failed to notice the none too friendly atmosphere in the hall.

In the intermission I was introduced to Joyce. "I," he said gruffly, "shave with a straight razor and no mirror"— a risky business in view of his impaired vision, he was almost blind. I was stunned. His tone was as hostile as if I had attacked him personally. The idea of prohibiting mirrors was central to the play; it occurred to me that this must have exasperated him because of his weak eyes. For a whole hour he had been exposed to Viennese dialect which, despite his linguistic virtuosity, he did not understand. Only one scene had been spoken in literary German, and that was where he had caught the bit about shaving in front of mirrors. This is what his wretched comment had referred to.

Evidently the linguist's frustration at failing to understand Viennese exacerbated his annoyance, in the one scene he understood, with the idea that mirrors were indispensable. This section, to which he seemed to object on moral grounds, he took personally and reacted by assuring me that *he* needed no mirror for shaving, that even though he used a straight razor, there was no danger of his cutting his throat. His outburst of male vanity might have been taken from the play. How stupid of me, I thought uncomfortably, to inflict *this* play on him. It was what I *wanted* to read, but I should have warned my hosts. Instead, I was glad when Joyce accepted their invitation and realized only when it was too late what havoc I had wreaked with my mirrors. His "no mirror" was a declaration of war. To my own consternation I felt ashamed for him, for his compulsive sensibility, which lowered him in my esteem. He left the auditorium at once; perhaps he thought the mirror play would be continued after the intermission. Someone in the audience told me to take it as an honor that he had come in the first place, and assured me that he had been expected to make some cutting remark.

I was introduced to several distinguished people, but the intermission was not long and I didn't catch the prevailing mood. My impression was that the people had shown and were still showing curiosity, and that they had not yet made up their minds. I pinned my hopes on the second part of my reading, for which I had chosen the "Kind Father" chapter from the novel that was soon to be titled *Die Blendung* (*Auto-da-Fé*). I had often read this chapter in Vienna, to both small and larger groups, and I felt as sure of it as if it had been an integral part of a generally known and widely read book. But as far as the public was concerned, that book did not yet exist, and while in Vienna there was already some talk of it, here it hit the audience with the shock of the totally unknown.

I had hardly spoken the last sentence when Max Pulver, who had come in a dinner jacket, bobbed up like a jack-in-the-box and sang out merrily: "Sadism at night is a bit of all right." The spell was broken, after that everyone felt free to express his distaste. The guests stayed awhile, I met almost all of them, and each in his own way told me how much the second part in particular had riled him. The more kindly souls represented me indulgently as a young writer, not entirely devoid of talent, but needful of guidance.

Wolfgang Pauli, the physicist, whom I greatly respected, was one of these. He gave me a benevolent little lecture, to the effect that my ideas were aberrant. Then, rather more sternly, he bade me listen to him, since after all he had listened to me. It is true that I hadn't been listening and consequently cannot repeat what he said, but the reason why my ears were closed to him was something he could never have guessed: he reminded me of Franz Werfel, though only in appearance of course, and in view of what Werfel had put me through exactly a year before, the resemblance was bound to shake me. But the manner of speaking was quite different, benevolent rather than hostile; I think—I may be mistaken—that he was trying to educate me along Jungian lines. After his admonition I managed to get hold of myself. I listened with apparent attention to the end, I even thanked him for his interesting observations, and we parted on the best of terms.

Bernard von Brentano, who had been sitting in the first row, exposed to the full force of my acoustic masks, seemed disgruntled. All he said, in his toneless way, was "I could never do that, stand up and act in front of all those people." The vitality of the characters had got on his nerves, he thought me an exhibitionist and exhibitionism was offensive to his secretive nature.

One after another was at pains to acquaint me with his disapproval; since many of these people were famous, the proceedings amounted to a sort of public trial. Each of them thought it important to demonstrate that he had been present, and since this was an established fact and could not be denied, to demonstrate his rejection in his own way. The hall had been full; there would be many names to mention; if I knew that any one among them was still alive I would mention him and at least clear him of any imputation of premature approval. The host, who felt sorry for me, finally led me to a gentleman whose name I have forgotten, a graphic artist, and said to me on the way: "You'll be pleased with what he has to say. Come." It was then that I heard the one positive statement of the evening. "It makes me think of Goya," said the artist. But there was no need of this consolation, which I mention only for fairness' sake, for I didn't feel shattered or even dejected. I was overpowered by the characters of my *Comedy*, their ruthlessness, their—I can find no other way of saying it—their truth; and as always after such a reading, I felt buoyant and happy. All the disapproval I had been subjected to merely intensified this feeling; I had felt surer of myself than ever before, and to this feeling the presence of Joyce, in spite of his absurd remark, actually contributed.

During the social part of the evening, which went on for some time, the mood changed for the better. Some erstwhile listeners even managed to talk about themselves so well that they became centers of attraction after all. The most striking of these was Max Pulver, who had already distinguished himself by being the only dinner-jacketed gentleman present and by his little quip about my sadism. He had a few confidential communications to make that attracted general attention. As a writer, he could not have meant much to this distinguished gathering, but for some time he had been busying himself with graphology. His recently published *The Symbolism of Handwriting* was being much discussed; it was thought to be the most important work on graphology since Klages.

He asked me if I knew whose handwriting had been submitted to him for an opinion. I had no idea, but at the time I took an interest in graphology and showed a satisfactory amount of curiosity. He didn't keep me on tenterhooks for long; in a voice loud enough for all to hear, he said something about "world-political importance."

"I shouldn't talk about it," he went on, "but I will all the same. I have specimens of Goebbels's and Göring's handwriting at my place, and that's not all. Oh yes, there's yet another, you can imagine who, but it's a deep secret. Himmler sent them to me for my opinion."

I was so impressed that for a moment I forgot my reading and asked: "And what do they show?"

This was six months after the Röhm putsch. Hitler had been in power for two years. The naïveté of my question matched the childlike pride of his announcement. His tone was unchanged in his answer to my question, which sounded affable rather than boastful, with something almost Viennese about it (he had lived for a time in Vienna).

"Very interesting, really," he said apologetically. "I'd be glad to tell you. But I'm pledged to strictest secrecy. Like a doctor, don't you know."

By then the whole company had been alerted to the dangerous names he had mentioned. The lady of the house joined our group. She knew what was going on and she said with a nod of the head in Max Pulver's direction: "He's going to talk himself into trouble one of these days."

Whereupon he declared that he was well able to keep his mouth shut, or they wouldn't send him such things.

"No one will ever get anything out of me."

I would give more today than I would have then to know how he worded his analyses.

The list of persons invited included C. G. Jung and Thomas Mann, neither of whom had come. I wondered if Pulver would have boasted to Thomas Mann of the handwriting specimens the Gestapo had commissioned him to analyze. The presence of refugees didn't seem to trouble him. There were many in the hall: Bernard von Brentano was thought to be one, and Kurt Hirschfeld of the Schauspielhaus was there. I even had the impression that their presence had prompted Pulver to make his "revelations." I was tempted to throw his "sadism" back in his face, but I was too shy and too unknown.

The actual star of the evening was the lady of the house. Her friendship with Joyce was well known. There was hardly a writer, painter or composer of repute who didn't come to her house. She was intelligent, one could talk to her, she understood something of what such men said to her, she was able without presumption to talk to them. She took an interest in dreams; that brought her close to Jung, and it was said that even Joyce told her some of his dreams. She had made herself a home in Comologno, a refuge for artists, who could go there to work. Very much a woman, she did things that were not merely calculated to further her own glory. I compared her in my thoughts with the noisy, witless woman in Vienna, who dominated the scene through boasting, greed and liquor. True, I knew that one better, I'd known her for years, and it's amazing how much you find out when you've known someone a long time. Still, I feel justified in comparing her with my hostess of that evening to the latter's advantage, and if my hostess is still alive, I hope she gets wind of my good opinion.

It was at her house that evening, among her guests who listened to me with disapproval, possibly because they only half understood me, that I recovered my self-confidence. Only a few days before, I had been ashamed to subordinate myself to a composer. Though I respected him, I had reason to doubt that he regarded me as an equal. At the house of this woman in Val Onsernone I had felt this to be a humiliation, though no one was to blame. Now in her Zurich town house she gave me an opportunity to read my latest work, which meant a great deal to me, to people more than one of whom I admired, and to suffer a defeat which was all my own and against which I could pit all my strength and conviction.

The Benefactor

Jean Hoepffner was the owner of the *Strassburger Neueste Nachrichten,* the most widely read of Alsatian dailies. It was published in German and French, gave offense to no one and stepped on nobody's toes. It provided all the news needed in Alsace but seldom went beyond matters of regional interest, except in the financial section. Everyone I knew in Strasbourg subscribed, it had by far the largest circulation of any daily, you saw it wherever you went. It wasn't the least bit stimulating, the cultural section was utterly undistinguished; anyone interested in such matters read the big Paris papers.

The printshop and offices were in the rear of the building on Blauwolkenstrasse (rue de la Nuée Bleue), but the thumping of the presses could be heard in every room front and back. Jean Hoepffner didn't live there, but he had a two-room apartment on the third floor, which he let out-of-town friends use. It was crammed full of old furniture, for he had a passion for rummaging in junk shops. He was overjoyed when he thought he had made a find and immediately moved it into his guest apartment, which became, as it were, his own private junk shop, except that nothing was for sale. This shop was visited only by the friends who were privileged to stay there, and when Jean Hoepffner's shining eyes opened wide and came to rest on something which he lavishly and unsuspectingly praised, one didn't have the heart to tell him the truth, namely, that one didn't like it at all. One just smiled, shared his pleasure and changed the subject as soon as possible.

When one stayed there for several weeks, as I did, one had to deal with this problem day after day, because in addition to the large stock that was already there, new pieces kept arriving; almost every day he appeared with something new, usually something small; he seemed to feel that he had to contribute to his guest's comfort by bringing in more and more new and startling objects. The apartment was full, it was no easy matter to find room for anything new, but he found it. I think I have never lived anywhere where the furnishings were less to my taste; everything looked dusty and unused; though the place was cleaned every day, one wouldn't have been surprised to find mold on everything, but it would have been a purely symbolic mold, because when you looked closely the place was scrupulously clean; it was more the nature of the objects and the fact that nothing went with anything else that gave the impression of mold.

The most amiable conversations were held in these rooms, where I slept and had my breakfast. In the morning, before going to his second-floor office, Herr Hoepffner dropped in to see me and kept me company at breakfast. He had his favorite writers, whom he read over and over again, whom he could not get enough of, and he liked to talk about them. In particular, there was Adalbert Stifter, practically all of whom he had read; some of his stories, he told me, which he was especially fond of, he had read more than a hundred times. In the evening, when he went home from his office, he would be looking forward to his Stifter. He was a bachelor and lived alone with his poodle; an old Alsatian woman, who had been with him for years, cooked and kept house for him. He wasted no time on superfluities; he appreciated the meal that his kindly housekeeper prepared for him, drank his wine with it and then, after playing awhile with his poodle, took up his Stifter, whom he could not praise enough. Of him he spoke more earnestly than of the junk he sometimes brought with him. But between his antiques and Stifter there was obviously a connection, which he wouldn't have thought of denying.

I once asked him why he kept reading the same things. He didn't resent the question, but it surprised him. What else was there to read? He couldn't bear modern writing, everything was so gloomy and hopeless, never a single good person. It just wasn't true, he said, he had seen something of life, he had met lots of people in his work, and he had never come across a single bad person. You had to see people as they are and not impute evil intentions to them. The writer who had seen this most clearly was Stifter, and ever since Jean Hoepffner discovered that, all other writers had bored him or given him a headache.

At first I had the impression that he had read nothing else. But there I was wrong, for it turned out that he had another favorite book which he had read no less often. It might come as a surprise to me, he said. He seemed to feel the need of apologizing before confiding the name. We should know, he explained, what the world would be like if there were bad people. It was an experience we needed, though of course it was an illusory experience. He had had this experience. Even though he knew that the picture this book painted was totally untrue, it was written so wonderfully that one had to read it, and he read it over and over again. Just as there are people who read crime novels for the pleasure of recovering from them, so to speak, of returning to the real world, he read his Stendhal, *The Charterhouse of Parma*. I admitted that Stendhal was my favorite French author, I had looked upon him as my master and tried to learn from him. "Learn from him?" he said. "The only thing you can learn is that fortunately the world is not like that."

He was convinced that *The Charterhouse of Parma* was a masterpiece, but a masterpiece of *deterrence*, and his conviction was so pure that I felt abashed in his presence. Something made me speak truthfully of myself, and I soon told him what I had written. I told him the story of *Kant Catches Fire*, and he listened with interest. "That sounds like even better deterrence than *The Charterhouse of Parma*. I'll never read it. But it's good such a book exists. It will have a good effect. The people who read it will wake up as from a nightmare and be thankful that reality is different." But he could see why no publisher, not even those who had spoken respectfully of the manuscript, had dared publish it. It took courage to publish such a book, and that was a rare commodity.

I believe he wanted to help me and disguised his wish with exquisite tact. He himself wouldn't read such a thing, my account of it had been too repellent. But he had heard from our friend Madame Hatt that I had not yet published a book, and that seemed unfortunate for a writer who was almost thirty. Since it wasn't exactly his cup of tea, he thought up an educational justification for the existence of such a novel: deterrence. Without transition and without hesitation, in the course of the same conversation, he suggested that I look around for a good publisher who believed in the book. Then he, Jean Hoepffner, would guarantee the publisher against loss. "But," I objected, "it's quite possible that no one will want to read my book."

"Then I'll make good the publisher's loss," he said. "I'm much too well off, and I have no family to support." He made it sound like the most natural thing in the world. He had soon convinced me that there was nothing he would rather do, nothing simpler, and at the same time he proved to me that the world wasn't the least bit like my book, that there were good people in it. He was certain that anyone who read my book would return with renewed confidence to the real world of good people.

On my return to Vienna I had a lot to talk about. My travels had taken me to Comologno and Zurich, Paris and Strasbourg; unusual things had happened and I had met remarkable people. When I reported to Broch, his candid response, proffered with less hesitation than usual for him, was that he envied me for just one thing, my meeting with James Joyce. Now, I had no reason at all to be so pleased with that meeting. His rudely macho remark—"I shave with a straight razor and no mirror"—had struck me as contemptuous and hostile. Broch disagreed; in his opinion it showed that my reading had touched a chord. Joyce, he assured me, was incapable of stupidity and with those words he had laid himself bare. Would I have preferred some smooth, meaningless remark? Broch turned the sentence round and round and tried various interpretations. Its contradictory character appealed to him, and when I accused him of treating this banal and utterly uninteresting sentence as an oracle, he agreed without hesitation; yes, that's just what it was, and he went on looking for interpretations.

If the *Comedy* had disconcerted Joyce, Broch went on, that was all to the good. Of course he had understood it perfectly; did I imagine that a man of his stamp could live so long in Trieste without mastering the Austrian dialects? When he kept interrupting all my attempts to tell him more about my trip with further talk about Joyce—another possible interpretation had occurred to him—I realized that for him Joyce had become a paragon, a figure one tries to emulate and from whom one can never quite dissociate oneself. Broch, who was himself the soul of kindness, refused to be put off by anything I said about Joyce's cruel arrogance. He insisted that this seeming cruelty resulted from his many eye operations and couldn't be taken seriously. What interested him, Broch, was the self-assurance with which Joyce carried his fame; no one else's fame was as distinguished, as elegant as his. This was the only kind of fame Broch cared about, and nothing would have made him happier than to be noticed by Joyce. Years later the hope of producing a work remotely comparable to Joyce was to play an important part in his conception of *The Death of Virgil.*

All the same, he was delighted when I told him about Jean Hoepffner and was no less amazed than I at his offer. A man who read hardly anything but Stifter, who rejected modern literature en bloc, who after the first few pages would have put aside *Kant Catches Fire* with horror, had offered to provide for the publication of this same book. "Once it's published," said Broch, "it will make its way. It's too intense, too gruesome perhaps to be forgotten. Whether you'll be doing your readers a good turn with this book, I don't dare decide. But there's no doubt that your friend is doing a good deed. He is acting contrary to his prejudice. It's a book he couldn't possibly understand. But he'll never read it. He's not even doing it to curry favor with posterity. He just has a hunch that you are a gifted writer and he somehow wants to do literature a good turn, because it has done so much for him with Stifter. What I like best about him is the way he lives in disguise. The director of a printing press and newspaper. What greater disguise could there be? You'll easily find a publisher."

He was right, and in a way he helped, though not in exactly the way he intended. A few days later he saw Stefan Zweig, who was in Vienna for two reasons. He was having extensive dental work done, and he was setting up a new publishing house for his books, which the Insel

Verlag in Germany was no longer able to publish. I believe
nearly all his teeth were extracted. A friend of his, Herbert
Reichner, was publishing a magazine called *Philobiblon*,
which was not at all bad. Zweig decided to let Reichner
publish his books and to find him a few other presentable
works for window dressing.

Soon after my return I ran into Zweig at the Café
Imperial. He was sitting alone in one of the back rooms,
holding his hand over his mouth to hide the absence of
teeth. Though he did not like to be seen in that condition,
he beckoned me over to his table and bade me be seated.
"I've heard the whole story from Broch," he said. "You've
met Joyce. If you have someone who will guarantee your
book, I can recommend it to my friend Reichner. Get
Joyce to write a preface. Then your book will get attention."

I told him at once that this was out of the question,
that I couldn't make such a request of Joyce, that he
hadn't seen the manuscript, that he was almost blind and
couldn't be expected to read such a thing, but that even
if he could read as easily as anyone else, I'd never ask
such a favor of him. I went on to say that I wouldn't ask
anyone to write a preface, that the book should be read
for its own sake. It needed no crutches.

All this sounded so harsh that I myself was rather taken
aback. "I only wanted to help you," said Zweig. "But if
you don't wish . . ." Back went his hand over his mouth,
and that was the end of our exchange. I went my way
without the least regret that I had turned down his
proposal so firmly. I had saved my pride and lost nothing.
Even had it been possible—in my opinion it was not—the
thought of publishing my book with a preface by Joyce,
regardless of what it said, stuck in my craw. I despised
Zweig for suggesting it. But fortunately, perhaps, I didn't
despise him so very much, for when a few days later I
received a letter from the Herbert Reichner Verlag,

speaking, it's true, of the guarantee but making no mention of a preface, and asking me to submit my manuscript, I took counsel with Broch, who advised me to send it in. And so I did.

An Audience

The first consequence of my increased self-assurance was my reading at the Schwarzwald School on April 17, 1935.

I had been to see Frau Dr. Schwarzwald, but not very often. Maria Lazar, to whom I also owed my friendship with Broch, had brought me. The legendary educator was an enormous talker; the first time she saw me she pressed me to her bosom as if I had been her pupil from infancy and had poured out my heart to her innumerable times. But despite her overflowing friendliness, I preferred the taciturn Dr. Schwarzwald, a small, slightly crippled man, who hobbled in on a cane and then sat morosely in a corner, where he submitted to the visitors' interminable, and the Frau Doktor's even more interminable, chatter. His head, which may be known to the reader because of a portrait by Kokoschka, looked, as Broch once remarked, like a root.

The smallish room in which visitors were received was even more legendary than Frau Dr. Schwarzwald, because it would be hard to think of a celebrity who had not been there at one time or another. Vienna's truly great had sat there long before they gained general recognition. Adolf Loos had come and brought young Kokoschka with him; so had Schönberg, Karl Kraus, Musil and any number of others. It is interesting to note that all these men, whose work would withstand the test of time, gathered there. But it should not be thought that any of them took a particular interest in Frau Dr. Schwarzwald's conversation. She was regarded as an impassioned educator with modern, liberal ideas; she was helpful and indulgent and her pupils idolized her, but since her talk was a hopeless jumble, her intellectual callers found her not only uninteresting but downright tedious. She was looked upon as a well-intentioned bore, but the people one met at her house were not bores, and there were never too many at a time. I listened to them and watched them closely, they imprinted themselves on my mind as if they had come to sit for their portraits. In a way, perhaps, I usurped the role of the great portraitist who made their acquaintance there and really did paint their portraits.

Whoever might be present, the most unforgettable was the taciturn Dr. Schwarzwald; his silent severity seemed to obliterate his wife's chatter. And then there was a person whom one felt to be the heart of the household, the marvelous Mariedl Stiasny, Dr. Schwarzwald's friend, who took care of him and not of him alone, for she managed the school and ran the household. She was a beautiful, radiant woman of lively intelligence, neither talkative nor silent, her laughter was like fresh air to all those who lived in the house or merely went in and out. When you dropped in for a visit, she wouldn't just be sitting there, she was always busy, but she would look in from time to time to see how things were going, and whoever might be in attendance, whatever kings of the intellect you had just met, you caught yourself waiting for Mariedl Stiasny to appear. When the door opened, everyone hoped it would be she, and some of us, I'm afraid, would have been slightly disappointed if it had been God the Father instead. In the rather ridiculous argument I had had with Broch about the "good" person, we had not, inconceivable as it may seem, thought of any woman, for if either of us had mentioned this particular woman, that would have been the end of our argument.

As might be expected, Fritz Wotruba had long been visiting the Schwarzwalds. He came irregularly and never stayed long, but what drove him away was not Frau Dr. Schwarzwald's chatter, he was used to that from Marian, his wife; it was his intense restlessness, his passion for the streets of this neighborhood not far from Florianigasse, which were his true home. He always felt better out of doors than in, and after the obligatory first visit was paid, it was not easy to get him to make another. When I told him, not without pride, about the unanimously unfavorable reaction of my Zurich audience, he said: "Those people don't understand the Viennese language. You must give a big reading here." It was the Viennese voices that had drawn him to the *Comedy*, and he thought I owed it to myself to read it to a Viennese audience.

It may have been his wife, the practical Marian, who thought of the large auditorium at the Schwarzwald School. Though my reading was not to be taken as a school function, the Schwarzwalds agreed to provide the hall. Everything else was handled by Marian Wotruba, handled with a vengeance. The hall was packed. Most if not all the members of the Sezession and the Hagenbund were there, painters and sculptors, the architects of the Neuer Werkbund, a few of whom were known to me. Marian must have talked them all, singly and collectively, into a stupor. But there were also people who were not in her province, writers and others who meant a good deal to me.

I must mention the two I esteemed most highly. One was the angel Gabriel, as I privately called Dr. Sonne, and as secret as this name, which he bore only for me and which I am now revealing for the first and only time, was his presence. He managed to be seen by no one and yet I felt protected by his sword. The other was Robert Musil, who came with his wife and with Franz and Valerie Zeis, who were good friends of his, as they were of mine, and who for some time had been tactfully laying the groundwork for this meeting. The presence of Musil meant more to me than had that of Joyce two months before in Zurich. For while Joyce was at the peak of his well-deserved fame, Musil, whom I had been reading seriously for only a year, struck me as equally deserving of fame; moreover, he was closer to me.

I read the same passages as in Zurich but in inverse order, starting with the "Kind Father" chapter of the novel and ending with the first part of *The Comedy of Vanity*. This may have been the better order, but I don't believe that alone was responsible for the different reception. Wotruba was right in saying that nothing was more authentically Vienna than what I had chosen for this reading. Besides, the audience *expected* more. In Zurich no one but my hosts had ever heard of me, for all the others I was an unknown quantity. And then, without explanation, to be assailed by this fairground, these voices, these characters. Here quite a few of the people knew who I was, and Marian had given those who didn't a good talking-to. In Zurich the quick shifts from one to another of these very divergent characters supposedly all talking at once made my head reel and kept me too busy to watch for reactions, as one ordinarily does when giving a reading. Consequently, it was only later, when it was all over, that I became aware of the total absence of understanding.

Here, from the very start, I sensed expectation and wonderment, which encouraged me to read as if my life depended on it. The gruesome "Kind Father" scene aroused horror, the Viennese knew the tyranny of their janitors and I don't believe any of my listeners would have dared doubt the veracity of this character as long as they were all sitting there together exposed to him. After this scene the *Comedy* began like a liberation from the

ghoulish janitor and then little by little developed a horror
of its own. If here again a few members of the audience
were horrified, they blamed the realities represented
rather than the author. I met with animosity only among
the close friends of the house, and the only real dressing-
down I got was from Karin Michaelis, a Danish writer,
who angrily accused me of inhumanity. While she was
talking, even Frau Dr. Schwarzwald fell silent for the first
and only time. She said nothing, she didn't even favor
me with her friendly chatter, for which I had been
prepared. Her silence contributed to the success of the
evening.

For I was full of the presence of Dr. Sonne and Musil.
I saw Musil facing me in the second row and felt a slight
twinge of fear that he would get up and go in the short
intermission I had arranged after the "Kind Father," just
as Joyce had done after the *Comedy* in Zurich. But he
didn't get up and he didn't go; on the contrary, he seemed
spellbound. Sitting as rigid as usual, he leaned slightly
forward; his head gave the impression of a projectile
aimed at me, but restrained by his prodigious self-control.
As I found out a little later, this impression, which
engraved itself forever on my memory, was not an illusion,
though the explanation, when I heard it, was bound to
surprise me.

Sonne, to whom I give second billing just this once, was
invisible. I knew I wouldn't find him, so I didn't look for
him. But for me this was a decisive moment in our
relationship. After all the conversations he had favored
me with for more than a year, this was his first encounter
with any of my writing. I had never shown him a manuscript; he had realized, though not a word had ever been
said about it, that I felt ashamed of not yet having
published a book, and that with him, who shunned all
publicity, but only with him, I lost this sense of shame.
He never asked me about it, he never said: "Wouldn't

you like to show me the novel Broch has told me about?"
He never said anything, because he knew that as soon as
the book was out and it was no longer possible to make
changes, I would bring it to him.

He also knew that I had to *protect* my manuscript from
his judgment, because a word from him, and from him
alone, could have destroyed it. To this danger, which I
clearly recognized, I exposed neither the novel nor the
two plays, and I did not regard this as cowardice, because
these three works, which I had not even managed to
publish, were all I had. I felt capable of protecting them
against anyone else. But against him I would have been
defenseless, because instinctively, but also very deliberately,
I had raised him up to be my supreme authority, to which
I would incline because I needed such an authority no
less than my awareness that my three works existed. But
now he had come, and oddly perhaps in view of the
foregoing, I felt no fear of his presence.

Broch was not in Vienna and Anna was taken up with
her sister Manon, who was gravely ill. None of those who
had inflicted the humiliation of the year before was
present. Not once did Werfel's "Give it up!" cross my
mind, though the sting of hatred was still in me. Those
words were intended as a curse on all my future writing,
and although I set no store by them, they *acted* as a curse,
for they were flung at the *Comedy*, which I firmly believed
in. The Zsolnay world, which I had never taken seriously,
was far away; here I was confronted with what I regarded
as the real, authentic Vienna, which I had faith in and
which, I was sure, would be the Vienna of the future.

The painters, a compact band led by Wotruba, were
unstinting in their applause, which contributed no little
to the outward success of my reading. Perhaps it was their
applause more than anything else which gave me the
impression that the *Comedy* had at last found its audience.
A mistake, as it later turned out, but a forgivable one.

Just this once I was able to indulge the feeling that the *Comedy* had been understood and might exert an influence on the generation for which it was written.

The moment it was over, Musil came up to me and it seems to me that he spoke to me warmly, without the reserve for which he was known. I was confused and intoxicated. His face, not his back, was turned toward me. I saw his face close to mine and I was too overwhelmed to catch what he was saying. Besides, he had little time to say anything, for already a powerful hand had taken me by the shoulder, I was turned around and hugged tight— it was Wotruba, whose brotherly enthusiasm stopped at nothing. I struggled free and introduced him to Musil. It was in that passionate moment that the seeds of their friendship were sown, and though their friendship was to be so eventful that they forgot this isolated moment, it has remained one of the luminous occasions of my life. I have not forgotten it.

We were separated; others crowded around, including many whom I was seeing for the first time. Then someone announced that we were going to the Steindl-Keller, that a room had been reserved on the second floor. It was a long, straggling procession that made its way through the streets; when I arrived and looked into the room that had been set aside for us, a good many people were already seated at the long horseshoe-shaped table. Musil was standing undecided in the doorway with his wife. Franz Zeis, whom he trusted, was trying to persuade him to go in and sit down. He hesitated, looked into the room, but did not move. When I went up to them and respectfully invited him to join us, he excused himself; there were too many people, he said, the room was too crowded. He still seemed undecided, but it was hard for him to reverse himself after expressly declining. In the end he found a table outside the room, and there he installed himself with his wife and the two Zeises.

Perhaps it was better so, for how could I have felt free in his presence? It would have been inappropriate to have him sitting there, hemmed in by all these people, who had come to eat, drink and make noise in honor of a young writer. I had to invite him when I saw him standing in the doorway and sensed his indecision; to accept his exclusion would have been more tactless than to invite him. And quite possibly he had waited for an invitation before declining. All Musil's defensive gestures, which I saw directed at myself or others, struck me as invariably right. I would hate to lose the memory of them. If this had been my only meeting with him (which was luckily not the case), I would nevertheless have the feeling that I had known him in a precise, appropriate way, compatible with the language of his work.

The atmosphere in the inner room was boisterous. A few of the painters were there, and they didn't have to be taught how to celebrate. I said to myself that not one person was there whose presence I would have been ashamed of. Fortunately, one does not look at things too closely on such occasions. But especially when toasts began going around, I felt that something was missing. I hesitated, as though I should wait a moment before drinking. I didn't know why, for I had forgotten the all-important. Perhaps amid this general rejoicing, which had taken hold of me too, I was afraid to tell myself that the decision, the crux, was still to come. I must have expected the judgment, but I wasn't looking for it. I was not in a state of mind to notice exactly who was there. Little by little, they would all speak up, I could rely on that. But once, just once, I felt that someone was looking at me. No one called out to me. I glanced, without searching, in a certain direction. At some distance from me, frail, rather squeezed in, in total silence, sat Dr. Sonne. As soon as he found my eyes, he raised his glass very gently, smiled and drank my health. It seemed to me that his lips moved, I could hear nothing, there was something unreal about hand and glass; they hovered motionless, as in a painting.

He said no more to me, not even in the following days when we again sat together at one of the round marble tables at the Café Museum. He had spoken to me by raising his glass, by holding it aloft; that meant more to me than any audible words. Since he had heard only parts and no complete work, he didn't wish to speak. But he hadn't barred my way, he hadn't warned me of any danger he had sighted. He had left me a free passage, in his considerate way that respected all life. I interpreted as approval what may even then have been more.

One of those who had come to the Steindl-Keller was Ernst Bloch. I had heard of his *Thomas Münzer* but had never looked into it. His presence at the reading was noticed by quite a few people, including, as I later found out, Musil. Musil declined my invitation, I went into the inner room. Bloch, who had just found himself a seat, stood up and came over to me. As far as possible in such a crowd, he took me aside and set out to tell me exactly what he thought. He began with an eloquent gesture. "First impression," he said, and raised both hands, at some distance from each other but palms facing, to slightly above shoulder level. Then with rhythmic emphasis he said: "It—towers." The interval after the "it" was as striking as the elevation of the hands. The "towers," so long after the indefinite "it," was as startling and lofty as a Gothic spire. I looked in amazement at the gnarled, slightly elongated face, the lines of which were brought out by the towering hands. After that he said things that proved he had understood the *Comedy*. He knew its implications, predicted what would inevitably happen in the second part, and hit the nail on the head. It was a thorough, perfectly organized statement; I could have hoped for nothing better. But it might all have been spoken in a foreign language. "It—towers!" is all that has stayed with me.

The evening had an epilogue that I don't wish to pass over in silence, though to me it was rather embarrassing. It has to do with Musil and what he was really thinking during the reading, something I could not have suspected and which, in my delight at his presence and friendly treatment of me, would have been lost forever if Franz Zeis hadn't told me about it some days later.

Franz Zeis was a high official in the patent office and had known Musil a long time. He was a loyal friend, who early recognized his worth. At that time there were perhaps a dozen creative artists whom it was meritorious to stand up for, because it brought no advantage but, if anything, trouble. Some of these banded together in small groups, Schönberg and his disciples for instance; others were isolated. Franz Zeis knew them all and helped them all. He had a fine instinct for their loneliness. He realized that they needed solitude, but he also knew how deeply they suffered from it. He knew Musil best, his touchiness, the distrustfulness of Martha, his wife, who kept watch with Argus eyes lest anyone come too close to him—in short, every particular of this constellation indispensable to so outstanding a mind. Zeis knew all about Musil's most secret reactions and he was shrewd enough to keep them in mind in his efforts to help Musil.

I told him what I thought about Musil, and once he was convinced of the depth and solidity of my admiration, he told Musil, who took a close look at admiration before accepting it. Franz Zeis always had to submit to an interrogation; every statement he relayed was weighed in the balance and usually found wanting. But if Zeis thought some little thing he heard might meet with Musil's approval, he could not be discouraged from repeating it. There are two kinds of tale bearers. There are those who do what they can to foment strife, who pass on every pejorative remark they hear, exaggerate it by taking it out of context, so arousing hostile reactions, which they carry back to the original denigrator, and so back and forth until they have completely alienated good friends. This little game gives them an enjoyable sense of power and sometimes they even manage to fill the place of one of the dislodged friends. The other sort of tale bearers—a lot rarer—are those who bear only good tales, do their best to palliate the effects of unfriendly remarks by neglecting to mention them, promote curiosity and, little by little, confidence, until inevitably the time comes when the persons involved, whose meeting has been so patiently prepared for, meet in reality. Franz Zeis was one of these, and I believe he was really eager to relieve Musil's sense of isolation and to give me the pleasure of knowing him better.

That is just what Zeis did by persuading Musil to attend my reading. Afterward he saw fit to describe Musil's reactions, and the next time we met he told me things that startled me not a little. First Musil had expressed surprise: "He's got a good audience," he had said, and mentioned a few names such as Ernst Bloch and Otto Stoessl. That had impressed him. Then, while I was reading "The Kind Father," he had suddenly gripped the arms of his chair and said: "He reads better than I do!" Of course, this was far from the truth, everyone knew what a fine reader Musil was; the interesting part of this remark was not its truth content but the form in which he made it. It bore witness to what I later regarded as Musil's *competitiveness*. He measured himself against others; to him a mere reading was what an athletic contest was to the Greeks. This struck me as almost insane, it would never have occurred to me to measure myself against him, I put him far above myself. And yet, though I was unaware of it at the time, it may have been a necessity for me, after the humiliation of the year before, to give battle before a better audience and to win.

The Funeral of an Angel

For almost a year she had been presented in a wheelchair, attractively dressed, her face carefully made up, a costly rug over her knees, her waxen face alive with false hope. Real hope, she had none. Her voice was unimpaired, it dated back to the days of innocence, when she tripped about on the feet of a doe and was regarded by visitors as the opposite of her mother. Now the contrast, which had always seemed incredible, was even greater. The mother, who went on living in her usual way, thought better of herself because of her beloved child's misfortune. The daughter, though paralyzed, was still capable of saying yes; she was engaged to be married.

This engagement was intended to be useful. The choice fell on a young secretary of the Patriotic Front, a protégé of the professor of moral theology who directed the conscience of the regal lady of the house. The young man, who had no compunctions about getting engaged to a woman who had only a short while to live, moved freely about the house when he called on his fiancée. By the side of her wheelchair he became acquainted with all the celebrities who came for the same purpose. With his ingratiating grin, his well-mannered bows and tremulous voice, he became a much discussed figure: the promising young man, whom no one had ever heard of before, who sacrificed himself, his looks, his increasingly valuable time, to give the angel the illusion of a possible recovery. Being betrothed gave her reason to hope that she would marry.

It made quite an impression when the dinner-jacketed young man kissed his fiancée's hand. As often as Viennese men say *"Küss die Hand"*—which rolls so easily off the tongue—he actually did it. When he straightened up with the pleasant feeling that he had been *seen* doing it, that in this house nothing was done in vain, credit was given for everything, especially for depositing a kiss on this hand, when for a moment he prolonged his bewitching bow to his paralytic fiancée, he was *standing* for both of them. There were some who shared the mother's belief in a miracle and said: "She will recover. The joy her fiancé gives her will make her well."

But there were others who looked with anger and disgust on this disgraceful spectacle and cherished very different hopes. They, and I was one of them, wished for just one thing: that mother and fiancé should be struck by lightning, which would not kill but paralyze them, and that the sick girl would jump up from her wheelchair in a panic and be *cured*. From then on her mother would be wheeled about in her stead, just as attractively dressed, just as carefully made up, with the same high-priced rug over her knees; the fiancé, standing but on roller skates, would be pulled toward her on a chain and would try unsuccessfully to bow and kiss the old woman's hand. Of course, the girl would put all her purity and kindness into trying to make her mother a present of her recovery and resume her former condition in her stead, but would be prevented by the perpetually unsuccessful bowing and hand kissing. Thus the three of them would be frozen into a waxworks group, which could be set in motion now and then, providing for all time a picture of the state of affairs on Hohe Warte.

But reality knows no justice, and it was the impeccably dinner-jacketed secretary who followed the funeral service leaning on a column in the Heiligenstadt Church. That was the end of his engagement to Manon Gropius; she died as had been foreseen and instead of a wedding he had to content himself with a funeral.

She was buried in Grinzing cemetery. Here again every

last possibility of effect was exploited. All Vienna was there, or at least everyone eligible to be received on Hohe Warte. Others came who longed to be invited but never were; you couldn't keep anyone away from a funeral by force. A long line of cars filed up the narrow road to the cemetery; actually it was more a path than a road; no matter how frantic the passengers of a car might be for a place of honor, passing was unthinkable. In unchanging order, the long file struggled up the hill.

I was sitting in one of these cars, a taxi, with Wotruba and Marian. Marian was in a frenzy of excitement and kept screaming to the driver: "Faster, faster. We've got to be up front. Can't you drive faster? We're way in back. We've got to be up front. Faster, faster!" Her phrases snapped like whips, but it wasn't a horse she was whipping, it was a taxi driver, and the harder she lashed, the calmer he became. "It can't be done, lady, it can't be done." "It's got to be done," Marian screamed. "We've got to be up front." Her excitement came out in sobs. "We'll be there at the tail end. Oh, this is disgraceful!"

I'd never seen her in such a state; neither had Wotruba. She had long been trying to get him a commission to do a Mahler monument. They kept asking him for new sketches. They kept putting him off on senseless pretexts. Anna, his pupil, had interceded with her mother. Carl Moll had been running himself ragged in Wotruba's behalf. He had once brought his influence to bear for Kokoschka, and took no less trouble for Wotruba. But always at the last moment something went wrong. I suspected the all-powerful widow, and indeed it was she who sabotaged Wotruba's candidacy. Alma Mahler had a crush on him, but since Marian was always nearby, she had little opportunity for ensnaring him. She went to his studio with enormous bologna sausages under her arm, and then, after beating a disappointed retreat, she would say to her daughter: "He's not right for Mahler. He's too

low-class." Marian, meanwhile, besieged every government bureau that could have the slightest influence on
the decision. Her enthusiasm for "Mahler," as the two of
them called the monument, reached its climax on this
ride to the funeral of Manon Gropius, who had very little,
and in death nothing at all, to do with Mahler.

But Marian Wotruba fumed, and since the car advanced
very slowly on its way to the cemetery, she had plenty of
time for fuming. "Now you can do it. Try it now. We've
got to get ahead. Look, we're the last in line. We've got
to get ahead." Wotruba looked at me as if to say: "She's
off her rocker," but was careful not to say it out loud, for
Marian could have transferred her fury from the driver
to him. Not that the matter left him indifferent. He too
would have preferred to be further forward, closer to the
Mahler monument. To a sculptor there is a close connection between tombs and statuary. A cemetery undoubtedly
represents the earliest assemblage of stone blocks in his
experience, and when the posthumous stepdaughter of a
monument-worthy man is concerned, the tie becomes
indissoluble.

I don't remember our arrival. Marian must have pro-
pelled us forward through the dense throng of tomb
lovers; in the end we were standing not far from the open
grave, and I heard the stirring oration of Hollensteiner,
custodian of the grieving mother's heart. She was weeping.
It struck me that even her tears were of unusual size.
There weren't many of them, but she managed to weep
in such a way that droplets merged into larger-than-life
accretions, tears such as I had never seen, enormous
pearls, priceless jewels. I couldn't look at her without
gasping in wonderment at so much mother love.

True, the child, as Hollensteiner eloquently pointed
out, had borne her sufferings with superhuman patience,
but no less great were the sufferings of the mother, who
had lived through her ordeal before the eyes of the whole

world, which had been kept constantly informed. Meanwhile all sorts of things had been happening in the world, other mothers had been killed, their children had starved to death, but none had suffered what this woman had suffered, she had suffered for each and all, she had not faltered, even now at the graveside she stood firm, a voluptuous but aging penitent, a Magdalen rather than a Mary, equipped with swollen tears rather than contrition, magnificent specimens such as no painter had yet produced. With every word of her orating lover, they went on gushing until at length they festooned her fat cheeks like clusters of grapes. That was how she wanted to be seen, and that was how she was seen. And all those present were at pains to be seen by her. That's what they had come for, to give her grief the public recognition it deserved. It did their hearts good to be there, on one of Vienna's last great days before it staggered to its doom and the new masters turned it into a province.

But there was another who distinguished herself on this occasion. Though somewhat removed from the rest, she was hardly inconspicuous; not content to share the glory of the bereaved mother, she managed to display her own no less public sorrow. On a fresh grave mound, not too near but not too far away, knelt Martha, the widow of Jakob Wassermann, who had died a year before while still almost at the height of his fame. Deep in fervent prayer, she had chosen her grave mound wisely, it could be seen from everywhere. Her gaunt hands were clasped, now and then they trembled with emotion, her tightly closed eyes, much as they would have liked to observe the effect of her retreat, saw nothing of this world. A little less rigorous, her sorrow might have been credible. In this attitude of fervid prayer the narrow face was meant to suggest a careworn peasant woman, shrewd calculation had shaped her hat to look like a headscarf. The whole performance was just a bit overdone; if the hands had quivered a little less, if the eyes had opened now and then, if the freshly filled grave, which couldn't very well be the angel's, had not been so obviously well placed, one might have been tempted to take her emotion at face value. But it was all too good to be true; one didn't even stop to wonder whom Martha might be praying for: for her late cardiac husband, who had worked himself to death, for the angel, who was beyond the reach of Hollensteiner's unction and her mother's stupendous tears, or for her own writing: she thought herself superior to her husband and after his death was grimly determined to prove it to the world.

The whole wretched performance in Grinzing cemetery was redeemed in my eyes by the opportunity to observe these two characters, the kneeling Martha, whom I saw as she was getting ready to kneel but not as she arose; the mother, whose great heart managed to produce such enormous tears. I did my best not to think of the victim, whom all had loved.

High Authority

In mid-October 1935 *Auto-da-Fé* appeared. In September we had moved to Himmelstrasse, halfway up the vine-clad slopes above Grinzing. It was a relief to be up here, away from the gloom of Ferdinandstrasse and at the same time to hold in my hands this novel sprung from the darkest aspects of Vienna. Himmelstrasse [Heaven Street] led to a hamlet known as Am Himmel [In Heaven], and I was so amused at the name that when Veza had stationery printed for me she gave the address as "Am Himmel 30" instead of "Himmelstrasse 30."

To her, our move and the publication of my novel meant escape from the world of the novel, which had depressed her. She knew that I would never break away from it, and as long as I had the thick manuscript in my house, she saw it as a threat. She was convinced that while I was working on it something had snapped inside me and that *The Comedy of Vanity,* which she preferred to my other works, gave a better idea of what I could do. Tactfully, thinking I didn't notice, she made it her business to find out to whom I was sending autographed copies of *Auto-da-Fé.* She saw I was sending only a few, hardly more than a dozen, and she was glad of that. She thought it inevitable that the critics would massacre me, but hated to see me alienate friends who thought well of me—there weren't many—by giving them this depressing novel to read.

She expatiated on the difference between public readings and reading to oneself. Apart from the obligatory "Kind Father," I had given readings of "The Morning Walk" (the first chapter) and some of the second part: "The Stars of Heaven" and "The Hump." The main character in these passages was Fischerle, whose manic exuberance was always infectious. But audiences were also moved by "The Kind Father," one could always feel pity for the tormented daughter. Some people might have been glad to read more, but the book was not in existence and thus they had been unable to subject themselves to the intolerably detailed presentation of the struggle between Kien and Therese. Having no reason for resentment against the author, they came to the next reading, which corroborated their previous opinion. Among the small groups of Viennese interested in modern literature, a deceptive reputation had been growing up; now, with the appearance of the book, it would receive a deathblow.

I myself had no fears, it was as if Veza had taken them all upon herself. My faith in the book had been reinforced by every publisher's rejection. I felt certain that the book would be a success, though perhaps not an immediate one. I don't know what gave me this certainty. Perhaps one defends oneself against the hostility of one's contemporaries by unhesitatingly appointing posterity as one's judge. That puts an end to all petty misgivings. One stops asking oneself what this one and that one are likely to say. Since it doesn't matter, one prefers not to think about it. Nor does one stop to recall what in times past contemporaries said about the books one loves. One sees them for themselves, detached from all the bothersome trivia in which their authors were involved in their lifetime. In some cases the books themselves have become gods, which means not only that they will always be around but also that they always have been around.

One cannot be absolutely sure about this gratifying posterity. Here again there are judges, but they are hard to find, and some unfortunate writers may never meet the man whom they can with a good conscience appoint as their posterity expert. I had met such a man, and after long talks with him over a period of a year and a half my respect for him was so great that if he had sentenced *Auto-da-Fé* to death I would have accepted his verdict. I lived for five weeks in expectation of his sentence.

I had inscribed his copy with words which no one else could have understood.

"For Dr. Sonne [Sun], to me still more. E.C."

In the copies I had sent to Broch, Alban Berg and Musil, I was not chary of expressions of esteem; I wrote clearly and plainly what I felt, in terms intelligible to all. With Dr. Sonne it was different. Since an "intimate" word had never been spoken between us, I had never dared tell him how greatly I honored him. I never mentioned his name to anyone without the "Dr." This should not be taken to mean that the title meant anything to me, practically everyone you met in Vienna called himself "Dr." The word merely served as a kind of buffer. One didn't just come out with the man's name, I prepared the way with a neutral, colorless word, which made it clear that I was not entitled to intimacy, that the name would always keep its distance. And it was thanks to this distancing title that so sacred a word as *Sonne*, luminous, searing, winged, source and (as still believed at that time) end of all life, did not for all its roundness and smoothness become a household word. I didn't even *think* the name without the title; whether I was alone or with others, it was always "Dr. Sonne," and only now after almost fifty years has the title begun to seem too stiff and formal. I shall not use it very often from now on.

At that time only the man to whom my inscription was addressed could understand that he meant more to me than the sun. For no one else did I reduce my own name to initials. The handwriting—witness the size of the letters—remained incorrigibly self-assured; this was not a man who wanted to disappear; with this book, which for years had existed only in secret, he was at last challenging the public. But he wished to disappear in the presence of *him*, the man who was concerned not with himself but only with ideas.

One afternoon in mid-October, at the Café Museum, I handed Dr. Sonne the book which he had never seen in manuscript, which I had never mentioned to him, of which he had heard only an isolated chapter at a reading. He may have heard more about it from others, perhaps from Broch or Merkel. Broch's opinion in literary matters may well have meant something to him, but he would not have taken it on faith. He trusted only his own judgment, though he would never have dreamed of saying so. After that I saw him as usual every day. Every afternoon I went to the Museum and sat down with him, he made no secret of the fact that he was waiting for me. The conversations to which I owed my rebirth at the age of thirty continued. Nothing changed; true, every conversation was new, but not new in a *different way*. His words offered no indication that he had been reading my novel. On that subject he remained obstinately silent, and so did I. I burned to know if he had *begun*, at least *begun*, but I never once asked him. I had learned to respect every corner of his silence, for only when he began unexpectedly to speak of something was he at his true level. His independence, which he maintained quite openly, but always with tact and gentleness, taught me the meaning of an independent mind, and in my dealings with him I was certainly not going to disregard what I had learned from him.

Week after week went by. I kept my impatience under control. A rejection from him, however fully documented, however compellingly reasoned, would have destroyed me. It was to him alone that I accorded the right to pass an intellectual death sentence on me. He kept silent, and evening after evening when I came home to Himmel-strasse, Veza, from whom I couldn't very well conceal anything so all-important, asked me: "Did he say anything?" I replied: "No, I don't think he's had time to look at it." "What! He hasn't had time? When every day he spends two hours at the café with you." I would affect indifference and toss out lightly: "We've talked about dozens of 'auto-da-fés,' " or try to divert her in some other way. Then she would lose her temper and cry out: "You're a slave. That's what he's done for you. I'd never have expected you to choose a master! At last the book is out, but you've turned into a slave!"

No, I was not his slave. If he had done or said something contemptible, I would not have gone along with him. From him least of all would I have accepted anything base or contemptible. But I was absolutely sure that he was incapable of doing anything stupid or base. It was this absolute, though open-eyed trust that Veza regarded as slavery. It was a feeling she knew very well, because it was how she felt about me. In this feeling she now felt justified by three valid works. But what works had Dr. Sonne ever produced? If any, he had known how to conceal them. Why would he do that? Did he think them unworthy of the few people with whom he associated? She was well aware that what Broch, Merkel and others most admired in him was his self-abnegation. But it seemed inhuman that he should carry self-abnegation so far as to keep silent for weeks about my book, though we saw each other every day. She didn't mince words. She attacked him in every way. Her usually ready wit seemed to forsake her when she spoke of him. Since she herself didn't feel sure about the book, she was afraid his silence meant condemnation and she knew what an effect that would have on me.

One afternoon at the Café Museum—we had just exchanged greetings and sat down—Sonne said without preamble, without apology, that he had read my novel; would I like to know what he thought of it? And he proceeded to talk for two hours; that afternoon we spoke of nothing else. He illuminated the book from every angle, he established connections I had not suspected. He dealt with it as a book that had existed for a long time and would continue to exist. He explained where it came from and showed where it would inevitably lead. If he had contented himself with vague compliments, I would have been pleased after waiting for five weeks, for I would have known his approval was sincere. But he did far more. He brought up particulars which I had indeed written but could not explain and showed me why they were right and could not have been different.

He spoke as though taking me with him on a voyage of discovery. I learned from him as if I were someone else, not the author; what he set before me was so startling I would hardly have recognized it as my own. It was amazing enough that he had every slightest detail at his command, as though commenting on some ancient text before a classroom. The distance he thus created between me and my book was greater than the four years during which the manuscript had lain in my drawer. I saw before me an edifice thought out in every detail, which carried its dignity and justification within itself. I was fascinated by every one of his ideas, each one came as a surprise, and my only wish was that he would never stop talking.

Little by little, I became aware of the intention behind his words; he knew the book would have a hard life and he was arming me against the attacks that were to be expected.

After a number of observations that had no bearing on this purpose, he began to formulate the criticisms for which we should be prepared. Among other things, he said, it would be attacked as the book of an old and sexless man. Very meticulously he proved the contrary. It would be argued that my portrayal of the Jew Fischerle lent itself to misuse by racist propaganda. But, said Sonne, the character was true to life, as true to life as the narrow-minded provincial housekeeper or the brutal janitor. When the catastrophe had passed, the labels would fall from these characters, and they would stand there as the types that had brought about the catastrophe. I am stressing this particular, because in the course of subsequent events I often felt uneasy about Fischerle. And then I found comfort in what Sonne had said that day.

Far more important were the profound connections he revealed to me. Of these I say nothing. In the fifty years that have elapsed many of these have been discussed in print. It would seem as though *Auto-da-Fé* contained a reservoir of secrets, which would be tapped little by little until all were drawn off and explained. This time, I'm afraid, has not yet come. I still preserve intact within me a good part of the treasure Sonne gave me then. Some people are surprised that I still respond with wonderment to every new reaction. The reason is to be sought in this treasure, the one treasure in my life that I like to keep an eye on and that I knowingly administer.

The attacks I still get from outraged readers do not really touch me, even when they are made by friends whom I love for their innocence and whom for that reason I had warned against reading the book. Sometimes I succeed with earnest pleas in keeping someone away from it. But even for close friends whom I have been unable to deter from reading it, I am no longer the same man. I have a feeling that they expect to find the evil the book is replete with in *me*. I also know that they don't find it, for it is not the evil I have in me now, but a different kind. I can't help them, for how can I possibly explain to them that on that afternoon Sonne relieved me of *that* evil by picking it before my eyes from every nook and cranny of the book and piecing it together again at a salutary distance from myself?

PART FOUR

Grinzing

Himmelstrasse

While searching Grinzing for something that money cannot buy, I came across Fräulein Delug, who was to be our landlady for three years. We moved into the apartment, the best I had ever had, on a temporary basis, until someone should turn up who was prepared to rent the whole apartment. We had the use of four rooms including a large studio, and we had our own entrance. The four remaining rooms were unoccupied. We showed our visitors the whole apartment, including the empty rooms, and they were entranced by the location, the size and number of the rooms and the varied views from the different windows.

The unoccupied rooms were much coveted, but they were not for rent. Fräulein Delug's unswerving honesty was our defense. She had rented us the part we lived in on one condition, namely, that if anyone should want the whole apartment, which was rather expensive, we would have to move. In the meantime we were left alone; she refused to move other people in with us, though it had often been suggested; she didn't even tell us about such proposals, we heard of them only indirectly. Without hesitation she said no, though such an arrangement would have doubled her rent. That wasn't what had been agreed between us, she said, and it wouldn't be right. She was no great talker but one of the few words she used frequently was "right"; she said it with a guttural "r," she was from the Tyrol, her dialect was something like Swiss, and that was one of my reasons for liking her. She was a small woman with an enormous bundle of keys; I couldn't say how many rooms, occupied and unoccupied, there were

in the building, which was originally planned as an art
academy; her daily rounds took her to all of them, except
when, as in our case, she was afraid of disturbing someone.
Then she would announce her visit the day before. All
the dimensions of this building were large. The entrance
and the stairway with its comfortable low steps received
you like a palace. But no lord and master was in command;
the authority here was a small, stooped, white-haired old
woman, who dragged herself about with a bundle of keys,
and far too seldom gave voice to a few guttural syllables,
which sounded harsh but were meant kindly.

She was all alone in the world; I never saw anyone who
seemed connected with her; she may have had relatives
in the South Tyrol, but if so, she never mentioned them;
she never said anything to suggest that she had any ties
at all. We saw her only in the house and garden, never
on Himmelstrasse, the street that led to the village, and
never in any shop; there was nothing to indicate that she
ever went shopping, she carried a bag only when she went
out to the garden for vegetables. We came to the conclusion that she lived on fruit and vegetables; she could get
milk from the tenant who lived on the garden side of the
ground floor, and he may have brought her bread as well.
It was only when she paid the rent that Veza saw the big
tower room where Fräulein Delug lived. There were a lot
of antiques in it that might have come from a fine Tyrolean
house, but they were jumbled all together, as though she
had had to move them here for lack of space anywhere
else, and yet there were quite a few large empty rooms
in the house. The tower room was the nucleus, the nerve
center so to speak, where Fräulein Delug labored to keep
things together, an endeavor that was far beyond her
strength. The building was more than twenty years old
and every corner of it cried out for repairs. These she
had to pay for out of the rents, for painter Delug had
evidently spent all his money building the Academy, his
lifelong dream. She never talked about her troubles. She

never complained. At the most she would remark now and then that a lot of things needed repairing. As a peasant woman tries to keep up her farm, so she tried to preserve her brother's dream. She was all alone and probably thought of nothing else.

The imposing building halfway up Himmelstrasse had been planned as an academy of art but had never served that purpose. Construction had barely been completed when Delug died, and the struggle to keep the property intact devolved on his sister. Six large apartments, three in each wing, were laid out for rental purposes, but there were also outbuildings and modest basement rooms. The garden, which extended on three sides, was subdivided here and there by beautiful stairways and adorned with sculptures, which were meant to look like time-scarred antiquities. As to their value as works of art, opinions may have varied, but the garden as a whole, copied from an Italian model, was most attractive. As it was surrounded by vineyards, it did not seem out of place, and precisely because it was an imitation it had the charm of the artificial. From a small lateral terrace reached by way of weather-beaten, moss-covered steps, one had a view extending from the houses of Vienna over the seemingly endless Danube plain.

All in all a delightful place, but the most delightful thing about it was its situation halfway between the Grinzing terminus of the No. 38 streetcar and the woods farther up the hill. You could climb the second half of Himmelstrasse, past more modest villas, to Am Himmel, above Sievering, not far from which the woods began. Or if you weren't in the mood for woods, you could take the relatively narrow road leading in a wide arc to Kobenzl; there again you had a wide view of the plain, but near at hand you could look across vineyards to the proud Academy building, where we had the good fortune to be living.

Diagonally across from the Academy, a little farther

down on Himmelstrasse, lived Ernst Benedikt, who until recently had been owner and publisher of the *Neue Freie Presse*. I had long known of him as a character in *Die Fackel*, though I had heard more about his father, Moritz Benedikt, who was one of *Die Fackel*'s prime monsters. We had already moved into our new lodgings when I found out about this; it was too late to back down, but I can still feel the shudder that ran through me when Anna, who had come to look at the studio we had said so much about, showed me the Benedikt house. We were standing on the garden terrace; I wanted to show her the view of the plain, she had a liking for open space, but to my surprise she pointed at a house not far away and said: "That's the Benedikts' house." She hadn't been there very often. She didn't take it very seriously. The power of the *Neue Freie Presse* had indeed been great, but that of Anna's mother was now greater. She may have known that thanks to *Die Fackel* the name of Benedikt had taken on a diabolical quality over the years, but to her it meant nothing; nothing was more alien to her than satire, and it is certain that she never read a whole sentence, let alone a page, of *Die Fackel*. She said "the Benedikts' house" as if the Benedikts were just anybody, and she was not a little astonished when in response to her harmless remark I showed every sign of horror and asked to know more about that ghoulish family.

"Is it really *the* Benedikts?" I asked more than once. "Right next door to us!"

"You don't have to look at them," she said.

I turned away in consternation and went back indoors. Anything rather than the view of that accursed house.

"He's uninteresting," said Anna. "He has four daughters and he plays the violin, not badly by the way. He has a mouth like a tadpole and a rather foolish way of speaking. He talks much too much. But no one listens. He's always trying to show how well informed he is on every possible subject, but he's just boring."

"And he publishes the *Neue Freie Presse?*"

"No, he's sold it. He has nothing to do with it anymore."

"What does he do now?"

"He writes. About history. The publisher didn't want any of his stuff. The readers said it was no good."

I asked more questions, but to no purpose. I was only talking to hide my excitement, but it was too great to hide. I felt as a believer must have felt in olden times when he heard that a heretic was living next door, an abominable creature all contact with whom was to be dreaded, and a moment later he's told that it's not a heretic, or anything else that endangers the hope of salvation, but a harmless, rather foolish individual, whom no one takes seriously.

I was too upset about this neighbor to let the figure whom Karl Kraus had built up over the years be taken from me at once. But I kept asking questions because I didn't want Anna to notice that this diabolical neighbor frightened me in some way. She noticed it, though, but she didn't make fun of me, she never really made fun of anyone. She thought mockery unaesthetic as well as indiscreet, and after what she had been through with her mother she had a special horror of it. But she must have thought it unworthy of me to waste more than a passing thought on this neighbor, and she may also have been eager to calm me down and change the subject, for we usually found more interesting and important things to talk about.

I adjusted to the situation in my usual way. I cast an interdict on the Benedikt house and from then on I *didn't see it.* I couldn't have seen it anyway from the window of the room where I wrote and where I kept my books, which looked out on the front yard and on Himmelstrasse. The Benedikt house was farther down and its number was 55. It couldn't be seen from *any* room in our apartment, not even from the unoccupied ones. To see the interdicted house you had to go out to the garden terrace,

where I had taken Anna. I had taken her exclamation as
a threat and from then on I stayed away from the terrace.
Besides, it was rather out of the way and there were
plenty of other things to show visitors in the large and
varied garden. And when I went down to the village,
usually to take the streetcar, I automatically turned my
face to the left until No. 55 was behind me.

It was early September when we moved in and for a
good four months, until well into the winter, this protection was adequate. At the back of my mind I had an exact
picture of the Benedikt house. I knew the open veranda
on the second floor, looking out on the street, the location
of the windows, the type of roof, the steps leading to the
front door. I don't believe I had so accurate a mental
image of any other house in the vicinity; though always a
poor draftsman, I could have drawn a picture of it, but I
never looked in that direction. I always looked toward
the houses on the other side of the street. When and on
what occasion I had formed my accurate picture of that
house—before setting foot in it—will always be a mystery
to me. I needed my image of it in order to cast an *interdict*
on it.

I had told Veza about it during Anna's visit, and she
laughed at me for being so upset. She had been no less
addicted to *Die Fackel* but only as long as she was sitting
in the hall facing Karl Kraus, not a moment longer. After
that, she read what she felt like reading, undeterred by
his anathemas, she made the acquaintance of people, saw
them through her own eyes, as though Karl Kraus had
never said a word against them. In the present juncture
she didn't give a thought to our pestiferous neighbor, in
fact she seemed pleased at the presence of four young
girls, the Benedikt daughters. She was curious about them,
as she would have been about any other young girls, made
fun of me for being so upset, and asked if they were
pretty—a question to which Anna could give no definite
answer—and asked Anna which of them I was likely to

fall in love with. Anna said she thought it unlikely that I would fall for any of them, they were silly little geese, you couldn't even talk with them. They took after their amiable, rather simple mother, not their idiotic father. But Veza didn't keep up her joking too long. Once she had established her independence, she made it clear that she would stand by me, and when I had pronounced my interdict on the house, she promised to help me and not to complicate matters for me with her girlish curiosity.

I myself wasted no thought on trying to figure out how these girls might look. Since they were born of the *Neue Freie Presse*, it went without saying that they were corrupt to the core.

On the way down Himmelstrasse to the village, I often saw the same people coming up at the same hour. I had an advantage over them, because they were slowed by the climb and I was moving faster than they were; they seemed to offer themselves to my inspection, while I hurried past them with a superior air. But sometimes a young girl coming up the hill passed me in great haste, and then I would slow down. Open light-colored coat, loose pitch-black hair, breathing heavily, dark eyes directed at a goal unknown to me, very young, perhaps seventeen. If her breathing hadn't been so loud, she'd have been as beautiful as a dark fish. There was something Oriental in her features (but she was too tall and too heavily built for a Japanese girl of her age). She ran furiously, almost blindly; I hesitated, fearing that she would run into me, but one glance from her sufficed to avoid a collision. That glance, which could mean nothing but flight, escape, hit me hard. She radiated tempestuous life. She seemed so young that I would have been ashamed to look after her, so I never found out where she was running to, but she must have belonged in one of the houses farther up Himmelstrasse.

She only appeared at the noon hour, and I can't imagine

what she had to do in the village at that time of day. After a few encounters with the dark-haired girl's intriguing haste, I found myself almost daily on the street. It never dawned on me that I was there on her account, though I was careful not to arrive at the corner of Strassergasse too soon, because that was where she came from and I would not be going that way. Thus I didn't take a single step out of my way because of her, I wasn't going out of my way for her, because I was *going my way*, it was her own passionate will that made her come running along; if I went this way almost every day at the same hour, it had nothing to do with her.

Her name? Any name would have disappointed me unless it had been Oriental. At that time I was seeing a good deal of Japanese color woodcuts. They fascinated me, as did the Kabuki theater, which I had seen during a week of guest performances at the Volksoper. I was especially fond of Sharaku's woodcuts of Kabuki actors, because on seven successive evenings I had had occasion to appreciate the effectiveness of Kabuki plays. But in these plays the female roles were played by men, and I'm sure there was no one resembling my daily apparition in any of Sharaku's woodcuts. But since the impetuousness that overwhelmed me in the girl rushing up the hill was common to them all, I now believe it was for the sake of this fascinating breathlessness that I made my way to the village at that particular time of day. It was then—about one o'clock—that the performance began, and I was its punctual audience. I was not tempted to look behind the scenes, I had no desire to find out anything, but I wouldn't have missed that entrance, that one scene, for the world.

Winter was coming on, and as the weather grew colder, the scenes became more dramatic, for the girl literally steamed. Her coat was more open than ever, she seemed to be in even more of a hurry, her violent bursts of breath became clouds in the cold air. The air was colder, more steam escaped from her open mouth; as she passed close to me, I could hear her panting.

When her time approached, I stopped work, laid my pencil down, jumped up and left the apartment unobserved through a door that led directly from my room to the vestibule. I went down the broad stairway with the low steps, crossed the front yard, looked up at my windows on the second floor as if I were still up there, and then I was on the street. I was always in some fear that my Kabuki figure, my Oriental girl, might have passed, but she never had, I had time to avoid the sight of No. 55 by looking to the left in obedience to the interdict I had cast upon it. Then, invariably, between No. 55 and Strassergasse, the wild girl would come running toward me, giving off waves of excitement. I absorbed as much of it as I could; any more would have lasted me beyond the next day. I used to inquire about many of the people in the vicinity. About the hill climber I did not. Boisterous and outgoing as she seemed, to me she remained a mystery.

The Final Version

Veza and I had married while we were still living on Ferdinandstrasse, a year and a half before moving to Grinzing. I had kept our marriage secret from my mother in Paris; later she may have suspected the implications of the new Himmelstrasse address, but nothing was said. When my brother Georg, from whom it could not be kept a secret, found out, he, who knew my mother best, had kept it secret. She had finally heard about it along with the book, which came as a big surprise to her, and while she was talking about the book, talking in a conciliatory vein most unusual for her, she had glossed over our marriage as a nonessential part of the overall news picture. I began to hope that the worst between us was over, that she would now be ready to forget the years during which (to protect Veza and spare my mother) I had concealed from her the seriousness and permanence of my relationship with Veza.

In her high-handed way she had shown me recognition. The book, she said, was just as if she had written it, it could have been by her, I had made no mistake in wanting to write, I had done right to put everything else aside. What could chemistry mean to a writer? Bother chemistry; I had fought resolutely against it, shown my strength even in opposition to her. With this book I had justified my ambition. This was the kind of thing she wrote me, but then when I saw her in Paris and tried to defend myself against this new submissiveness, which I had never met with in her and found hard to bear, more and more followed.

Suddenly she started talking about my father and about his death, which had changed our whole existence. For the first time I learned what ever since then—more than twenty-three years had elapsed—she had concealed under frequently changing versions.

While taking the cure in Reichenhall, she had met a doctor who spoke *her* language, whose every word had its hard contours. She felt challenged to give answers and found within herself daring, unexpected drives. He introduced her to Strindberg, whose devoted reader she had been ever since, for he thought as ill of women as she did. To this doctor she confided that her ideal, her "saint," was Coriolanus, and he had not found this odd, but admired her for it. He didn't ask how she as a woman could choose such a model, but, moved by her pride and beauty, avowed his tender feelings for her. She adored listening to him, but she did not give in to his pleas. She allowed him to say what he wished, but she said nothing relating to him. He had no place in her conversation, she talked about the books he gave her to read and about the people whom he as a physician knew. She marveled at the things he said to her but made no concessions. He persisted in urging her to leave my father and to marry him. He was entranced by her German, she spoke German, he said, like no one else, the English language would never mean as much to her. Twice she asked my father to let her prolong her cure, which was doing her good, and he consented. She blossomed in Reichenhall, but she knew quite well what was doing her so much good: the doctor's words. When she asked for a third extension, my father refused and insisted on her coming straight home.

She came. Not for a moment had she thought of giving in to the doctor. And not for a moment did she hesitate to tell my father everything. She was with him again, her triumph was his. She brought herself and what had happened to her and laid it—those were her very words—at my father's feet. She repeated the doctor's words of admiration and couldn't understand my father's mounting agitation. He wanted to know more and more, he wanted to know everything; when there was nothing more to know, he kept on asking. He wanted a confession and she had none to make. He didn't believe her. How could the doctor have proposed marriage to a married woman with three children if nothing had happened? She saw nothing surprising because she knew how it had all developed from their conversations.

She regretted nothing, she retracted nothing, she told him over and over again how much good the doctor had done her; her health was restored, that's what she had gone there for, and she was glad to be home again. But my father asked her strange questions:

"Did he examine you?"

"But he was my doctor!"

"Did he talk German to you?"

"Of course. What would you have him speak?"

He asked if the doctor knew French. She said she thought so, they had talked about French books. Why hadn't they spoken French together? This question of my father's she had never understood. What could have given him the idea that a doctor in Reichenhall should speak any other language than German to her, whose language was German?

I was amazed at her failure to realize what she had done. Her infidelity had consisted in speaking German, the intimate language between her and my father, with a man who was courting her. All the important events of their love life, their engagement, their marriage, their liberation from my grandfather's tyranny, had taken place in German. Possibly she had lost sight of this because in Manchester her husband had taken so much trouble to learn English. But he was well aware that she had reverted passionately to German, and he had no doubt of what this must have led to. He refused to speak to her until she confessed; for a whole night he kept silent and again in the morning he maintained his silence, convinced that she had been unfaithful to him.

I hadn't the heart to tell her that she was guilty in spite of her innocence, because she had listened to words she should never have allowed, spoken in this language. She had carried on these conversations for weeks and, as she owned to me, she had even concealed one detail—Coriolanus—from my father.

He wouldn't have understood, she said. They had been so young when they talked about the Burgtheater together. When they were adolescents living in Vienna, they hadn't known each other, but they had often attended the same performances. They had discussed them later on, and then it had seemed to them that they had been there together. His idol was Sonnenthal, hers was Wolter. He was more interested in actors than she was; he imitated them, she preferred to talk about them. He hadn't much to say about the plays, she read them all over again at home; he liked to declaim. He would have been a better actor than she. She *thought* too much, she preferred to be serious. She cared less for comedies than he did. It was through the plays they had both seen that they got to know each other well. He had never seen *Coriolanus*, he wouldn't have liked it. He had no use for proud, heartless people. He had a hard time with her family because of their pride; her family had opposed the marriage. He would have been hurt to learn that of all Shakespeare's characters Coriolanus was her favorite. Only when she suddenly started talking about Coriolanus in Reichenhall had it dawned on her that she had always avoided mentioning him in conversations with my father.

Had she been dissatisfied in some way? Did my father hurt her feelings in some way? I didn't ask many questions, she needed no prodding, nothing could have diverted the flood that had been storing up inside her for so long. But this question tormented me and it was good that I asked it. No, he had never hurt her feelings, never once. She had been bitter about Manchester because it wasn't Vienna. She hadn't said a word when my father brought me English books to read and discussed them with me in English. That was why she had withdrawn from me at that time. My father had been enthusiastic about England. He had been right. There were distinguished, cultivated English people. If she had only known more of them. But she lived among the members of her family with their ridiculous lack of education. There was no one she could have a real conversation with. That's what had made her ill, not the climate. That is why Reichenhall, especially her conversations with the doctor, had helped her so much. But it was a *cure*. It had served its purpose. She would have liked to go there once a year. My father's jealousy had ruined everything. Had she been wrong to tell him the truth?

She meant the question seriously and wanted an answer from me. She put as much urgency into it as if all this had just happened. She retracted nothing about her meeting with the doctor. She didn't ask whether she should have refused to listen to him. She thought it enough that she had been deaf to his entreaties. I gave her the answer she didn't want. "You shouldn't," I said, "have shown how much it meant to you." I said it hesitantly, but it sounded like blame. "You shouldn't have bragged about it. You should have said it casually."

"But I *was* glad," she said vehemently. "I'm still glad. Do you think I'd have come to Strindberg otherwise? I'd be a different woman, you wouldn't have written your book. You'd never have gone beyond your wretched poems. You'd never have amounted to anything. Strindberg is your father. You're my son by Strindberg. I've made you into his son. If I had disowned Reichenhall, you'd never have amounted to anything. You write German because I took you away from England. You've become Vienna even more than I have. It's in Vienna that you found your Karl Kraus, whom I couldn't bear. You've married a Viennese woman. And now you're even living in the midst of Viennese vineyards. You seem to like it. As soon as I'm feeling better, I'll come and see you. Tell Veza she needn't be afraid of me. You'll leave her just as you left me. The stories you made up for me will come true. You *have* to make up stories, you're a writer. That's why I believed you. Whom is one to believe if not writers? Businessmen? Politicians? I only believe writers. But they have to be distrustful like Strindberg, they have to see through women. One can't think ill enough of people. And yet I wouldn't give up a single hour of my life. Let them be bad! It's wonderful to be alive. It's wonderful to see through all their villainy and yet to go on living."

From such speeches I learned what had happened to my father. He felt she had deserted him, while she thought she had done no wrong. A confession of the usual sort might not have hit him so hard. She was not fully aware of her own state of mind; else she wouldn't have bludgeoned him with her happiness. She wasn't shameless, she wouldn't have spoken so freely if she had seen any impropriety in her behavior. How could he have accepted what had happened? To him the German words they used with each other were sacred. She had profaned these words, this language. As he saw it, everything they had seen on the stage had turned into love. They had talked to each other about it innumerable times; these words had helped them to bear the narrowness of their daily lives. As a child I was consumed with envy over these foreign words, they made me feel superfluous. The moment they began talking German, no one else existed for them. My feeling of exclusion threw me into a panic; in the next room, I would desperately practice saying the German words I did not understand.

Her confession left me embittered, because she had deceived me. Over the years I had heard version after version; each time she seemed to give a different explanation for my father's death. What she represented as consideration for my tender years was in reality a changing insight into the extent of her guilt. In the nights after my father's death, when I had to restrain her from killing herself, her sense of guilt was so strong that she wanted to die. She took us to Vienna to be nearer the place from which her first conversations with my father had drawn their nourishment. On the way to Vienna she stopped in Lausanne and hit me over the head with the language which up until then I had not been allowed to understand.

On the evenings when she read to me in Vienna, the evenings that gave me my being, she recapitulated those early conversations with him, but added *Coriolanus*, the mark of her guilt. In our apartment on Scheuchzerstrasse in Zurich she drowned herself every evening in the yellow Strindberg volumes I presented her with one after another. Then I would hear her singing softly at the piano, talking with my father and weeping. Did she pronounce the name of the author whom she read so avidly and whom he had not known? Now she saw me as the child of her infidelity and threw it up to me. What was my father now?

In such moments she *tore* everything, she was as reckless as she would have been if she had been leading her true life. She had a right to see herself in my book, to say that she herself would have written like that, that she *was* my book. That was why she recovered her magnanimity, why she accepted Veza and forgot that I had deceived her for so long about Veza. But she combined her magnanimity with a dire prophecy: just as I had deserted her, so I would desert Veza. She couldn't live without thoughts of revenge. She said she would come to see us, imagining that she would then see her prophecy come true. She was quick and impetuous and took it for certain that with the publication of my book, which obsessed her, a time of triumph was sure to set in. She saw me surrounded by women, who would worship me for the "misogyny" of *Auto-da-Fé* and long to let me chastise them for being women. She saw a fast-moving procession of bewitching beauties at my home in Grinzing, and in the end she saw Veza banished and forgotten in a tiny apartment just like her own in Paris. The inventions by which I had taken her mind off Veza had come true; the chronology didn't matter. I had merely predicted something, I hadn't deceived her and she hadn't let herself be deceived; no one could hide his wickedness from her, she had the gift of seeing through people, and she had passed it on to me. I *was* her son.

I left Paris thinking she had resigned herself to our marriage, that in a way she felt sorry for Veza, precisely because Veza had a dark future ahead of her. It comforted her to think she knew Veza's inevitable fate, which Veza herself was not yet prepared to acknowledge. I thought up conversations between them and felt relieved. They may have offered me some compensation for the terrible story I had heard about my father's end.

But things turned out differently. I was all wrong, I underestimated her emotional instability, which now surpassed all bounds. I had failed to consider how it would affect her to have told me the truth at last. Up until then she had put me off. In all the years of our early life together, when I had thought our relations so frank and open, she had diverted me with one version after another and guarded her secret. Now she had revealed it and asked me for my opinion. Sensitive as I was to words, I had found fault with her, not for what had happened, but for not having *spared* my father, for not realizing what she was doing to him with her boastful story. The outburst with which she reacted to my words had not troubled me, but had confirmed me in my belief that she was unchanged, indestructible, and that she had masterfully put an end to the long struggle between us, though aware of its necessity.

What I had not foreseen came a few months later. Before the year was out, her feelings against me hardened and without denigrating or accusing Veza, as she had done in the past, she wrote that she never wanted to see me again.

Alban Berg

Today I have been looking with emotion at pictures of Alban Berg. I don't yet feel up to saying what my acquaintance with him meant to me. I shall try only to touch quite superficially on a few meetings with him.

I saw him last at the Café Museum a few weeks before his death. It was a short meeting, at night after a concert. I thanked him for a beautiful letter, he asked me if my book had been reviewed. I said it was still too soon; he disagreed and was full of concern. He didn't quite come out with it but hinted that I should be prepared for the worst. He, who was himself in danger, wanted to protect me. I sensed the affection he had had for me since our first meeting. "What can happen," I asked, "now that I've got this letter from you?" He made a disparaging gesture, though I could see he was pleased. "You make it sound like a letter from Schönberg. It's only from me."

He wasn't lacking in self-esteem. He knew very well who he was. But there was one living man whom he never ceased to place high above himself: Schönberg. I loved him for being capable of such veneration. But I had many other reasons for loving him.

I didn't know at the time that he had been suffering for months from furunculosis; I didn't know that he had only a few weeks to live. On Christmas Day, I suddenly heard from Anna that he had died the day before. On December 28 I went to his funeral in Hietzing cemetery. At the cemetery I saw no such movement as I had expected, no group of people going in a certain direction. I asked a small misshapen gravedigger where Alban Berg was being buried. "The Berg body is up there on the

left," he croaked. Those words gave me a jolt, but I went
in the direction indicated and found a group of perhaps
thirty people. Among them were Ernst Krenek, Egon
Wellesz and Willi Reich. All I remember of the speeches
is that Willi Reich spoke of the deceased as his teacher,
expressing himself in the manner of a devoted pupil. He
said little, but there was humility in his feeling for his
dead teacher, and his was the only address that did not
grate on me at the time. To others who spoke more
cleverly and coherently I did not listen; I didn't want to
hear what they said, because I was in no condition to
realize where we were.

I saw him before me at a concert, reeling slightly when
moved by some Debussy songs. He was a tall man and
when he walked he leaned forward; when this reeling set
in, he made me think of a tall blade of grass swaying in
the wind. When he said "wonderful," half the word
seemed to stay in his mouth, he seemed drunk. It was
babbled praise, reeling wonderment.

When I first went to see him at his home—I had been
recommended to him by H.—I was struck by his serenity.
Famous in the outside world, in Vienna a leper—I had
expected grim defiance. I had thought of him far from
his home in Hietzing and didn't stop to ask myself why
he lived here. I didn't connect him with Vienna, except
insofar as he, a great composer, was here to incur the
contempt of the far-famed city of music. I thought this
had to be so, that serious work could be done only in a
hostile environment; I drew no distinction between composers and writers; it seemed to me that the resistance
which made them was in both cases the same. This
resistance, I thought, drew its strength from one and the
same source, from Karl Kraus.

I knew how much Karl Kraus meant to Schönberg and
his students. This may have been responsible at first for
my own good opinion. But in Berg's case there was

something more: that he had chosen *Wozzeck* as the subject of an opera. I came to Berg with the greatest expectations, I had imagined him quite different from what he was—does one ever form a correct picture of a great man? But he is the only one I expected so much of who did not disappoint me.

I couldn't get over his simplicity. He made no great pronouncements. He was curious because he knew nothing about me. He asked what I had done, if there was anything of mine he could read. I said there was no book; only the stage script of *The Wedding*. In that moment his heart went out to me. This I understood only later; what I sensed at the time was a sudden warmth, when he said: "Nobody dared. Would you let me read it in that form?" There was no particular emphasis on the question, but there was no room for doubt that he meant it, for he added encouragingly: "It was the same with me. Then there must be something in it." He didn't demean himself with this association, but he gave me expectation, the best thing in the world. It wasn't H.'s organized expectation, that left one cold or depressed, it wasn't the expectation that Scherchen quickly converted into power. It was something personal and simple; he obviously wanted nothing in return though he had made a request. I promised him the script and took his interest as seriously as it was meant.

I told him in what state of mind I had come across *Wozzeck* at the age of twenty-six and how I had kept reading and reading the fragment all through the night. It turned out that he had been twenty-nine when he attended the first night of Büchner's play in Vienna. He had seen it many times and decided at once to make it into an opera. I also told him how *Wozzeck* had led to *The Wedding*, though there was no direct connection between them, and I alone knew how one had brought me to the other.

In the further course of our conversation I made some
impertinent remarks about Wagner, for which he gently
but firmly reproved me. His love of *Tristan* seemed
imperturbable. "You're not a musician," he said, "or you
wouldn't say such things." I was ashamed of my impertinence, but I wasn't too unhappy about it, I felt rather
like a schoolboy who had given a wrong answer. My gaffe
didn't seem to diminish his interest in me. And indeed,
to help me out of my embarrassment, he repeated his
request for my play.

This was not the only occasion when he sensed what
was going on inside me. Unlike many musicians, he was
not deaf to words; on the contrary, he was almost as
receptive to them as to music. He understood people as
well as he did instruments. After this first meeting I
realized that he was one of the handful of musicians
whose perception of people is the same as writers'. And
having come to him as a total stranger, I also sensed his
love of people, which was so strong that his only defense
against it was his inclination to satire. His lips and eyes
never lost their look of mockery, and he could easily have
used his irony as a defense against his warmheartedness.
He preferred to make use of the great satirists, to whom
he remained devoted as long as he lived.

I would like to speak of every single meeting I had with
him; they were rather frequent in the few years of our
acquaintance. But his early death cast its shadow on them
all; like Gustav Mahler, he was not yet fifty-one when he
died. It discolored every conversation I had with him and
I am afraid of letting the grief I still feel for him rub off
on his serenity. I am reminded of a sentence in a letter
to a student, which I learned about only later. "I have
one or two months yet to live, but what then?—I can
think or combine no more than this—and so I'm pro-
foundly depressed." This sentence did not refer to his
illness but to the threat of imminent *destitution*. At the

same time he wrote me a wonderful letter about *Auto-da-Fé*, which he had read in that same mood. He was in severe pain and in fear of losing his life, but he did not thrust the book aside, he let it depress him, he was determined to do the author justice. He did just that and consequently this first letter I received about the novel has remained the most precious of all to me.

His wife, Helene, survived him by more than forty years. Some people ridicule her for "keeping contact" with him all this time. Even if she was deluding herself, even if he spoke inside her and not from outside, this remains a form of survival that fills me with awe and admiration. I saw her again thirty years later, after a lecture given by Adorno in Vienna. Small and shrunken, she came out of the hall, a very old woman, so absent that it cost me an effort to speak to her. She didn't recognize me, but when I told her my name, she said: "Ah, Herr C.! That was a long time ago. Alban still speaks of you."

I was embarrassed and so moved that I soon took my leave. I forwent calling on her. I'd have been glad to revisit the house in Hietzing, where she was still living, but I didn't wish to intrude on the intimacy of the conversations she was always carrying on. Everything that had ever happened between them was still in progress. Where his works were involved, she asked him for advice and he gave her the answer she expected. Does anyone suppose that others were better acquainted with his wishes? It takes a great deal of love to create a dead man who never dies, to listen to him and to speak to him, and find out his wishes, which he will always have because one has created him.

Meeting in the Liliput Bar

H. was back in Vienna that winter. We arranged to meet in town late one night. A new bar had been opened on Naglergasse, not far from Kohlmarkt. Marion Marx, a singer who was also the owner, aimed at an avant-garde clientele. She was a tall, warmhearted woman with a deep voice which filled her Liliput Bar, as the place was called, with gaiety. She made a fuss over young writers, whom she valued for the boldness of their projects, the bolder the better. They felt good in her place. The figure on the check which the waiter brought them before they left was fictitious, she didn't want them to feel embarrassed in front of wealthy customers; actually they didn't pay at all. It was this tact that won me to Marion. I didn't ordinarily go to bars, but to Marion's I went.

I took H. there, he enjoyed nightclubs after a hard day's work. The place was packed, not a table to be had. Marion caught sight of me; she broke off her song before the last verse, welcomed me effusively and led us to a table. "These are good friends of mine, they'll put you at your ease. I'll introduce you." Two chairs were produced from somewhere and we squeezed ourselves in. H., usually so high and mighty, had no objection; to my surprise he didn't seem to mind sharing a table with strangers. He liked Marion, but he liked the table even more. Marion introduced H. and me. And then in her warmest Hungarian manner: "This is my friend Irma Benedikt, with her daughter and son-in-law."

"We've known you for ages," said the lady, "from seeing you pass our house. You always look the other way, like your Professor Kien. My daughter is only nineteen but she has already read your book. Perhaps a little young for it, but she's been talking about it day and night. She tyrannizes us with your characters, she imitates them. She calls me Therese. She says that's the worst thing she could possibly say to me."

The woman seemed open and unassuming, almost childlike at, I should guess, forty-five, neither snobbish nor decadent, the opposite of everything the name of Benedikt had stood for in my imagination. I was rather alarmed at the thought that the characters of *Auto-da-Fé* practically lived in her house, as she put it. I had looked the other way to avoid all contact with its inhabitants, who, I was convinced, gave off some sort of infection, and now it turned out that Kien and Therese, who were a lot less sociable than I, seemed to feel at home there. The son-in-law, a big clod not much younger than the mother, didn't say a word, his features were as smooth and well groomed as the suit he was wearing, he didn't once open his mouth, and he seemed put out about something. Though it didn't dawn on me for quite some time, the nineteen-year-old daughter who had read *Auto-da-Fé* too soon was his wife, but wished she weren't, for she sat with her back turned to him and didn't address a single word to him. They seemed to have quarreled and now they were carrying on their quarrel in silence.

There was a brightness about her; she tried to say something and her eyes became brighter and brighter. She made several tries, and as not a word came out, I looked at her longer and perhaps more intensely than usual. Thus it could not escape me that she had green eyes. They did not captivate me, for I was still under the sway of Anna's orbs.

"She's not usually so quiet," said Frau Irma, her mother, while the wooden son-in-law nodded from the waist up. "She's afraid of you. Say something to her, her name is Friedl. That will break the spell."

"I'm not the sinologist," I said. "There's really no need to be afraid of me."

"And I'm not Therese," she said. "I'd like to be your pupil. I want to learn to write."

"It can't be learned. Have you written anything?"

"She does nothing else," said her mother. "She's run away from her husband in Pressburg [Bratislava] and come home to us in Grinzing. She has nothing against her husband but she doesn't want to keep house, she wants to write. Now he's here to take her back. She says she won't go."

The mother brought out these indiscretions in all innocence; she sounded almost like a child speaking of an older sister. As though to confirm the intention imputed to him, the clod put his hand on Friedl's shoulder.

"Take your hand away," she snapped. While issuing this brief command she looked in his direction. Then she turned to me, beaming—or so it seemed—and said: "He can't arrest me. He can't do a thing to me. Am I right?"

This marriage was over before it had begun, and what had happened seemed so irrevocable that I felt no embarrassment. I didn't even feel sorry for the clod. How quickly he had removed his hand. This creature radiant with expectation wasn't for him, she was a good twenty years younger. Why had she married him?

"She wanted to get away from home," said Frau Irma, "and now she never stirs out of the house. But that's because of our illustrious neighbor."

It was meant in jest, but it sounded serious, so serious that H. had enough. He was used to being the center of attraction, and now someone had usurped his role. He called attention to himself in his brutal way by coming to the forlorn husband's assistance.

"Have you ever thought of giving her a good thrashing?" he asked. "That's what she wants."

But this was too much even for the luckless husband,

and in a disagreement between men he could take care of himself. "What do you know about it?" he rasped. "You don't know Friedl. Friedl is special."

With that he suddenly had everyone on his side and H.'s attempt to get attention had failed. But Frau Irma, who had entertained any number of musicians as well as artists in her house, knew what was proper. She turned to the conductor and said apologetically that she had not been to any of his concerts, because her poor head simply couldn't follow modern music.

"That can be learned," said H. encouragingly. "You just have to begin." Whereupon Friedl nonchalantly turned the conversation away from him.

"*I'm* interested in learning to write. Will you take me as a pupil?"

She was back where she had started. I had to give her the same answer a little more fully. I told her I had no pupils and didn't think writing could be learned. Had she tried anyone else?

"No living writer," she said. "I'd like to learn from a living writer."

What was her favorite reading?

"Dostoevsky," she said without a moment's hesitation. "He was my first teacher."

"You couldn't very well show *him* your work."

"No, I couldn't. Anyway, it wouldn't have done any good."

"Why not?"

"Because it's exactly like what he writes. He wouldn't have noticed that it's not by him. He would have thought I'd copied it somewhere."

"You don't think much of yourself, do you?"

"I couldn't think less of myself. With you that wouldn't happen. No one could copy from you. No one can write as angrily as you."

"Is that what you like about my writing?"

"Yes, I like Therese. That's what all women are like."

"Are you a woman hater? I'm nothing of the kind, you know."

"I'm a housewife hater, that's what I am."

"She's thinking of me," said her mother, and again her tone was so charmingly simple that she almost won my heart, even if she was married to a Benedikt.

"She can't possibly be thinking of you, *gnädige Frau.*"

"Oh yes, I am," said Friedl. "It's deceptive. Wait till you hear her talking to the chauffeur. She'll sound entirely different."

H. got up to go. He saw no reason to spend the night in a bar listening to family squabbles. But it was rather embarrassing, although I was pleased in a way by the young creature's extravagant devotion to me in the presence of witnesses. No one had ever set such high hopes on me, an author whose book expressed nothing but horror.

I was glad to be going. Frau Irma asked me to come and see her; after all, we were neighbors. Friedl said something about Himmelstrasse, she seemed distressed that we were leaving and apparently placed her hopes in Himmelstrasse, the street that went down to the streetcar. That was the only word I understood in her last sentence. The clod neither stood up nor said goodbye. He had a right to be rude, because H. didn't offer to shake hands with anyone.

Outside he said to me: "Cute chick. And already so screwy. A pretty mess you've got yourself into, C." But he hadn't finished with me yet. Before we separated he said: "Four sisters, I hear. You can expect the worst. All you need to do is write something nasty enough and you'll have four sisters on your neck." I'd never had so much sympathy from him. Himmelstrasse was beginning to interest him and he made a note of our new half-empty apartment.

The Exorcism

It was amazing how often I ran into Friedl from then on. I'd take my seat in the empty No. 38 streetcar, look up, and there she'd be sitting across the aisle from me. She always rode as far as Schottentor, just as I did. I went to the Schottentor Café. When I entered, she was already there, sitting at a table with friends. She greeted me, but stayed with her friends and didn't disturb me. On the way back, she was already in the car, this time in a corner, a little farther from me, but not so far that I wasn't exposed to her glances. I buried myself in a book and paid no attention to her. But when I started up the hill in Grinzing, she was suddenly by my side. She greeted me and hurried past. Up until then I had received little attention from women, and from young girls none at all, so I thought nothing of these frequent encounters. But all of a sudden Himmelstrasse seemed infested with her and her sisters. One of these had the gall to introduce herself with the words: "I beg your pardon, I'm Friedl Benedikt's sister." "Oh!" I said, without raising my eyes until she had passed. But usually it was Friedl herself who turned up. She came running, she was always in a hurry. The sound of her light footfalls became familiar to me. Not once did I get to the streetcar stop without her overtaking me and passing me by. Her greeting was not obtrusive, but there was always a note of supplication in it, which I noticed without admitting it to myself. If she hadn't been so unassuming, I'd have been angry, for it happened just too often, two or three times a day, and seldom did a day pass when she didn't come running past me or toward me or take the same car.

I was always deep in thought, but she didn't often disturb me. I didn't mind her running through my thoughts, because she didn't stop running or take up too much room.

And then one day she rang up. Veza, who had been expecting her to call, picked up the phone. Could she speak to me? Veza thought it wisest to ask her to tea, without even consulting me. "Come and have tea with me," she said. "C. never knows in advance whether he'll be busy or not. Just come and see me and maybe he'll have time for us." I was rather annoyed at being presented with a *fait accompli*. But Veza convinced me that it was all for the best. "You can't go on living in this state of siege. Something must be done. And there's nothing you can do until we get to know her a little. Maybe it's just a crush. But maybe she really wants to write and thinks you can help her."

So I went and joined them while they were drinking tea in Veza's small, paneled room. I had barely sat down when Friedl spilled her whole cup of tea on the table and floor. In that rather dainty room it seemed most ill-bred, as though she weren't even capable of holding a teacup properly. Instead of apologizing, she said: "No breakage. I'm so excited that you've come." "It's nothing to get excited about," said Veza. "He always comes to tea. He likes this room. It's just that one can't make appointments for him." "It must be wonderful," Friedl said to her with no sign of embarrassment, as if I weren't there, "to be able to talk to him." "Don't you talk at home?" "Oh yes. They never stop. But what they say doesn't interest me. My parents are always giving receptions. Nothing but famous people. If you're not famous, you don't get invited. Don't you think famous people are boring?"

It soon became clear that she wasn't at all as I had imagined a daughter of that house. She didn't regard her father as a father, she paid so little attention to him that she wasn't even rebellious. He seemed to have opinions on everything under the sun; he spread himself too thin, if I understood her right, so that nothing had *weight* for him. He jumped from one thing to another and thought he was impressing people, but he only seemed silly. He was good-natured, he was fond of his children, but they didn't interest him. He didn't want to be bothered with them and left them entirely to their mother. They did as they pleased, and attended the constant dinner parties only singly and not very often. What Friedl had to say of her home was frank and vivid, but her language was so primitive one would never have imagined that she wanted to write, let alone that she had ever written anything.

She took some papers out of her handbag. Would I care to read something of hers? It was very bad, she knew that, and if I thought it was pointless for her to write, she would give it up. She never showed her father anything, he talked everything to death, and when he was done you knew less than before. He didn't know anything about people. Anyone could talk him into anything and they all cheated him. She wanted awfully to study writing with me.

It appealed to me that she felt repelled by the flabbiness of her home. It was also plain that she was pursuing me for the sake of her writing and for no other reason. Veza thought so too. I took Friedl's papers and began to read. "You won't take me as a pupil," she said rather despondently. "It's not good enough. But tell me at least if I should give it up or if there's any point in my going on with it."

This obsession with writing as well as her desire to hear the truth from me must have appealed to me, though I wouldn't have admitted it. For I went straight to my room and read her pages. I couldn't believe my eyes: she had copied fifty whole pages of Dostoevsky and represented them as her own work. The story was exciting in a way, but rather empty; I had never seen it; it must have been a discarded draft.

I hated having to see her again and tell her. If only for Dostoevsky's sake, I couldn't just let it go at that. What annoyed me most was her lack of respect for him. But I was also vexed that she should think I wouldn't notice. It was obvious; no one who had ever read a single book by Dostoevsky could fail to notice; you didn't have to be a writer or a professor. I told her just that when she stood before me on the landing two days later. I was so annoyed that I wasn't going to ask her into my room.

"Is it very bad?" she asked.

"It's neither bad nor good," I said. "It's Dostoevsky. Where did you get hold of it?"

"I wrote it myself."

"Copied it, you mean. Which of his books did you take it from? After the first paragraph one knows who wrote it. But I've never read the book you took it from."

"It's not from any book. I wrote it myself."

She stuck obstinately to her story and I got angry. I harangued her and she listened. She seemed to enjoy it. Instead of confessing, she kept right on denying; she made me so furious that I lost self-control and began to shout. She wanted to write? What did she think writing was? Did she really think it began with stealing? What's more, so clumsily that any idiot would notice. And quite aside from the disrespect she was showing a great author, what was the sense of it? Everybody learns to read and write. Could it be the influence of journalism that she'd absorbed since childhood from the *Neue Freie Presse*?

She was radiant, she was savoring every word. "Oh," she cried out, "how wonderful it is when you shout! Do you often shout like that?" "No," I said. "Never. And I won't say another word to you until you tell me where you got that from."

Luckily Veza came in just then; she saw me looking

THE PLAY OF THE EYES

happily for more words of rage. I don't know what would
have happened next without Veza's intercession. As she
told me later on, she suspected that I was accusing the
girl unjustly, though she couldn't make out why Friedl
seemed so happy about it. She took Friedl into her paneled
room. To me she said: "I'll clear this up. Calm yourself.
Go out for an hour and come back."

I took her advice. It turned out that the fifty controversial pages had really been written by Friedl; they had
not been copied. Not for nothing had they struck me as
empty. Not for nothing had I been unable to say which
of Dostoevsky's books they came from. They came from
none. Friedl had devoured all Dostoevsky and could write
nothing else. She wrote like Dostoevsky but she had
nothing to say. What could she have had to say at the age
of nineteen? In a state of incredible emptiness she turned
out page after page; her output looked like Dostoevsky
but was not a parody. She was possessed in a way known
to us from the stories of hysterical nuns. I had recently
read the story of Urbain Grandier and the nuns of
Loudun. Just as they were possessed by Urbain Grandier,
so Friedl was possessed by Dostoevsky, no less a devil and
no less complicated than Grandier.

"You'll have to play the exorcist," said Veza. "You'll
have to cast out Dostoevsky. Luckily he's dead, so he can't
be burned at the stake. And all four sisters aren't possessed
with him, only one, the others aren't interested. Even so,
it won't be easy."

From then on Veza, who was sufficiently independent-
minded to defend herself against any influence that ran
counter to her inclinations or judgment, took the girl in
hand. She thought her gifted, though in an unusual way.
Whether she would ever do anything worth mentioning,
Veza thought, would depend on whose influence she came
under. The girl was making a desperate effort not to

resemble her father, not to be a cultural potpourri or a social center; she was in constant motion, a bundle of human contradictions, and could be influenced only by the one person to whom, thanks to some inexplicable whim, she felt drawn. Since *Auto-da-Fé* had come her way, this person was me. Did I think it right to disavow the influence of my own book? "You like to take walks. Take her with you now and then. She's light and gay, the opposite of what she writes. She gets comical ideas. I think she has a gift for the grotesque. Make her tell you about the dinner parties at home. They're very different from what *Die Fackel* would lead one to think. They're more like Gogol."

"Impossible," I said, but Veza knew my weakness. The idea that this charming, cheerful creature had grown up in a Gogol-like atmosphere and was now possessed by Dostoevsky, who "like all of us was descended from *The Overcoat*," struck me as a highly original version of a well-known literary phenomenon. Just that, I thought, might give me a chance to free her from her "devil." Veza had thought up a gratifying role for me; there was nothing I would not have undertaken for the greater glory of Gogol. I also felt that in her tactful way Veza was making her peace with *Auto-da-Fé*, for it, too, "like all of us was descended from *The Overcoat*." To my relief, she was no longer quite so worried about the fate of the book. She recognized the book's effect on Friedl, took it seriously and asked me to help.

When Veza's sound instinct went hand in hand with her warmth, she was irresistible. She had soon won me over and I took Friedl on walks. Writing was one thing that could not be learned; but one could go walking with this girl and find out what she had in her. She was in high spirits; sometimes she ran a few steps ahead and waited for me to catch up. "I have to let my feelings out," she said. "I'm so glad you're letting me come with you."

I got her to talk about herself. She talked freely, she never stopped talking, always about people she knew at home. For some time she had been allowed to be present at soirées. She hadn't the slightest respect for the distinguished guests and saw them as they were. Some of her comical remarks amazed me and I pretended not to believe her, I said she must be exaggerating, that such things were impossible. At that she laid it on so thick that I couldn't stop laughing, and once I started to laugh she invented more and more. Then I too started inventing. Which is just what she had wanted, a contest in inventing.

I gave her "tests." I asked her about the people we passed on our walks, especially those she did not know. She was to tell me what she thought of them, and their story as well if something good occurred to her. There I had something to go by, because I too saw these people and was able to judge what she perceived in them and what escaped her. I corrected her, not by finding fault with an oversight or imprecision, but by giving her my version. This sort of competition became a passion with her, but what interested her was not so much her own inventions as my stories. These talks of ours were very spontaneous and lively. I could tell when something troubled her, because then she fell silent and sometimes, luckily not very often, she was taken with despondency. "I'll never be able to write. I'm too sloppy and I don't get enough ideas." Sloppy she was, but she had ideas to burn. Her leaning toward fantasy didn't trouble me in the least. That is just what was most lacking in most of the young writers I knew.

I sometimes asked her to make up names for people we saw. That was not her forte and she didn't especially enjoy it. She preferred talking about what people did and talked about at home. Sometimes it was harmless chatter and revealed little more than her undeniable gift of imitation. But then suddenly she would amaze me with something monstrous. She would say it as though it didn't shock her in the least; she didn't suspect how strange it was and that it didn't at all fit in with her childlike sparkle and her light step.

Apart from the few days of her marriage she had always lived in Grinzing. She had been born in a motorcar. When her mother felt her labor pains coming on, her father had sat her down in his car and had her driven to the hospital. As usual he had talked nonstop. When they got to the hospital, the baby was lying on the floor of the car, it had come into the world without either of them noticing. Friedl attributed her restlessness to being born in a moving car. She was always having to go away, she couldn't stand it anywhere; when her husband, who was an engineer, went to the factory, she couldn't bear waiting at home for him. On one of the first mornings, she ran away, left the house, left Pressburg, and came home to Grinzing. There she knew every pathway. She would often run off into the woods. She liked meadows even better. She would squat down to pick flowers and disappear in the grass. On our walks I sometimes noticed the longing looks she cast at the meadows, but she controlled herself, because one of us would be telling a story, and that meant even more to her than her freedom. She was attracted most to small, unimpressive things, but she was not unreceptive to views, especially when there was a bench to sit on and a table to go with it, and one could order something to drink.

But what interested her most was what could be communicated in words. I have never known a child to listen more avidly. After I had challenged her in every possible way, our duel always ended in my telling her a story, and the excitement with which she took in every word moved me more deeply than I would have been willing to admit.

The Fragility of the Spirit

It was a varied life that I led in those few years in Grinzing. It contained so many contradictory elements that it would be hard for me to describe them all. I lived them all with equal intensity, and though there was no ground for satisfaction, I did not feel threatened. I stuck obstinately to my main project. I read abundantly, took notes for my book about crowds and discussed the subject with anyone worth talking to. Seldom has anyone clung so tenaciously to a project. It was not possible to understand what was going on—a great deal was going on, and a lot more was moving rapidly to center stage—on the basis of any of the current theories.

We were living in an imperial capital, which was no longer imperial, but which had attracted the notice of the world with daring, carefully thought-out social projects. New and exemplary things had been done. They had been done without violence, one could be proud of them and live in the illusion that they would endure, while in nearby Germany the great madness spread like wildfire and its adherents seized all the commanding positions. Then in February 1934 the power of the Vienna municipal government was broken. Its leaders were despondent. It was as though all their work had been in vain. What was new and original in Vienna had been wiped out. What remained was the memory of an earlier Vienna, which was not far enough back to be exonerated from its share of guilt for the First World War, into which it had maneuvered itself. The local hope that had stood up to poverty and unemployment was gone. Many who could not live in such a void were infected with the German plague and hoped to achieve a better life by being absorbed into the larger country. Most failed to see that the actual consequence could only be a new war, and when the few who saw clearly pointed this out, they refused to believe it.

My own life, I repeat, was varied and throve on its contradictions. I found justification in my ambitious project, but I did nothing to hasten its execution. Everything that happened in the world contributed to the experience that went into it. This was no superficial experience, for it went beyond the reading of newspapers. Everything that happened was discussed with Sonne as soon as I heard about it. He commented on the events in different ways, frequently changing his vantage point as a means of seeing more clearly, and ended by presenting a résumé of the various perspectives, in which the weights were equitably distributed. These were the most important hours of my day, a continuous initiation into world affairs, their complexities, crises and surprises. They never discouraged me from going on with my own studies, in ethnology, for example, which I pursued more systematically than before. If only because of the humility I felt in Sonne's presence, I seldom let myself be tempted to speak to him of an idea that I regarded as new and important; still, we found common ground in conversations on the history of religions, a field in which his knowledge was overpowering and mine had developed little by little to the point where I could always understand him and was in a position to question ideas that did not satisfy me.

He showed no impatience when I spoke of my own intention of elucidating the behavior of crowds. He listened to what I had to say, thought about it and said nothing. He did not interfere with my burgeoning thoughts. It would have been easy for him to ridicule my concept of the crowd, which was becoming increasingly rich and complex and could not be subsumed in any definition. In a single hour he could have demolished what I regarded as my lifework. He never discussed the matter with me, but neither did he discourage me and try (like Broch) to get me to abandon my undertaking. He was careful not to help me; he never became my teacher in any matter bearing on crowds. Once when I nevertheless broached the subject, hesitantly and in a way reluctantly, for his opposition could have imperiled my whole project, he listened to me calmly and earnestly, kept silent for longer than usual in our discussions and then said almost tenderly: "You've opened a door. Now you must go in. Don't look for help. One must do that kind of thing alone."

He seldom said that, and was careful to say no more. He didn't mean that he refused to help me. If I had asked him, he would not have withheld his help. But I had asked him no questions when I began. I had spoken of what already seemed clear to me; perhaps I had only wanted him to puncture my idea if he thought it wrong. In speaking of a "door," he had shown that he did not think it wrong. He had merely warned me, as was his way, with a gentle hint. "One must do that kind of thing alone." With that he had warned me against the theories that were going around and that explained nothing. He knew better than anyone that they barred the way to an understanding of public affairs. He was friends with Broch, whom he respected and perhaps even loved. When they spoke together, the conversation undoubtedly turned to Freud, with whom Broch was obsessed. How Sonne bore this without making insulting comments I would have been glad to know, but it was quite impossible to ask him so personal a question. That he had weighty objections to Freud I had discovered on one occasion when I came out violently against the "death instinct." "Even if it were true, he would have no right to say so. But it's not true. Things would be much too simple if that were true."

I looked on the exchange between Sonne and myself as the true substance of my day; it meant more to me than what I myself was writing. I was in no hurry to finish anything I was then working on. For this there were several reasons, the most important being my awareness that I didn't know enough. I was far from regarding my project as pointless; my belief in the necessity of discovering and applying the laws governing mass behavior and power over the masses was unshaken. But with the events that were descending on us, the scope of my project kept expanding. My conversations with Sonne sharpened my sense of what was to come. Far from minimizing the threat, he made me more and more aware of it, as though providing me with a unique telescope, which he alone was able to adjust properly. At the same time I came to realize how contemptibly little I knew. Ideas alone were not enough. The sudden illuminations that I was rather proud of might even bar my way to the truth. There was danger in intellectual *vanity*. Originality wasn't everything, nor was strength or the devastating recklessness I had learned from Karl Kraus.

I was extremely critical of the literary pieces I was then working on and left them unfinished. I didn't abandon them forever, I pushed them aside. This was no doubt what most worried Veza. Once in a serious conversation she went so far as to say that Sonne's influence on other people's minds made them sterile. He was indeed the best of critics, she had finally come to recognize that, but one should consult him only if one had a finished piece of work to show. One should not associate with him day after day. He was a man of renunciation, perhaps a pure ascetic and sage. He foresaw the worst but did not fight against it. What good did that do me? When I came home from a meeting with him, I seemed paralyzed; she could hardly get me to open my mouth. Sometimes, in fact— and this was a severe blow to me—she had the impression that he was making me *cautious;* I'd stopped reading her the things I was working on. I had no chapter of a new novel, no new play to show her. When she tactfully asked me, my answer was always: "It's not good enough for you, it needs more work." Why had everything been good enough for her in the past? Why had I been more daring?

It had begun, she said, with Anna's humiliation of me; that had been as clear as day to her, and she had long dreaded my reading of the *Comedy* on Maxingstrasse. That was why she had made friends with Anna—to find out what she was actually like; for I had idealized her and glorified her, if only by contrasting her to her mother. She now knew Anna well enough to realize that in connection with her one couldn't speak of a defeat, she didn't love like other women and certainly not like her mother. She had her own optical laws, you could gaze on her and admire her, you could regard her eyes as supremely beautiful, but you should not suppose that they saw you. When once her eyes had fallen on someone, she had to play with that person and win that person for herself, like a ball of wool, an object, not like a living creature. This play of the eyes was the only dangerous thing about her, otherwise she was a good friend, trusting, generous, even reliable. The one thing you must not do was try to *bind* her. Without her freedom she could not live, she needed it for her eye-play, if for nothing else, but that was her deepest need, it would never change, not even in old age; a woman endowed with such eyes couldn't help herself, she was a slave to the needs of her eyes, not as victim but as huntress.

I was amused at Veza's eye mythology. I knew there was a good deal of truth in it and I knew how much Veza had helped me by making friends with Anna. But I also knew how mistaken she was in another point: my friendship with Sonne had *not* sprung from my bad luck with Anna; it was *sovereign*, the purest need of my nature, which was ashamed of its dross and could only improve or at least justify itself by earnest dialogue with a far superior mind.

Invitation to the Benedikts'

What I had liked about Frau Irma, Friedl's mother, when I first met her at the Liliput Bar, was her simple, unpretentious way of talking; you had no hesitation in believing what she said. Her face had a kind of roundness I had never seen before, but it was not a Slavic face, though that too would have been attractive. Then I heard from Friedl that her mother was half Finnish. She had been born in Vienna but from childhood on had paid frequent visits to her mother's family in Finland.

One of her aunts, whom they often spoke of in the family, had distinguished herself by her independent life and intellectual achievements. Aunt Aline had lived in Florence for years and had translated Dante into Swedish. She owned an island off the coast of Finland and often went there to write. Pride and the desire to keep herself free for intellectual pursuits had stopped her from marrying. Friedl was her favorite niece and she intended to leave her her island. I enjoyed hearing Friedl talk about this island. She cared nothing for possessions, but she delighted in the idea of having an island of her own. She had never been there but she had no trouble visualizing it, especially during winter storms, when one would be wholly cut off from the mainland. She never mentioned the island without solemnly offering it to me as a trifling gift, her only way of expressing her veneration for her literary mentor.

Sometimes I accepted the island, sometimes I didn't. After all, Aunt Aline had worked on the Swedish Dante there. A generous gift, I was pleased with it, especially as it seemed to imply a long life for me. In the course of Friedl's talk about the beauty and solitude of the island, I learned, quite incidentally, something about her that impressed me far more—to wit, that her godmother had been Frieda Strindberg, Strindberg's second wife, who had been a childhood friend of her mother. It was from her that Friedl got her name and something else as well. When her mother was in despair over her sloppiness, she would say: "You've inherited that from your godmother, Frieda. Apparently one can inherit character traits by way of one's name." Frieda Strindberg was thought to be the sloppiest person in the world. Friedl as a child had been taken to see her. The disorder in the house had made such an impression on her that often when left alone she had done her best to copy it in her room at home. She had opened all the drawers and closets, thrown her clothes all over the place, and gleefully sat down on the mess, thinking that now she had a room like her godmother's. But she had never admitted to her mother how she came by her brilliant idea. That was her biggest secret, which is why she had to confide it to me. I must never come into her room unexpectedly, for if I once caught sight of that mess I'd be so horrified that I wouldn't take her on any more walks. I had no intention of dropping into her room, so I thought no more about it, but the Strindberg connection intrigued me and I believe that was what gave the Benedikt household a new dimension for me.

Friedl must have seriously pestered her mother over the choice of guests with a view to luring me to one of their lunches. For boring as she herself found these affairs, rarely as she consented to attend them, she had soon gathered from our conversations that I suspected something evil and unsavory where she saw only stiffness and boredom. From childhood on, she had heard only famous names. For a time—she was already going to school—she imagined that all grown-ups were famous, which to her mind was no particular recommendation for either category. If a new name was mentioned frequently in the house, there could be only two explanations: Either someone had suddenly become famous—in that case, how do you get him to accept an invitation? Or someone who had long—always, it seemed to her—been famous had arrived in Vienna and *of course* he would come and dine with them. It had never occurred to her that there might be any other possibility; it was always the same, and that's why it was so boring. But now, when we saw each other and she mentioned a certain person who came to the house, she sensed my surprise. And then I would ask: "What! *He* comes to your house?" As if it were forbidden to set foot in her house. She noticed that to certain other names I did not react at all, that their coming did not surprise me, that according to *Die Fackel*'s rules they were the right people for this house. But she began to take an interest in others, the ones who shocked me. She realized that with them she could lure me to her house. But it took time and elaborate preparations.

"Thomas Mann came to lunch yesterday," she said, and gave me an expectant look.

"What does he talk about with your father?"

That just popped out of me, and it came to me only afterward how tactless my question had been, as it showed in what contempt I held her father. Evidently I thought him incapable of carrying on a conversation with Thomas Mann.

"Music," she said. "They talked about music the whole time, especially Bruno Walter."

She added that, knowing nothing about music, she

could not report the conversation in detail. Why wouldn't I come and listen for myself? Her mother would be so glad to invite me, but she didn't dare. I seemed so standoffish; they all thought I was like Kien in my novel, a grumpy misogynist. "I'm always telling her what amusing things you say. But my mother says: 'He despises us. I can't understand why he goes walking with you.' "

After various attempts Friedl finally inveigled me into accepting an invitation. Of the three leading lights of the Viennese *décadence* at the turn of the century—Schnitzler, Hofmannsthal and Beer-Hofmann—only the last was still alive. Having written very little, he passed as the most exclusive. For decades he had been working on *one* play. It seems he was never satisfied with it and no one could persuade him to finish it. In Vienna in those days there was something puzzling about such parsimony. One wondered how with so little work to show he had come by his lofty reputation. I imagined that he avoided all "noxious" company and associated only with his equals. What did he do now that the two others were dead? And then I heard from Friedl that he was a frequent guest in her house, a corpulent, sociable old man with a beautiful wife who was about twenty years younger than he and seemed even younger than that. This sounded tempting, but what overcame all my resistance was the latest coup. Emil Ludwig, the success story of the day, who wrote a whole book in three or four weeks and boasted about it, had announced his intention of visiting the Benedikts in order to make the acquaintance of the revered Richard Beer-Hofmann. Everyone, said Friedl, was looking forward to this confrontation, it was sure to be great fun and I really mustn't miss it. She had persuaded her mother to invite me, I could expect her phone call that same day. My curiosity was aroused, I thanked her and accepted.

Instead of the maid, it was Friedl who opened the door; she had seen me from the window. As though addressing a fellow conspirator, she said: "They've both come. They're already here!" In the drawing room her father welcomed me in a few effusively flattering words, relevant to nothing in particular. He hadn't read my book yet, it had been going the rounds—the young ladies, his wife—just today he had finally wrested it away from them. There it was—he pointed at the table—and this time he would hold on to it; he would start reading it this very afternoon, he was fortifying himself by conversing with the author before embarking on this perilous adventure; he had heard that my book was exciting but wicked—one wouldn't suppose that from a glance at the author. I was rather taken aback by his apparent inoffensiveness, and he felt the same way about me. After what he had heard about *Auto-da-Fé*, he expected a *poète maudit*.

He took me over to Beer-Hofmann, the most distinguished of his guests, the man who wrote no more than two lines a year. The portly old gentleman kept his seat and said ponderously: "Young man, I shall not stand up, I'm sure you don't expect me to?" I uttered a few syllables of acquiescence, such as he no doubt expected, and already I was being led to a weedy, explosive little man. He took no notice of my hand, so I didn't have to hold it out to him, and a moment later I could hear him overwhelming Beer-Hofmann with foaming admiration. This was Emil Ludwig, protesting how long—since his infancy?—he had admired Beer-Hofmann. The word "master" emerged several times from the flood, also "perfection," even "finish"—a rather tactless word to a man who claimed to require decades for a play of average length. Beer-Hofmann wagged his head thoughtfully, he was definitely listening, he didn't miss a word, he seemed exceedingly self-assured, and who would not have felt secure in the presence of this promiscuous interviewer, this most prolific and best-selling of writers—as self-assured as a heavyweight confronted by a featherweight—but the corpulent old gentleman cannot have felt really at ease, for the contrast between his dignified verbal constipation and the weedy little man's published logorrhea was too glaring— after all, other people were listening. He finally inter- rupted the sycophantic whining and said regretfully but firmly: "It's too little."

He had written so little that he *had* to say that, and who could have answered him? There were perhaps a dozen persons in the room and all held their breath. But even to that Emil Ludwig had an answer, this time a single sentence: "Would Shakespeare have been less Shakespeare if he had only written *Hamlet*?"

This bit of effrontery left everyone speechless. Beer- Hofmann stopped wagging his head. To this day I cherish the hope that Beer-Hofmann, for all his self-assurance, did not give himself credit for a *Hamlet*.

During luncheon, which soon followed, Emil Ludwig, after so much self-effacement, turned his attention to Number One; he praised his fertility, his fluency, his far- flung experience, his highly placed friends and admirers all over the world. He knew everyone from Goethe to Mussolini. Stirringly he contrasted Goethe's—as he put it—simple dwelling in Weimar with the enormous recep- tion hall of the Palazzo Venezia in Rome. Traversing the breadth of the hall, which he likened to an imperial continent, he had come tripping up to Mussolini, who was resolutely waiting for him behind his vast desk at the far end of the room. Mussolini knew who was approach- ing. When after his long march Ludwig finally reached the desk (which was probably the biggest desk in the world, bigger than his own in Ascona), he was welcomed with flattering words, which his modesty forbade him to repeat. Instinctively recognizing Ludwig's importance, Mussolini had favored him with several long interviews, which were published in all the world's leading newspapers and, it goes without saying, in book form. But that was in the past. Since then seven or eight new books had appeared, the most recent being *The Nile*. But Ludwig didn't stop at that, he burbled on, sometimes in rather veiled terms, about his next three or four projects. And after that? No, he had no more to say, after all he was not the only guest of honor. "And our healthy self-esteem—only scoundrels are modest—has not made us forget the man at this festive board who stands for the priceless Young Vienna group of the turn of the century, the sole surviving representative of an undying tradition, and the greatest."

This was pretty steep, but it was the opinion of this assembly, and possibly what Beer-Hofmann thought of himself. For otherwise he would have found it hard to justify his withdrawal from the world. Later on I was more than once to hear him intimating that Hofmannsthal had too often given in to the seductions of the world; he regarded Hofmannsthal's whole connection with Salzburg, his libretti, his interest in opera, as an aberration. In his heart of hearts he must have loathed Emil Ludwig, as did all those sitting at the table with the exception of the host—but it cannot have left him unmoved to be proclaimed the greatest of the Young Vienna three.

It did not take Ludwig long to get back to himself. He owed it to Vienna to show himself at the opera, and he had reserved a box for that same evening; but he did not wish to go alone, he wished to be accompanied by the most beautiful of the four daughters of the house. Friedl sat across the table from him, listening to him with apparent interest. She didn't interrupt him, she didn't once laugh; he felt admired by her, and indeed it was she who by her deceptive attentiveness encouraged him to go on with his endless effusions about himself. And so he asked her to attend the opera with him. She was well aware of my dislike for the man. I am sure she asked herself whether it would impair her standing with me if she accepted. Her instinct no doubt told her that her standing could not be very high, since she was the daughter of an accursed house. And she relied on the ridiculous behavior that was to be expected of Ludwig at the opera and on the lively report she would entertain me with. She accepted Ludwig's invitation and told me all about it on our next walk.

Ludwig had kept jumping up in his box to make himself visible to as many people as possible. He had serenaded Friedl with arias, humming them at first, but then singing louder and louder. The occupants of the neighboring boxes were furious, but that's just what he had been counting on. He heeded no protests, he seemed in a trance, captivated by his young companion. The rest of the audience had started looking at the box instead of the stage. When at length someone went out and asked the attendant to do something about the objectionable noises, he discovered the identity of this little man who kept jumping up, leaning over the front of his box, singing and gesticulating. Why, it was Emil Ludwig in person! The news spread like wildfire and when it was certain that the whole house knew, the noises suddenly stopped. I forget what the opera was, but Friedl told me that when it was over he bowed instead of clapping and took the applause for himself. It was only after she remarked on the impropriety of his behavior that he had morosely clapped once or twice.

"I am looking for my peers"

On my second visit to the Benedikts' something happened which transformed this erstwhile abode of the Devil into an Oriental theater. I had climbed the outside steps and rung the bell when I heard hurried, slightly stumbling steps behind me; surprised, because such steps could hardly belong to an adult guest, I turned around. Who should be standing there before me but the breathless "Japanese girl," as I called her in my thoughts, the girl whom I had been seeing on Himmelstrasse for months, with the open coat, the strand of black hair over her face, in violent mimetic motion, as in one of Sharaku's portraits of actors or in a Kabuki play. Another guest? This young girl? I was so overcome at the thought that I forgot to bid her good day. She nodded but said nothing. Friedl opened the door as she had the first time and laughed when she saw us standing side by side on the doormat. "Oh, Susi," she said. "Susi, this is Herr C. This is my youngest sister, Susi."

I had good reason for embarrassment, but she too felt awkward. Though I meant nothing to her, she was well aware that we had been seeing each other day after day on Himmelstrasse. She wasn't a guest, she had come from school and was late as usual; hence her breathless haste. When a moment later she vanished up the stairs, Friedl said in surprise: "So you've seen Susi often. You never told me."

"I didn't know who it was. You said your youngest sister was fourteen."

"She is. But she looks eighteen."

"I thought she was Japanese."

"She does look exotic. No one knows how she got into our family."

Then I entered the drawing room. But for a while I felt rather uncomfortable. It had finally dawned on me that I had *sought* these meetings on Himmelstrasse; I had always gone down at the same time and made sure not to miss her as she came out of Strassergasse. A fourteen-year-old schoolgirl on her way home from school. Her breathlessness, her excitement, which had communicated themselves to me, had meant nothing: just a schoolgirl afraid of being late for lunch. True, the Japanese actors, whom I had not forgotten, contributed to this impression, as had my love for Sharaku's woodcuts. But why did she look like an actor in one of those woodcuts? She was fascinatingly foreign-looking, and Friedl, who embodied the lightness and exuberance of Vienna, couldn't bear comparison with her inexplicable beauty. I felt this so strongly that I never mentioned it; none of the sisters ever found out that from then on it was the thought of this youngest sister and her secret that attracted me more and more to the house.

I asked Friedl whether she could hear several things at once; if, for example, she was sitting in a crowded café and people were talking, arguing and singing all around her. She said she didn't see how it was possible to listen to more than one thing at a time without missing something. I explained that if you had one, two, three or four voices ringing in your ears, the interplay among them produced the most surprising effects. The voices paid no attention to one another; each started off in its own way and proceeded undeviatingly like clockwork, but when you took them in all together, the strangest thing happened; it was as though you had a special key, which opened up an overall effect unknown to the voices themselves.

I promised to give her a demonstration; she would just

have to try it a few times, at first she would listen through my ears as it were, and after a while she would be able to do it by herself, it would become an indispensable habit.

Late one night I took her to a café on Kobenzlgasse, where people went after the *Heurigen* had closed and the last No. 38 streetcar had left Grinzing. The crowd was more mixed than at the *Heurigen*. The first to arrive were those for whom midnight had come too soon and who wanted to round out their evening. Then came locals who had been serving wine until then and who now after work wanted to relax in a different, but not foreign, atmosphere. These set the tone; the *Heurigen* clientele were no longer in the majority, they no longer received special attention. Little by little, as the night advanced, they ceased to be active participants and became mere onlookers. The *Heurigen* singers, to whose songs they had drunk and in which they had joined, gave way to genuine Grinzingers, figures more original and more striking than anything one was likely to find in the best of the *Heurigen*. Here more could happen in an hour than elsewhere in a whole evening.

It was fairly late when we got there. I had wanted Friedl to get the full effect of many discordant voices while her expectation was still at its height. The café was packed, smoke and noise hit us full in the face as we entered. There wasn't a seat available, but when they saw Friedl, whose entrance was like a breath of fresh air—she leapt into the tumult like a cat, her eyes sparkled—the people somehow made room and forced seats on us instead of our having to fight for them. "I don't understand a thing," said Friedl. "I hear it all but I don't understand a word." "Hearing is half the battle," I said. "Soon something will happen that will straighten everything out."

I was counting on the arrival of a man whom I had seen and heard a few times. Thus far he had always come on Saturdays and then I had thought about him all week. Sure enough, the door soon opened, admitting a gaunt,

rather tall figure with a dark birdlike head and piercing
eyes. With a hopping step he made his way to the middle
of the room, not actually pushing but clearing a path for
himself with his elbows. Then, raising his hands in supplication, he began to whirl about and to chant the words:
"I am looking for my peers. I am looking for my peers."
The "my" had a lofty ring like a potentate's "I" or "we."
His hands clutched someone who was not there, a "peer"
no doubt. Over and over again he whirled, letting no one
approach his hands, chanting all the while: "I am looking
for my peers"—the mournful, insistent cry of a long-
legged bird.

"Why, that's Leimer," said Friedl. She knew him, but
how had she recognized him? She knew him by day, she
had never seen him at night when he went among men
with his majestic plaint. His days were spent at the
Grinzing swimming pool, which belonged to him and his
brothers and sisters. He would guide customers to their
cabins or sit at the cashier's desk. Sometimes, when he
was in the mood, he gave swimming lessons. He could
afford his moods, because the pool was a popular attraction, often so full that customers had to be turned away.
People came from all over Vienna to the Grinzing swimming pool; the Leimers were believed to be one of the
richest families in Grinzing if not *the* richest. They owed
their prosperity to their energetic mother, who toward
the end of the past century—when she was still young
and beautiful—had stationed herself in the path of the
Emperor Francis Joseph's carriage and tossed a petition
through the window, in which the Leimer family requested
permission to draw the water needed for the installation
of a swimming pool. The aqueduct carrying the finest
mountain water to Vienna had just been built, and the
enterprising woman had struck while the iron was hot.
The emperor had granted her petition, and thanks to his
favor the Grinzing swimming pool and the Leimer family
had flourished.

This was generally known, for everyone went to the swimming pool. What was not known to the daytime public was the way in which the emperor's favor had affected one member of the family in this emperorless period. "I am looking for my peers!" Thus written out, this monarchistic plaint may sound ridiculous. It did not sound ridiculous when accompanied by the movements of this man who chanted it late at night, always slowly and always drawing out the syllables to maximum length.

Full of longing for his peers, he circled between the tables and around the narrow middle area; he spoke to no one, no one spoke to him, not for the world would he have interrupted his chant. No one made fun of him. No one tried to divert him from his search. All had witnessed his act before and despite his seriousness it didn't seem to bother anyone. As lord of so much water, he was a respected figure, but his dance introduced a somber note into the café. He made his way to the door and his chant died down. He was gone, but the chant still echoed in one's ears.

Then a winegrower sitting beside me said: "The Frenchman's coming." Another, across from him, took up the words and repeated them with enthusiasm. This was something new to me, something I didn't understand and couldn't explain to my companion. People at the other tables also seemed to be expecting "the Frenchman." I knew of no Frenchman in Grinzing, but the locals all seemed to know what they meant, in their mouths the word suggested one of the seasons. When Friedl had heard the cry a few times—"The Frenchman's coming! The Frenchman's coming!"—she was so excited by its air of expectancy that she turned to the jolly drunk beside her—though she hardly wanted to encourage him, as she was having to ward off his attentions—and asked: "When is this Frenchman coming?" and he replied: "He's coming, he's coming. He's coming right now."

A moment later a blond giant appeared; he seemed to

be a head taller than anyone else in the bar. A young woman clung fast to him and a whole retinue followed. "The Frenchman's here! The Frenchman's here!" That was the Frenchman, but his whole retinue consisted of locals. The woman was another Leimer, the sister of the man who had been looking for his peers. The giant led his retinue in, it was amazing how many people poured into the place that was already full. They all sat down at a long table; the people who had been there before had evacuated it and squeezed their way into seats at other tables. The Leimer sister was still beside the Frenchman, still clinging to him, but now it was clear that she was holding him back from something that hadn't happened yet and that she didn't want to happen. I now learned that she was his wife, that she had married him in France. She came home to Grinzing once a year and brought her Frenchman with her. He was a sailor on a submarine, though no one knew for sure whether this was still the case or whether it had been in the last war. I was puzzled and looked at him in amazement: such a big man in a submarine; I had always thought they picked little fellows.

Everyone spoke to him. He understood no German and the people at his table seemed to take no interest in anyone else. They didn't talk to one another, they talked only to him. They kept asking him questions he couldn't answer, they shouted at him to make him understand, it didn't help. He remained totally mute, he didn't even say anything in his own language, I'd never seen such a big silent Frenchman. The less he said, the more they shouted at him. People at other tables tried to goad him into saying something. At first his wife, who was acting as his interpreter—that was why she was clinging so close to him—pulled herself up to his level and attempted a few lip movements. But she soon gave up. It was hopeless; maybe her French wasn't good enough, but even if she had known it as well as her mother tongue, she couldn't have made any headway against that barrage of shouts. She clung tighter and tighter to his arm. The jumbled shouts rose to a roar. From all sides people were bellowing at the Frenchman. Even at our table the noise was deafening.

I could see him well and I kept my eyes glued to him. I was almost going to shout something at him in his own language, but the excitement had risen to such a pitch that my intervention couldn't have done much good. Suddenly he jumped up and roared: *"Je suis français!"* With a sweep of his arms he pushed aside all the people near him, took a gigantic leap that carried him over the table and landed on a pile of bodies. Assailed on all sides, he went on bellowing: *"Français! Français!"* With incredible strength he plowed through the heap, an amazing feat even for a man of his size. People had fastened on to him in clusters; clearing a way to the door, he dragged them with him. He had lost his wife, she was far behind with the retinue. She was doing her best to push through the hostile crowd that had fastened on to his arms and legs and refused to let him go. When he had fought clear, she managed to follow, but I couldn't see what happened in the street. Some returning eyewitnesses reported that his wife was taking him home. As a brother-in-law, he belonged to the swimming pool; no one seemed to question that.

Afterwards in the café no one spoke of anything else. Evidently the Frenchman came every year. The locals always knew he was coming, they were waiting for him and every year it ended the same way. I asked some of them why the Frenchman had suddenly jumped up like that. He did it every time; that was all they knew. At first he always sat there as silent as a carp. Did he understand what people were shouting at him? No, not a word. Why did they keep trying? That was part of the fun. Did he always bellow the same thing? Yes, always *"Je suis français!"*

They tried to imitate his pronunciation. You had to hand it to him, he was strong. But nobody could mess around with them.

I wondered how long a man squeezed in among strangers could be expected to listen to foreign, totally incomprehensible talk before going berserk.

A Letter from Thomas Mann

It was a long handwritten letter in the careful, well-balanced style known to us from his books. It said things that were bound to surprise and delight me. Exactly four years earlier, I had sent Thomas Mann the manuscript of my novel in three black linen binders—a trilogy, he must have thought—accompanied by a long dry letter explaining my plan for a "Human Comedy of Madmen." It was a proud letter, containing hardly a word of homage, and he must have wondered why I had written it to him rather than someone else.

Veza loved *Buddenbrooks* almost as much as *Anna Karenina*; when her enthusiasm rose to such heights, it often deterred me from reading the book. I had read *The Magic Mountain* instead, its atmosphere was familiar to me from what my mother told me about the Waldsanatorium in Arosa, where she had spent two years. The book had made a deep impression on me, if only because of its reflections on death, and although I felt differently about these matters, I thought the book offered a scrupulous treatment of them. At that time, October 1931, I saw no reason not to appeal first to Thomas Mann. I hadn't read Musil yet, and my only possible objection might have been that I had already read some things by Heinrich Mann, who was more to my liking than his brother. The astonishing part of it, in any case, was my self-confidence. This first letter didn't include the slightest homage to Thomas Mann, though having read *The Magic Mountain*, I might well have expressed my admiration. But it seemed to me that one look at my manuscript would suffice, and he would *have* to go on reading; I was convinced that a pessimistic author—as I thought him to be—would find this book irresistible. But the enormous package was returned unread with a polite letter pleading lack of sufficient time and strength. It was a hard blow, for who else would consent to read so depressing a book if *he* declined? I had expected not mere approval, but something more like enthusiasm. I felt sure that the right kind of statement from him, betokening conviction rather than a mere desire to be helpful, would clear the way for my book. I saw no obstacle in my path, and that may be why I took so presumptuous a tone.

His letter declining to read my manuscript was his answer to my presumption; it was probably not unjust, for he had not read the book. For four years my manuscript went unpublished. It is not hard to imagine how that affected my outward circumstances. But it meant still more to my pride. I felt that by declining to read my book he had abased it, and I accordingly decided to make no further attempt to publish it. Then little by little, as I won a few friends for it with my readings, I was persuaded to try a publisher or two. These attempts were fruitless, just as I had expected after the blow Thomas Mann had dealt me.

But now in October 1935 the book had appeared and I was determined to send it to Thomas Mann. The wound he had dealt me was still open. He alone could heal it by reading the book and admitting that he had been wrong, that he had rejected something deserving of his esteem.

The letter I wrote him now was not impertinent, I merely told him the whole story and thus effortlessly put him in the wrong. He wrote me a long letter in return. He was too conscientious and upright a man not to make amends for the "wrong" he had done. After all that had happened his letter made me very happy.

Just then a first review of the book appeared in the *Neue Freie Presse*. It was written in a tone of lavish enthusiasm, but by a writer whom I did not take seriously, who could not be taken seriously. Still, it had its effect, for when I went to the Café Herrenhof that same day (or possibly the day after), Musil came up to me. I had never seen him so cordial. He put out his hand, and instead of merely smiling he positively beamed, which delighted me because I had been led to believe that he didn't permit himself to beam in public. "Congratulations on your great success," he said, and added that he had only read part of the book, but that if it went on in the same way I *deserved* my success. The word "deserved" from his lips almost made me reel. He uttered a few more words of praise, which I shall not repeat because, in view of what happened next, he may have withdrawn them since. His praise deprived me of my reason. I suddenly realized how eagerly I had been waiting for his opinion, possibly no less than I had been for Sonne's. I was intoxicated and befuddled. I must have been very befuddled, for how otherwise could I have made such a gaffe as I did then?

The moment he stopped speaking, I said: "And just imagine, I've had a long letter from Thomas Mann." He changed in a flash, he seemed to jump back into himself, his face went gray. "Did you?" he said. He held out his hand partway, giving me only the tips of his fingers to shake, and turned brusquely about. With that I was dismissed.

Dismissed forever. He was a master of dismissal. He had ample practice. Once he had dismissed you, you stayed dismissed. When I saw him in company, which happened now and then in the next two years, he was polite but never addressed me, never entered into a conversation with me. When my name was mentioned in company, he said nothing, as though he didn't know who I was and had no desire to find out.

What had happened? What had I done? What was the unpardonable offense that he could never forgive? A moment after he, Musil, had accorded me his recognition I had uttered the name of Thomas Mann. I had spoken of a letter, a long letter, from Thomas Mann immediately after he, Musil, had congratulated me and explained his congratulations. He was bound to assume that I had sent the book to Thomas Mann, as I had to him, with a similar respectful inscription. He had no knowledge of what had gone before, he didn't know that I had sent Thomas Mann the book four years before. But even if he had known the whole story, he would have been no less offended. Musil was touchier in his self-esteem than anyone else I have known, and there can be no doubt that in my euphoric befuddlement I stepped on his toes. It was understandable that he should make me repent it. My penance was very painful to me, I never really got over his dismissal of me in the most exalted moment I had ever known with him. But because it was he who imposed my penance, I accepted it. I realized how deeply I had wounded him in the state of euphoria that goes hand in hand with sudden recognition, and I felt ashamed.

He must have thought that I held Thomas Mann in higher esteem than him. And this he could not accept from someone who had stated the contrary everywhere. As he saw it, respect had to be based on intellectual considerations, otherwise it could not be taken seriously. He always attached importance to a clear decision between himself and Thomas Mann. If someone like Stefan Zweig had been involved, someone who owed his reputation to sheer bustle, the question of a decision would never have arisen. But Musil knew quite well who Thomas Mann was, and what exasperated him most was that Thomas Mann's prestige was so much greater than his own. In his own way, he (unbeknownst to me) had courted Thomas Mann at about this time, but with the feeling that he himself had every right to *wrest* Thomas Mann's fame away from him. All Musil's letters suggesting help from Thomas Mann sound like *demands*. It was a very different matter when a young writer, who had assured him of his sincerest reverence, should, a moment after Musil had set his stamp of approval on this young writer's work, mention the name of the man whom Musil aspired to supplant, and whose entrenchments he was still trying in vain to storm. Such an action cast suspicion on all my previous expressions of reverence. I had committed a crime of lèse-majesté, and deserved to be punished by banishment.

It made me very unhappy to have Musil turn away from me. Seeing the purely physical act at the Herrenhof, I knew that something irreparable had happened.

After that I couldn't answer Thomas Mann's letter. Its effect on Musil paralyzed me. For a few days I couldn't even bring myself to pick it up. I delayed my thanks so long that to write a simple note of thanks seemed out of the question. Then I went back to the letter and read it with all the greater pleasure. As long as I failed to answer it, my pleasure remained fresh. Every day I felt as if I had just received it. Perhaps after waiting for four years I wanted to make Thomas Mann wait a while too, but this is an idea that came to me only recently. Friends who had heard about Thomas Mann's letter asked me what I had written in answer, and all I could say was: "Not yet, not yet." A few months later they asked: "How will you explain yourself? What explanation will you give for waiting so long to reply to such a letter?" And again I knew no answer.

In April 1936, after more than *five months*, I read in the newspapers that Thomas Mann was coming to Vienna to deliver a lecture on Freud. This seemed the last chance to make good my omission. I concocted the most effusive letter I have ever written; how else could I account for what I had done? I think it would embarrass me to read that letter today. For by the time I got around to writing it, I had read the work of a writer who meant more to me than Thomas Mann: the first two volumes of *The Man without Qualities* had appeared. I was really grateful to Thomas Mann, *that* wound had healed. He had said things in his letter that filled me with pride. Though I didn't admit it to myself, I had done the same as Thomas Mann: made good an omission. He had read *Auto-da-Fé* and given his opinion of it. I had replaced my presumptuous first letter with another, improving on the homage that I had owed him then.

I think it gave him pleasure. But the circle did not fully close. In my letter I wrote that I should be delighted to meet him during his stay in Vienna. He was invited to the Benedikts' for lunch. There he asked after me and said he would have been glad to see me. Broch, who was present, said I lived nearby and offered to run over and get me. I was out when he came, I had just gone to meet Sonne at the Café Museum. And so it came about that though I heard Thomas Mann lecture I never met him personally.

Ras Kassa. The Bellowers

One night a party of Indians came to a *Heurigen* on Kobenzlgasse. Five or six luxurious limousines unload outside, some thirty people, all Indians, come in, they want a whole room to themselves; the people sitting in the first room leave their seats and obligingly move into the second room. Youngish Indian men in fashionable European clothes, rings on their fingers sparkling with jewels, beautiful women in saris, every one of them dark-skinned, not a single white among them. Standoffish. Smiling but firm, they insist in English—none of them can speak German—on having a room to themselves.

Once they are all seated, the *Heurigen* musicians come in from the other room and prepare to sing for them. The Indian spokesman signals a decided no; they want to play their own music. A chirping is heard from one corner, a strange dark sound, all present fall silent. Then a singing that strikes the locals as gloomy, a kind of dirge here in a *Heurigen*. Is that what they've kept still for? What is it? they ask when the song is over. With a friendly smile the spokesman explains: "An Indian low song." No one understands. What's a low song? The atmosphere has become strangely tense since the Indians started supplying their own music. Heads appear in the doorway. None of the locals has entered the Indians' room, but people start pushing in from outside. Low song? Low song? Then someone, it may have been me, hits on the solution: love song, an Indian love song. Disappointment. "A love song? Call that a love song? The *Heurigen* music has to stop for that? Is that what they call a love song in their country?"

The Indians had expected applause. Instead they sense the hostility in the air. Shouts that seem to come from the *Heurigen* songs that feel offended and supplanted. The Indians hesitate, maybe they hadn't chosen the right song. They try another. The singer doesn't get very far, to unpracticed ears it sounds like the first. Locals from outside, who have been inspecting the big limousines with hatred, crowd into the room. The Indian spokesman is still smiling, but he is obviously uneasy as the inferiors come closer. The women are still seated, but huddled together, and they've stopped beaming, the voices of the intruders are getting louder and rougher; one Indian is still chirping. No one is listening. Suddenly someone in the middle of the room roars angrily: "Ras Kassa!"

Ras Kassa is an Abyssinian chief who is still resisting the Italians. Mussolini has invaded Abyssinia, which is fighting bare-handed, so to speak, against Italian tanks and bombers. Ras Kassa's picture is in all the papers. Everyone admires him for his bravery. His skin is dark. Apart from his dark skin, he has nothing in common with these Indians at the *Heurigen*. But once shouted, his name becomes a battle cry. The Indians understand it despite the Viennese pronunciation, but take it as some sort of threat. The chirping and singing are submerged by the rising tumult. The Indians stand up and head, first hesitantly, then more and more hurriedly, for the door. No one stops them from leaving. A few more shouts of "Ras Kassa." A crowd has gathered around the big cars. Admiration for so much wealth gives way to disgust at so much luxury. Hesitant hostility, not yet active but on the verge. Its slogan is Ras Kassa, which has now become an insult, something one would hardly have expected during the Abyssinian war. Everyone's sympathy, one might have thought, was with the weak, the victims of aggression, who had taken up arms in a hopeless struggle. "Ras Kassa! Ras Kassa!" The Indians vanish into their cars. All dark-skinned people are Ras Kassa now. The Indians drive away.

Often at night I went into the garden that extends far down the slope at the back of the house. In the early summer, the air was shot through with luminous trails, glowworms, I tried to follow them with my eyes, but lost them, there were too many. There was something sinister about their numbers, as though they had been sent by a secret power determined to abolish the night. I was fascinated by their light, but as their numbers swelled, it became overpowering. I was glad they stayed close to the ground, that they didn't rise higher or go farther afield.

I heard a bellowing in the distance, it came from all sides, too far away to be threatening, from the general direction of the village. It was the bellowing of drunks in the *Heurigen*, their songs which merged and could not be kept apart, not a howling of wolves, a sound between laughing and crying. It was the voice of a special variety of animal, which favored this locale, an animal that was content to sit there and wallow in self-pity; there was no great threat in its bellowing; it seemed, rather, to express a longing for happiness. Even people without the slightest aptitude for music could bathe in this fountain of youth and, as part of the *Heurigen* animal, bellow along with the rest.

Every night I listened to it from the garden of the house on Himmelstrasse. I could feel justified in living here as long as I took in this total bellowing. It filled me with a kind of despair, which, however, did not exclude the feeling that I overcame it by facing up to it.

This was a credible exemplar of what I later called a feast crowd. When I went down with friends and sat in one of the garden cafés, we became part of it in our way. We didn't bellow, but we drank and boasted. Other people were boasting at other tables. All sorts of things were said and all sorts of things were tolerated. Funny things and outrageous things, but we were free to be just as outrageous. The general tendency was toward expansion, but no one encroached on anyone else, there was no fighting; crude as people's desires might be, no one seemed to begrudge anyone else his expansion. The drinking, which never ceased, was the magic elixir of expansion, and as long as one drank, everything increased, there seemed to be no obstacles, prohibitions or enemies.

When I sat there with Wotruba, I was shown what gigantic stones he would someday hew. But he didn't bat an eyelash when a young architect who was with us begot whole cities. Wotruba even allowed himself to be bombarded with the name of Kokoschka—something that seldom ended well under other circumstances. That was the greatest name the painters and sculptors of Vienna could bandy at that time. Though he was in Prague just then and had turned his back on Vienna, everyone who was out for fame was proud of him, he seemed beyond emulation. When Wotruba's friends wanted to squelch Wotruba's self-assurance, they would bring up the name of Kokoschka, and although they had nothing whatever in common—Wotruba was the exact opposite of Austrian baroque—he came to regard that name as a club with which he was being hit on the head.

It struck me that he often seemed paralyzed by fear that he would never equal Kokoschka. This was quite unlike him and I tried to talk him out of overestimating Kokoschka, whose late work, as a matter of fact, he did not greatly admire. Only at the *Heurigen*, when he reveled in immense blocks of stone and told us how Michelangelo had longed to carve whole mountains in the region of Carrara, to make sculptures that could be seen from ships at sea instead of merely hewing blocks of stone for the Pope's tomb in Rome; when I saw how deeply he regretted Michelangelo's failure to realize this ambition, it sounded as if he were still trying to egg Michelangelo on, as if his own blocks of stone were suddenly mingled with Michelangelo's, and as if he were about to take the job out of Michelangelo's hands—only then did the name of Kokoschka, if anyone had been foolish enough to utter it, sound silly and lightweight, while Wotruba was a mighty mountain beside it.

In his case I literally saw expansion and aggrandizement; I saw his stones growing, I never heard him singing, let alone bellowing, at the most he growled, but then he was angry and that's not what he went to the *Heurigen* for.

But at night when I went into the garden alone, heard the bellowing, felt ashamed of living so close to it, but stayed there until I had taken all the bellowing into myself and overcome my sense of shame, I sometimes wondered whether there might be others like him sitting down there, others who did not go in for bellowing and who from the general expansiveness drew the strength for legitimate work. I never gave myself an answer. I could not possibly have profaned my faith in my friend's uniqueness, but the mere fact that I could ask such a question somewhat tempered my pride, and I no longer felt quite so superior to the bellowing.

From time to time—not often—I went to a *Heurigen* with friends and especially with visitors from abroad. It was hard to avoid doing the honors of Grinzing. And with the help of these foreign eyes I found out what they had to offer. In those *Heurigen* where the atmosphere was still authentically rustic, where one sat quietly in a garden with not too many people, visitors were often reminded of Netherlands painting, of Ostade or Teniers. There was something to be said for this view and it attenuated my distaste for the bellowing. With the help of this association I finally realized what really bothered me about this kind of merrymaking. I was as fond as ever of Brueghel, I loved his richness and scope, and always will. The fall from his immense general views to the small, banalized excerpts characteristic of Flemish genre painting was to me intolerable. Their attenuation and fragmentation of reality struck me as fraudulent. It was only in the event of certain scenes, such as when upper-class Indians tried to sing their love songs in one of these cafés, that the place suddenly looked real—like Brueghel—to me again.

The No. 38 Streetcar

It wasn't a long line. The ride from terminus to terminus took less than half an hour. But as far as I was concerned it could have taken longer, it was an interesting ride, and there was nothing I liked better than to settle myself in a car on the Grinzing loop. In the early afternoon the car was almost empty. I made myself at home and opened one of the several books I had with me. The squeaking of the wheels on the tracks was my musical accompaniment. It lulled me, and yet I was alert to every stop, I watched everyone who sat down on the opposite bench. It was the right distance to watch people from. At first they were only a sprinkling and loosely distributed. At every stop the space between them diminished. Those on my side of the aisle were lost to my view. The ones farther from me were hidden by those nearest me, I could look at them only as they got on or as they stood up to get off. But there were plenty of people on the opposite bench, and as they got on only one or two at a time, I was able to take them in at my leisure.

At Kaasgraben, the first stop, Zemlinsky got on; I knew him as a conductor, not as a composer; black birdlike head, jutting triangular nose, no chin. I saw him often, he paid no attention to me, he was really deep in thought, musical thought no doubt, while I was only pretending to read. Every time I saw him I looked for his chin. When he appeared in the doorway, I gave a little start and began to search. Will he have one this time? He never did, but even without a chin he led a full life. To me he was a substitute for Schönberg, who in my time was not in Vienna. Only two years younger than Zemlinsky, Schönberg had been his pupil and had shown him the reverence which was an essential part of his nature, and which Schönberg's own pupils Berg and Webern were to show him. Schönberg, who was poor, had led a hard life in Vienna. For years he had orchestrated operetta music; gnashing his teeth, he had contributed to the tawdry glitter of Vienna, he who was restoring Vienna's fame as the birthplace of great music. In Berlin he obtained regular employment as a teacher of music. When discharged for being Jewish, he emigrated to America. I never saw Zemlinsky without thinking of Schönberg; his sister had been Schönberg's wife for twenty-three years. The sight of him always intimidated me, I sensed his extreme concentration; his small, severe, almost emaciated face was marked by thought and showed no sign of the self-importance one would expect in a conductor. It may have been because of Schönberg's enormous reputation among serious-minded young music lovers that no one ever spoke of Zemlinsky's music; when I saw him on the streetcar, I didn't even suspect that he had composed anything. But I did know that Alban Berg had dedicated his *Lyrical Suite* to him. Berg was dead and Schönberg was not in Vienna; I was always moved when his vicar Zemlinsky entered the car at Kaasgraben.

But the ride could begin very differently; sometimes Emmy Wellesz, the wife of Egon Wellesz the composer, got on at Kaasgraben. Wellesz had won world fame with his research into Byzantine music and had been awarded an honorary degree by Oxford University. He had some reputation as a composer, but not as much of one as he would have wished. The musical public seemed to take it amiss that he had distinguished himself in another field. His wife was an art historian; I had been watching her in the car for some time when I met her at someone's home. She seemed intelligent and somewhat too meek; as though in an effort to overcome her natural aggressiveness, she had decided to be meek. But then in a long talk with her I found out where this meekness came from. She had known Hofmannsthal and was wildly enthusiastic about him. She told me how years ago she had caught sight of him while taking a walk, a supernatural vision. Her critical, intelligent features lit up, her voice cracked with emotion and she held back a tear. She spoke of that incident as if she had met Shakespeare. This struck me as absurd and from then on I did not take her seriously. It was only much later that I found out to what degree her ideas even then were in agreement with the century's academic opinion, and when I learned that the collected works were being prepared in one hundred eighty-eight volumes, I began to be ashamed of my shortsightedness. What I would give now to help that tear take form and to bathe in her meekness.

Not far from Wertheimstein Park, where the No. 39 line branches off to Sievering, a young painter who lived on nearby Hartäckerstrasse would sometimes get on. I had once called on him in his studio when he was showing his pictures. He was the lord and master of a strikingly beautiful woman with jet-black hair. She was as seductive as an early Indian Yakshini, though there was nothing in the least Indian about her, her name was Hilde and she came of correspondingly Germanic stock. She was devoted to him after the manner of a slave girl who looks languishingly about her for a liberator but who, when liberation beckons—considering her looks, nothing could have been simpler—reverts to her master's whip; never under any circumstances would she have let herself be liberated. She suffered from his hard rule, but she liked to suffer. I had heard about this unusual relationship and the girl's beauty, which may be why I accepted the invitation to visit the painter's studio, though I had never seen any of his pictures.

He was a cubist and had been influenced by Braque.

The paintings were shown in a rather ritualistic way. Slowly, impersonally, at regular intervals, with no attempt to influence the viewer by charm or flattery, he placed them on an easel; I thought it appropriate to react in the same way.

A writer who lived on the upper floor of the same house had come to the showing with his mistress. He attracted my notice with his grimacing features and long arms, an imposing figure. He stationed himself at the right distance from the easel. His inconspicuous, but in her own way just as devoted, girlfriend, a rather insipid-looking blonde, sat beside him. Whenever a new picture appeared, she smiled at him, but much more discreetly than her counterpart. The sweet sympathy they emanated exasperated me with its regularity; it showed the same well-tempered joy over every picture and as much fervor as if they were viewing one Fra Angelico after another at the church of San Marco in Florence. I was so fascinated by this regularly repeated reaction that I paid more attention to the writer than to the pictures and certainly failed to do them justice. This of course was just what the writer was aiming at. His little game became the center of attraction, no mean achievement in view of the house slave, who was doing her utmost to call attention to her oppressed condition.

With consummate self-assurance, as though on horseback, the writer smiled from on high, a knight who had never doubted his powers, an old familiar of death and the Devil, both of whom called him by his first name. But he did not see the slave, who writhed in chains not far from him; indeed, I had the impression that he didn't even see the pictures that were set before him, so prompt and unchanging was the smile with which he greeted them. When the showing was over, he thanked the artist fervently for the great pleasure. He didn't stay one minute more, the slave girl smiled in vain, he withdrew with his paramour, and it was only later that I heard his name, which struck me as rather ridiculous, though it went with his grimaces: it was Doderer.

(I saw him again twenty years later under very different circumstances. Now famous, he came to see me in London. Once fame has set in, he said, it's as irresistible as a dreadnought. He asked me if I had ever killed a man. When I answered in the negative, he said, grimacing with all the contempt of which he was capable: "Then you're a virgin!")

But it was the young painter who got on the No. 38 streetcar at that stop and greeted me in his colorlessly correct way. He was always alone. When I asked him about his girlfriend, he replied with the same reserve as he had shown in his greeting: "She's at home. She doesn't go out. She doesn't know how to behave." "And how is that writer with the long, apelike arms who lives upstairs?" He guessed what I was thinking. "He's a gentleman. He knows how to behave. He comes only when *I* invite him."

At Billrothstrasse more people got on; after that, as a rule, quiet observation was impossible. But for me this stretch had other, historic charms. After the Belt came Währingerstrasse and soon we passed the Chemical Institute, where I had spent several aimless and fruitless years. Not once did I neglect to look at the Institute, where I hadn't set foot since 1929. Each time I sighed with relief that I had escaped it. The car went quickly past, reenacting my flight, which I could never celebrate enough. How soon it becomes possible to look back on a past; with what joy one relives one's escape from it! With a sense of exaltation I arrived at Schottentor; it came to me every time I rode down Währingerstrasse. Broch, who visited us in Grinzing, asked me if that was why I chose to live in Grinzing. If he hadn't looked at me with the gimlet eye of a psychoanalyst, I might have admitted as much.

PART FIVE

The Entreaty

Unexpected Reunion

Ludwig Hardt, one of whose recitations I had attended in 1928 in Berlin, was now a refugee living in Prague. He performed in Vienna now and then. I attended one of his recitations, and was overwhelmed as I had been eight years before. I went backstage to thank him, though I was sure he wouldn't remember me, and had hardly opened my mouth when he came running up to me and startled me with a well-aimed dart: "You've lost your idol and you didn't even go to his funeral."

Karl Kraus had died recently and, true enough, I hadn't gone to his funeral. I had been terribly disillusioned after the events of February 1934. He had come out in support of Dollfuss and had not said a word in condemnation of the civil war in the streets of Vienna. All his followers, literally all, had dropped him. He still gave small, obscure readings that no one knew about; no one wanted to know about them, let alone attend them. It was as if Karl Kraus had ceased to exist. The old issues of *Die Fackel* were still on my shelf, but in these last two years I hadn't picked them up; he was obliterated from my mind and the minds of many others. It was as if he had gathered his followers together and attacked himself in one of his most eloquent and annihilating speeches. In these last two years of his life he was *mentioned* in conversations, but in hushed tones, as though he were dead. I heard the news of his actual death—he died in June 1936—without emotion. I didn't even take note of the date, and I had to look it up just now. Not for a moment did I consider going to his funeral. I saw no mention of it in the papers and I didn't feel that I was missing anything.

The first person to mention it in my presence was Ludwig Hardt. After eight years he had recognized me instantly and recalled a conversation in which I had made myself ridiculous with my blind admiration for my demi-god. He knew what had happened in the meantime and felt sure that I hadn't attended the funeral. For the first time I felt guilty about it. To make amends for the harm done by his words, he invited himself to call on us in Grinzing.

I expected a long and unpleasant argument, but I was so enchanted by Ludwig Hardt's artistry that I wanted to straighten things out with him. I couldn't believe that such a man merely wanted to show that he had been right. Perhaps he would condole with me and in return expect me to confess that I had been mistaken in Karl Kraus. But how was I to disavow the man to whom I owed *The Last Days of Mankind* and innumerable readings of Nestroy, of *King Lear, Timon of Athens, The Weavers,* and so on? These readings were a part of my being, and his unspeakable conduct a few years before his death defied explanation. A discussion was unthinkable; the only pos-sible reaction was silence. In all my thirty years I had never suffered such a disappointment; it had left me with a wound that would take more than thirty years to heal. There are wounds we carry about for the rest of our lives, and all we can do is conceal them from others. There can be no point in tearing them open in public.

I was not sure what attitude I should take in my conversation with Ludwig Hardt, but of one thing I was certain: never, under any circumstances, would I deny what Karl Kraus had meant to me. I had not overestimated him, no one had overestimated him, he had changed and, I assumed, that change had been the cause of his death.

Ludwig Hardt arrived. He didn't say one word about Karl Kraus. He didn't so much as allude to him. The words with which he had so startled me after his reading were merely a sign of recognition. Another man would have said: "I remember you well, though we haven't seen each other for eight years." He had to prove it in his light-footed way. I remembered him just as well, how at parties in Berlin he would jump up on the table and declaim Heine.

I took him straight to my study. For one thing, I didn't want to divert him with the landscape. From my study there was no view of vineyards, nor of the plain or the city; one saw only the garden gate and the short path leading to the house. I expected a confrontation, and I may have felt safer here. Also, I wanted him to see that my many books included the complete works of the man we would be arguing about. But he paid no attention to them; he talked about Prague. A small, graceful, uncommonly mobile man, he declined to sit down and didn't keep still for a moment. While pacing back and forth, he held his right hand deep in his jacket pocket, toying with an object that seemed to be a book. At length he produced it, it was indeed a book, he held it out to me with a grand gesture, and said: "Would you care to see my most precious possession? I carry it with me wherever I go, I wouldn't entrust it to anyone. When I go to bed I put it under my pillow."

It was a small edition of Hebel's *Treasure Chest,* dating from the past century. I opened it and read the inscription: "For Ludwig Hardt, to give Hebel pleasure, from Franz Kafka."

It was Kafka's own copy of *The Treasure Chest,* which he too had carried about with him. It seems that when he first heard Ludwig Hardt reciting Hebel, he was so moved that he inscribed his own copy and gave it to him. "Would you like to know what Kafka heard me recite?" Hardt asked. "Yes, indeed," I said. At that he recited, by heart as usual—I had the book in my hands—in this order: "The Sleepless Night of a Noblewoman," the two Suvarov pieces, "Misunderstanding," "Moses Mendelssohn," and, last, "Unexpected Reunion."

I wish everyone could have heard that last story. Twelve years after Kafka's death, I was hearing the very words that he had heard, from the same lips. When he had finished, we both fell silent, for we both realized that we had lived a new variation of the same story. Then Hardt said: "Would you care to hear what Kafka said about that?" and went on without waiting for my answer: "Kafka said: 'That's the most wonderful story in all the world.'" I had thought so myself and always will. But it was unusual to hear such a superlative from Kafka, and, what's more, quoted by a man who after reciting this story had been honored with the gift of *his Treasure Chest*. As everyone knows, Kafka's superlatives are numbered.

After that, my relationship with Ludwig Hardt changed. It took on an intimacy such as I have known with few people. From then on, whenever he was in Vienna, he came straight to our house. He spent many hours on Himmelstrasse, reciting almost uninterruptedly. His repertory was inexhaustible and I couldn't get enough of it. It was all stored up in his head and he no doubt had more in his head than I ever heard. My memory of that first recitation of Hebel has never paled. Sometimes, when his recitations put us into too solemn a mood, we went to Veza's paneled room, where he recited other things that Veza too was fond of, plenty of Goethe and always Lenz's Sesenheim poem "Love in the Country," which has Goethe in it and might have been written by Goethe. Then we talked enthusiastically about Lenz, whose life moved him no less than it did me. Once when I remarked that this poem was full of what Goethe had done to Lenz and that Lenz, like Friederike, was always waiting for Goethe, who couldn't bear it and for that reason destroyed him, Hardt jumped up and embraced me. For Veza and for me as well, he recited Heine, of whose worth he had convinced me in Berlin; just for Veza he recited Wedekind and Peter Altenberg.

We never let him go without reciting two poems, both by Claudius, "War Song"—

> *They've gone to war, O heavenly angel,*
> *Oh stop them in God's name.*
> *They've gone to war, and I must hope*
> *That I am not to blame.*

each of whose six stanzas I would like to copy out today— and the "Letter of a Hunted Stag to the Prince Who Was Hunting Him."

The recitation ended with the miracle of transformation that I can still call to mind, the transformation of Ludwig into a dying stag. If I had doubted that of all man's gifts transformation is the best, that after all the crimes he has committed it is his justification and crowning glory, I would have discovered it then. Hardt *was* the dying stag. When he had breathed his last, he came to life and was Ludwig Hardt again. I couldn't get over it. And though he enjoyed our amazement, the death of the hunted animal was always authentic, overwhelming, because the stag was also a human being, and a human being I loved because he was human.

The Spanish Civil War

Two years of my friendship with Sonne coincided with the Spanish Civil War. It was the main subject of our daily talks. All my friends sided with the Republicans.

Our sympathies with the Spanish government were un-
concealed and expressed with passion.

For the most part we simply discussed what we had
read in the papers that day. It was only in my conversations
with Sonne that we looked more deeply into what was
happening in Spain and considered its consequences for
the future of Europe. Sonne proved to be well versed in
Spanish history. He had studied every phase of the
centuries-long war between Christianity and Islam, of the
Moorish period and the Reconquista. He was as familiar
with the country's three cultures as if he had grown up
in all of them, as though they still existed and were
accessible through a knowledge of the three languages,
Spanish, Arabic and Hebrew, and of the corresponding
literatures. From him I learned something about Arabic
literature. He translated Moorish poems of the time as
easily as if he had been translating from the Bible, and
explained their influence on the European Middle Ages.
Though he never for a moment claimed to know Arabic,
it came out quite incidentally that he was fluent in that
language.

When I tried to explain certain events in the recent
and past history of Spain by the particular type of mass
movements specific to the Iberian peninsula, he listened
and did not try to discourage me. I had the impression
that if he expressed no reaction it was because he realized
my ideas were still fluid and that it would be better for
their future development if they were not yet solidified
by discussion.

It was only natural at that time that we should think of
Goya and his *Horrors of War* engravings. For it was his
experience of the cruel reality of his time that made this
first and greatest of modern artists what he was. "He
didn't look the other way," said Sonne. Those words were
spoken from the heart. How shattering to contrast the
rococo style of Goya's early works with *these* engravings

and the late paintings. Goya had his opinions, he was partisan; how could a man who saw the royal family with his eyes have failed to be partisan? But he saw what was happening as if he belonged to both camps, because his knowledge was a human knowledge. He detested war, more passionately perhaps than anyone before him or even today, for he knew that there is no such thing as a good war, since every war perpetuates the most evil and dangerous of human traditions. War cannot be abolished by war, which merely consolidates what is most detestable in man. Goya's value as a witness exceeded his partisanship; what he saw was monstrous, it was more than he had any desire to see. Since Grünewald's *Christ* no one had depicted horror as he did, no whit better than it was—sickening, crushing, cutting deeper than any promise of redemption—yet without succumbing to it. The pressure he put on the viewer, the undeviating direction he gave to his gaze, was the ultimate in hope, though no one would have dared call it by that name.

Those who had not forgotten the teachings of the First World War were in a state of grave spiritual torment. Sonne recognized the nature of the Spanish Civil War and knew what it would lead to. Though he hated war, he thought it necessary and indispensable that the Spanish Republic should defend itself. With Argus eyes he followed every move of the Western powers that were trying to prevent the war from spreading to Europe. He groaned to see the democratic powers reducing themselves to impotence with their nonintervention policy and knowingly letting the Fascists pull the wool over their eyes. He knew this weakness had its source in a dread of war, which he shared with them, but it also revealed ignorance of the enemy and terrifying shortsightedness. The pusillanimity of the Western powers encouraged Hitler, who was testing their reactions, trying to find out how far he could go; his enemies' dread of war confirmed him in his warlike plans. Sonne was convinced that nothing could be done to change Hitler's determination to make war, that it was his basic principle (derived from *his* experience of war), the principle by which he lived and through which he had come to power. Sonne regarded all attempts to influence Hitler as futile. But it was necessary to break off the chain of his successes before all anti-war sentiment had been suppressed in Germany. This sentiment could be encouraged only by unequivocal action outside of Germany. Hitler's triumphal march was a deadly threat to all, the Germans included. With his fanatical sense of historic mission Hitler was bound in the end to drag the whole world into this war, and how could Germany hope to defeat all the rest of the world?

Sonne's opinions were far in advance of the times. Politicians were staggering from one makeshift solution to the next. Though he saw the coming catastrophe more and more clearly, he took an interest in every least detail of the Spanish conflict. For to his lucid mind, oddly enough, nothing could be regarded as settled once and for all; an unforeseen event, however unimportant at first sight, could give rise to a new hope—and such hopes must not be overlooked, everything must be borne in mind, nothing was unimportant.

In the course of the civil war, Spanish names came up, the names of places to which some historical or literary memory attached. Sonne would speak to me of these memories and it will always be a source of amazement to me how late and with what a sense of urgency I became acquainted with Spain.

Up until then something had deterred me from taking a closer look at the Spanish Middle Ages. I had not forgotten the songs and sayings of my childhood, but they had led to nothing more, they had stuck fast inside me, congealed by the arrogance of my family, who claimed a right to all things Spanish, insofar as they served their caste pride. I knew Sephardic Jews who lived in Oriental sloth, outstripped in mental development by anyone who had gone to school in Vienna, asking nothing more of life than the right to feel superior to other Jews. Nor was I doing my mother an injustice when I observed that she was well read in all the literatures of Europe but knew next to nothing of Spanish literature. She had seen plays by Calderón at the Burgtheater, but it would never have occurred to her to read them in the original. To her, Spanish was not a literary language. What it had given her was the memory of a glorious medieval past and perhaps it was of value only because it was a *spoken* language and was the source of a certain disdain for the people around her. She could not provide me with an introduction to Spanish literature. There was something uncommonly Spanish about her pride, yet she derived her models for it from Shakespeare, in particular *Coriolanus*. Vienna, not her origins, had been the dominant influence in her upper-class education.

I was thirty when I was introduced to the poets who created what has remained of those early years in Spain. I heard about them from Sonne, a "Todesco"*—his family hailed from Austrian Galicia—to whom my mother would have denied any right to "our poets," whom she did not know at all. He translated them to me orally from the Hebrew and explained them, and sometimes on the same afternoon he would translate Moorish poems from Arabic and explain them. Since he showed me an overall picture, not something torn out of its temporal context for reasons of absurd vainglory, I put away my distrust of Ladino culture and viewed it with respect.

These were strange conversations. They started from news items about the war in Spain. How expertly Sonne dealt with the situation, the relative strength of the

* A German Jew. (Trans.)

opposing forces, the length of time it would take for expected help to reach them, the effect of a Republican retreat on foreign opinion—would it result in more aid or less?—the changes taking place in the Republican government, the increasing influence of *one* party, the role of regional autonomistic tendencies. Nothing was omitted, nothing forgotten. Often I had the impression of talking with a man who held the threads of history in his hands. But it was also quite evident that he was trying to give me the feeling that all these events were taking place in a country that should be familiar to me, and that he was therefore doing his utmost to make it familiar to me. With few words he transported me to the cultural spheres which, no less than this terrible war, were Spain.

I still remember how I was led to one work or another. The occasion was often a name that had come up in the news. The shock of a news item entered into such a book and it no longer existed by itself alone. The present events gave rise to a secret nucleus, its second, immutable structure.

It was then that Quevedo's *Dreams* came my way. Along with Swift and Aristophanes, Quevedo was one of my ancestors. A writer needs ancestors. He must know some of them by name. When he thinks he is going to choke on his own name, which he cannot get rid of, he harks back to ancestors, who bear happy, deathless names of their own. They may smile at his importunity, but they do not rebuff him. They too need others, in their case descendants. They have passed through thousands of hands; no one can hurt them; that's why they have become ancestors, because they have succeeded without a struggle in defending themselves against the weak. By giving strength to others, they grow stronger. But there are also ancestors who feel the need of resting awhile. They go to sleep for a century or two. They get woken, you can rely on that; all of a sudden they ring out like trumpets, only to yearn again for their forsaken slumbers.

Sonne may have found it unbearable to lose himself entirely in events. He may have been repelled by his powerlessness to influence them. In any case, he never missed an opportunity to call attention to my origins, precisely because I attached so little importance to them. He felt strongly that no part of a life must be lost. What a man touched upon, he should take with him. If he forgot it, he should be reminded. What gives a man worth is that he incorporates everything he has experienced. This includes the countries where he has lived, the people whose voices he has heard. It also takes in his origins, if he can find out something about them. By this he meant not only one's private experience but everything concerning the time and place of one's beginnings. The words of a language one may have spoken and heard only as a child imply the literature in which it flowered. The story of a banishment must include everything that happened before it as well as the rights subsequently claimed by the victims. Others had fallen before and in different ways; they too are part of the story. It is hard to evaluate the *justice* of such a claim to a history. To Sonne's mind history was eminently the area of guilt. We should know not only what happened to our fellow men in the past but also what they were capable of. We should know what we ourselves are capable of. For that, much knowledge is needed; from whatever direction, at whatever distance knowledge offers itself, one should reach out for it, keep it fresh, water it and fertilize it with new knowledge. The present civil war, which affected us even more deeply than what was happening in the city where we lived, provided Sonne with a means of entrenching me in my past, which now for the first time became real for me. It was thanks to him that when I had to leave Vienna shortly thereafter, there was more of me to go. He enabled me to take a language with me and to hold on to it so firmly that I would never under any circumstances be in danger of losing it.

I shall never forget the day when in a state of great agitation I came to meet Sonne at the Café Museum and he received me in total silence. The newspaper lay on the table in front of him, his hand lay on top of it, he didn't lift his hand to shake mine. I forgot to pronounce a greeting; the words I was going to fire at him stuck in my throat. He had turned to stone, I was delirious with excitement. The same news—the destruction of Guernica by German bombers—had affected us in very different ways. I wanted to hear a curse from his lips, a curse in the name of all Basques, all Spaniards, all mankind. I did not want to see him turned to stone. His helplessness was more than I could bear. I felt my anger turning against him. I stood waiting for a word from him. I couldn't sit down until he said something. He paid no attention to me. He looked drained; he looked desiccated, as though long dead. The thought passed through my head: A mummy. She's right. He *is* a mummy. That's what Veza called him when she was angry. I was sure he *felt* my condemnation, even if I hadn't said anything. But that too he disregarded. He said: "I tremble for the cities." It was hardly audible, but I knew I had heard right.

I didn't understand. Those words were then harder to understand than they would be today. He's befuddled, I thought, he doesn't know what he's saying. Guernica destroyed, and he talks about *cities*. I couldn't bear the thought of his being befuddled. His clarity had become the biggest thing in the world for me. Two disasters had hit me at once. A town destroyed by bombers. Sonne stricken with madness. I asked no questions. I offered no moral support. I said nothing and left. Even out on the street I felt no sympathy for him. I felt—it sickens me to say it—pity for myself. It was as though he had died in Guernica, as though I had lost everything and was trying to face up to it.

I hadn't gone far when it suddenly occurred to me that

he might be ill; he had looked frightfully pale. He couldn't
be dead, I thought, for he had spoken, I had heard his
words, what had hit me so hard was the absurdity of those
words. I turned back, he welcomed me with a smile, he
was the same as usual. I would gladly have forgotten the
incident, but he said: "You needed a breath of air. I can
see that. Maybe I need one myself." He stood up and I
left the café with him. Outside, we spoke as if nothing
had happened. He made no further reference to the
words that had so upset me. That may be why I have
never been able to forget them. Years later, in England
during the war, the scales fell from my eyes. We were far
apart, but he was still alive. He was in Jerusalem. We did
not correspond. I thought to myself: Never has there
been a more reluctant prophet. He saw what would
happen to the cities. And he had seen all the rest. He had
had plenty to tremble for. He didn't justify one atrocity
by another. He had left the blood feud of history behind
him.

Conference on Nussdorferstrasse

Hermann Scherchen was planning a journal in four
languages, to be called *Ars Viva* like the series of concerts
he was then giving in Vienna, for which he had recruited
a special orchestra. The journal was not to be devoted
solely to music; literature and the plastic arts were to be
represented on an equal footing. He asked me to propose
possible co-editors in Vienna, and I mentioned Musil and
Wotruba. Quick as usual to make up his mind, he suggested that the four of us should meet and discuss the

possibility of our putting out a journal together. It was to be a private meeting, without witnesses; in those times of political pressure a café seemed too exposed for the purpose. Wotruba had left the apartment on Florianigasse to his mother and sister, and moved to one of his own on Nussdorferstrasse. That seemed the best place for our meeting, for apart from being centrally located, it was neutral ground, so to speak. Himmelstrasse in Grinzing was too far out of the way. Scherchen and his Chinese wife were staying with us, but since I had offended Musil with my tactless remark about Thomas Mann, he had been cool to me and I could not invite him to my house. Wotruba had met him at my reading at the Schwarzwald School. That had been almost two years before. Since then they had exchanged greetings, but had not become friends. Nothing had happened between them that might have prevented Musil from accepting an invitation. After consultation with me Wotruba wrote a strong but respectful letter, and Musil agreed to come.

As might have been expected with Musil, there were complications from the start. As we knew he disliked going anywhere alone, the invitation included his wife. But in addition he brought two men who had not been invited. One was Franz Blei—gaunt, arrogant, precious—whom none of us would have wanted. The other was a young man unknown to us. Musil introduced him nonchalantly, almost gaily, as an admirer of *The Man without Qualities,* and Blei added: "From the Café Herrenhof." So there were the four of them. Musil seemed to feel at his ease under the protection of his wife, his old friend Blei and his young admirer, who didn't open his mouth but listened attentively. Blei spoke with authority, as though *he* were founding a journal, while Musil spoke his mind freely and without hesitation.

On the other side of the room, moroseness set in immediately. Blei's aesthetic pose was deeply repugnant to Wotruba. On entering the whitewashed room, Blei had noticed two Merkels on the wall. He hesitated a moment, then damned them with faint praise. "He's not without charm," he said. And after a short pause: "One of the younger lot?"

Quite rightly, Wotruba took the "younger" as a dig at himself, sensed that Blei knew nothing about him, regarded him as nothing more than "young." He replied with deliberate rudeness: "Hell, he's as old as you."

This was an exaggeration. Georg Merkel was not as old as Blei, but he belonged to the same generation as Musil, and Wotruba took the imputation that a picture hanging on his wall must necessarily be by "one of the younger lot" as an impertinence. A little later, when Marian came in with coffee, he blithely interrupted the conversation, saying in a loud voice: "Hey, Marian, do you know what Merkel is? He's one of the younger lot."

Scherchen began to unfold his plan for his review. What he wanted was originality and high quality; it should really be something new, no academic material would be considered. It should not be confined to any one modern trend, all would be given a chance to express themselves, regardless of language; translations could always be managed. Musil wanted to know the maximum length of contributions. He was pleased when Scherchen replied: "No limit. We could run a whole play; for instance, I'd welcome a play by my friend Canetti. True, he refuses to give me one. But we'll bring him around."

After more than three years he hadn't forgotten *The Wedding*. But I wished to publish it only in book form. It was hardly the right moment to discuss all this, but he wanted to make it known that he was not unacquainted with modern literature. *The Wedding* still struck him as something "new."

He had hardly spoken when Blei took the floor.

"Plays are not literature," he proclaimed. "Plays cannot be considered for a literary journal."

This he said with such an air of certainty that the three

of us, Scherchen, Wotruba and I, were dumbfounded. Musil smiled genially.

He was under the impression, I believe, that Blei was giving a good account of himself and had already taken over the management of our journal. Then came a long statement by Blei, which must have been prepared in advance, outlining the program of the projected journal. With every sentence he seemed surer of getting his way. To my amazement the ordinarily so dictatorial Scherchen let him talk. Wotruba's seething rage began to worry me. He'll pick him up and throw him out the window, I thought, and despite my own anger, I feared for the life of the distinguished intruder. If I had known that he was partly responsible for discovering Robert Walser, I'd have forgiven him his impertinence, and consideration for Musil would not have been my only reason for treating him with respect. Suddenly Scherchen cut him off:

"My young friends and I have entirely different ideas," he said. "Everything you say is contrary to our intentions. We want a living organ, not a scholastic petrifact. You come out for restrictions of every kind; we want *Ars Viva* to stand for expansion, and we are not afraid of the times. There are plenty of other journals for fossils."

For the first time in all the years I'd known him, Sch. had spoken after my own heart. Wotruba shouted furiously: "I'm not interested in Herr Blei's opinion. No one invited him. I want to know how Herr Musil feels about the journal."

Wotruba was famous for his rudeness and no one took it amiss. Anyone meeting him for the first time would have been disappointed if he had behaved differently. He was serious through and through. Worrying about good manners would have made him look ridiculous, as though he were trying to stammer in a foreign language. I felt that Musil liked him, and he didn't seem offended for Blei, though he had listened to Blei's disquisition with apparent approval.

Now he stepped, as it were, out of Blei's umbra and spoke as frankly as Wotruba himself. He wasn't sure, he hadn't made up his mind yet. He had an article on Rilke that might do for the journal. Perhaps he'd think of something else. His delivery was firm; not so the content of his remarks. He promised nothing. He was undecided. But he had been invited and received so deferentially that he couldn't just decline. He felt safe with his retinue. Blei was an old friend, but Blei was capricious and unpredictable, and moreover he had been responsible for suddenly elevating Broch's *Sleepwalkers* to Musil's high level. Broch had not been suggested for the new journal, he was not in Vienna at the time, and knowing how Musil felt about him, we had avoided mentioning him for the present. If one of us had done so, Musil would have declined forthwith and would not have attended the meeting. His rejections were harsh and cutting. Wotruba and I both delighted in the legends that were going around about his way of saying no.

Here, in the company of three acolytes and confronted by three men who were trying to enlist his support, he reacted with a different kind of no—the cautious hesitation of a man who didn't want to be taken advantage of, but didn't want to miss a good opportunity either. He wanted time to think, he said neither yes nor no, but tried to get more information. Sch., who had never been so retiring, who seldom said "I" and prefaced every sentence with "my young friends," was not to his liking. It was obvious to Musil that Scherchen knew nothing of literary matters and would rely on me. I had been rejected because of my heretical mention of Thomas Mann. The stubbornness with which I had nevertheless clung to my opinion that Musil was top man worked in my favor to the extent that he accepted my presence. To Wotruba he felt very much drawn. Wotruba had no connection with literature of any kind; but his words had power, they struck with the force of cannonballs. When Musil took a liking to someone, his face showed surprise—a controlled, moderate surprise. He had full control over his reactions and made no mistake. His astonishment was limited, but that did not detract from its purity. It was not subordinated to any purposes.

When he spoke now, he seemed to be waiting for one reaction, Wotruba's, as though no one else's counted. He didn't take Blei's orotund proclamation very seriously. He had known Blei's opinions for a long time and I had the impression that they bored him. He accepted the proclamation because it was made by a supporter, but he didn't come out in favor of it, he only smiled indulgently, which was a way of distancing himself from it. Wotruba's rude rejection of Blei, followed by his demand to hear what Musil himself had to say, pleased Musil; and he began quite candidly to examine the plan for a journal. He insisted that he wished to write on a poetic subject, and asked to know more of our intentions.

Sch. said this was lucky, because his wife, who was not present at the conference, took a special interest in poetry, which was quite in the Chinese tradition. Indeed, poetry meant even more to her than music. True, he had met her as a student in a conducting course he had given in Brussels, she had come from China to Brussels expressly to study under him, but he was becoming more and more convinced that poetry meant more to her. Now he was sorry he hadn't brought her to the meeting. She had given thought to the journal and drawn up suggestions relating exclusively to poetry, she called them her "list." She would have liked to bring them up at once, but she hadn't been told that Herr Musil was also a poet, so she had thought it inappropriate to speak of them at the very first meeting. But there was plenty of time, the project called for careful preparation. He would send Herr Musil his wife's suggestions along with a list of related topics, all of which merited consideration. Unfortunately, his wife spoke only French, he in a pinch could carry on a discussion with her, conversation with her was none too easy, that was another reason why he hadn't brought her, but her written French had been praised by everyone in Brussels, and Veza too had offered to look through her French notes, to make sure that Herr Musil would have no trouble with them.

It was not like Scherchen to deliver a lengthy plea of this sort. Ordinarily he contented himself with giving orders or explaining musical compositions. But he liked talking about his Chinese wife. He was proud of her, he attracted attention through her. She was an enchanting, highly cultivated woman of good family. She had lived through the Japanese invasion of China, and when she talked about it she acted out the terrible events. Sch. had fallen in love on seeing her, frail, slender, clad in Chinese silk, conducting Mozart in Brussels. But when she talked about war, you could hear the rat-tat-tat of machine guns. Back in Peking, she wrote to him. Sch. had called off all his concerts and taken the Trans-Siberian Railroad to China, planning to stay five days. He allowed no more than five days for wooing and wedding Shü-Hsien. When he got there, he was told that it couldn't be done so quickly, it took longer to get married, but there again he had won out by sheer force of will, and married Shü-Hsien within five days. Leaving her at home with her parents for the time being, he had jumped into the train and in little more than a month he was back in Europe giving his concerts.

Shü-Hsien arrived a few months later and the two of them came to live with us in Grinzing. There we witnessed the early days of their marriage; they had to communicate with each other in French, hers correct but delivered in a monosyllabic-sounding staccato, his an unspeakably barbaric Franco-German, larded with mistakes and to us totally incomprehensible. He put her right to work, all day she had to copy music for his orchestra. I can't help wondering when she had time to think up poetic themes for the projected journal. Perhaps she had once spoken to him of Chinese poetry. And then, since he made use of everything that came his way, he asked her to jot down a few ideas. This he now remembered at our conference, and it came in handy. It enabled him to promise Musil something, a list of topics that might appeal to him and that would give Shü-Hsien, who was well versed in French literature, no trouble. He was so full of his Chinese love that he was always glad to talk about her. I liked him at that time. The resentment I had carried about with me since our days in Strasbourg seemed to have evaporated. The new phase had begun with the sudden arrival of a wire from him asking me to meet him at such and such a time at the West Station, where he had an hour's wait between trains. More out of curiosity than affection, I went. His train pulled in, he leaned out of the window and said: "I'm on my way to Peking to get married."

Then on the platform he breathlessly told me the story. He spoke with rapture of his Chinese girl, told me how he had been overcome at the sight of her conducting Mozart in Chinese dress. He had words, ecstatic words, for a human being other than himself. He had promised to go and marry her as soon as he heard from her. Now she had written, and it was as though he, who was always issuing orders, were voluntarily submitting to an order from halfway around the world. I had never seen him like that, and as he went on with his breathless tale, I felt that I had suddenly begun to like him. It was almost unthinkable that this workhorse should call off all his concerts and rehearsals for five weeks.

In his haste to be married he had forgotten a few important things. Suddenly Dea Gombrich, the violinist, appeared on the platform. She too had been summoned to the West Station, and she was late. He told her only that he was going to Peking to be married, would she please run and buy him a tie, he needed one for his wedding. She hurried off and came back just as his train was pulling out. She handed him the tie through the window, he stood there smiling and thanked her; his lips were not as thin as usual. He was already on his way to Siberia when I told the story to Dea, who was still out of breath from running so fast.

I had seen him swept off his feet, and my new feeling for him lasted longer than one might have expected. The two of them stayed with us on Himmelstrasse for quite some time. Veza was entranced by Shü-Hsien, who had a good head and in spite of being in love saw Sch. as he was. She could even make fun of him.

Now, at the editorial conference, I didn't mind his using her as he used everything and everyone. I realized that he had to boast about her because he was still in love with her. Perhaps, I thought, there will be a miracle and it won't end as everything ends with him, perhaps he will stick to his Chinese woman. My love for things Chinese made me worry about her future. I worried more about her, who was a total stranger here, than I would have about any of his European women. But at this conference on Nussdorferstrasse she was suddenly very much present. Musil, whose main concern was obviously to avoid promising to give the journal a prose piece of any length, and who for that reason had brought up the possibility of poetic subjects, had conjured up Shü-Hsien with his suspicious questions. We had all heard of her, we enjoyed thinking about her, she was our real poetic theme. The magazine came to nothing, but thanks to Shü-Hsien I think we all preserved a pleasant memory of the founding conference.

Hudba. *Peasants Dancing*

My mother died on June 15, 1937.

A few weeks earlier, in May, I went to Prague for the first time. I still felt light and free. I took a room on the top floor of the Hotel Juliš on Wenceslas Square. From the wide terrace that went with the room I could look down on the traffic, and at night on the lights of the square—a view that seemed made to order for the painter who was living in the room next to mine: Oskar Kokoschka.

For his fiftieth birthday, a big exhibition was being given at the Museum of Applied Art on Stubenring in Vienna. Up until then I had seen only a few of his pictures here and there, but the show had given a powerful impression of his work as a whole. In Prague he was doing a portrait of President Masaryk and he had refused to go to Vienna for the opening. Carl Moll, his old champion in Vienna, had given me a letter for him and had asked me to tell him about the exhibition and remind him of how many admirers he had in Vienna. Moll told me of Kokoschka's deep resentment against official Austria, not only for its disregard of his work but also because he could not forget the events of February 1934. His mother, whom he had loved more than anyone in the world, had died of a broken heart as a result of the civil war being fought on the streets of Vienna. From her house in Liebhartstal she had seen guns firing at the new workers' apartment blocks. When buying a house for his mother, who had believed in him from the very first and taken a passionate interest in his painting, Kokoschka had chosen this location because of the view of Vienna. And what had become of that view!

She had been close enough to hear the gunfire. She couldn't tear herself away from the sight of the fighting. Soon afterward she had fallen ill and had never left her sickbed. Carl Moll had known Kokoschka's mother and was convinced that without her her son would never have found himself. Now that this woman, who had borne the wonderful name Romana, was gone, he felt that Kokoschka would break with Austria for good. The new regime in Germany regarded him as a degenerate artist; this was the moment for Austria to receive its greatest painter with open arms. But even if the Austrian authorities had been farsighted enough to ask him back with honor, how could he have returned to a country which he held responsible for his mother's death?

I had heard a good deal about Kokoschka. Anna had told me about a turbulent phase of his life. His passion for Alma Mahler had been made legendary by some of his first paintings. On my first visit to Hohe Warte I had seen a portrait of her as "Lucrezia Borgia," as she titled it. It was hung in the tireless widow's trophy room, where she displayed it to all comers with the observation that, sad to say, the artist, who had had talent in those days, had come to nothing and was only a poor refugee.

Now for the first time I saw the man himself, from terrace to terrace; his features were familiar to me from self-portraits. What surprised me most was his voice. He spoke so softly that I could hardly understand him. I paid close attention, but missed a good deal even so. Carl Moll had announced my coming in a letter, but it was by pure chance that I moved into the room next to his. He was not only quiet but self-effacing as well. Still under the sway of his exhibition, I was rather taken aback that he should treat me as an equal. He asked about my book, said he was meaning to read it, Moll had spoken highly of it. Here on the terrace I had the impression that he was curious about me. I felt his octopus eye on me, but it did not seem hostile.

He apologized for being busy that evening, as though he felt obliged to devote an evening to me. His gentleness seemed all the more astonishing when I thought of Anna's story from her early childhood, when she had answered to the name Gucki. Sitting on the floor in a corner of the studio, she had listened in horror to a jealous scene between Kokoschka and her mother. He had threatened to lock her mother up in the studio, once he may even have carried out his threat. Those scenes had made a lasting impression on Anna. In my imagination they were loud and violent, and I had expected an emotional man who would respond to my news of his show with an angry tirade against the Austrian government. He had only a few disparaging words, and these were softly spoken. His most aggressive feature, I thought, was his chin, which was quite pronounced, very much as he painted it in his self-portraits. But most impressive was his eye, motionless, opaque, undeviatingly on the lookout; strangely enough, I always thought of one eye, just as I have written here. His words came out blurred and toneless, as if he released them haphazardly and reluctantly. He gave me an appointment for the following day and left me in a state of confusion: neither his pictures nor anything I had heard about him seemed compatible with his muted manner.

Next day I met him at a café. He was with the philosopher Oskar Kraus, who was a faithful disciple of Franz Brentano. This Kraus, a professor of philosophy and a well-known figure in Prague, had been infected with his mentor's addiction to riddles. He was doing most of the talking. He managed to captivate Kokoschka with a variety of riddles and with talk relating exclusively to riddles; once again I had an impression of modesty, simplicity. In reality, as I realized only later, he was anything but simple, his mind often went devious ways. Nor was he modest; the truth of the matter was that in certain surroundings it pleased him to disappear, as though adapting to the ambient coloration. This opalescent quality was his special gift; here again, in his easy, natural way of changing color, he resembled an octopus, while his large eye, which I always thought of in the singular, scrutinized its prey without indulgence.

But in that café there was little for him to scrutinize. He knew old Professor Kraus well and could hardly have found the smugly garrulous philosopher very exciting. There was something servile about the way in which a man of his age kept referring to his master Franz Brentano, or so it seemed to me at the time, for I had hardly read Brentano and was not yet aware of how richly inspiring a thinker he was. I felt that Kraus with his perpetual chatter was being rude to Kokoschka, but Kokoschka seemed to enjoy it, he had no desire to say anything himself and persisted in his opalescent watchfulness.

All this time I was burning to hear him say something about Georg Trakl. I knew he had known Trakl and had taken the wonderful title of his picture *The Bride of the Wind* from Trakl. I was convinced that without the title the picture would not exist, that no one would have paid any attention to it if it had not been so titled. It was about that time that I fell under Trakl's spell; no other modern poet has meant so much to me. His tragic fate still moves me as deeply as when I first learned of it. Obviously there was no point in turning the conversation to Trakl in the presence of this unfeeling riddler. But that is just what I did. I quietly asked Kokoschka if he had known him. "I knew him well," he replied. He said no more; even if he had wanted to, he couldn't have said anything, for the professor was already bleating away at another riddle.

I had the impression that Vienna no longer counted for Kokoschka. In his early days, when he would suddenly turn up just about anywhere with Adolf Loos, Vienna had been something. But he had cast Vienna out rather than the other way around, and good old Moll, who had been running himself ragged for him for years, wasn't the man to revive his interest in Vienna. Gifted as he was at disappearing, I suspected that at present he was disappearing only because he wanted to be left in peace.

I had almost given up hope of having a real conversation with him when he suddenly warmed up and began talking about his mother and his brother Bohi. The house in Liebhartstal, where his brother was still living since his mother's death, was the only thing that still interested him in Vienna. He regarded his brother as a writer. Did I know him? He had written a great novel in four volumes. He had been a sailor and seen a good deal of the world. No one wanted to publish the book. Did I know of a publisher who might be interested? His brother had no luck in such matters. He was lacking, not in self-confidence, but in calculation. Kokoschka saw nothing shameful in Bohi's acceptance of his help. He was glad to support his brother and never uttered a word of complaint. He spoke of him with affection and respect. I was moved by this love for his brother, who had always believed in him but also in himself, and it struck me as an endearing trait in Kokoschka that he insisted on offering the world a picture of two equal brothers.

Among my friends in Vienna there had often been talk of this brother. Kokoschka's reputation was so great that any connection with him conferred a certain prestige. Walter Loos was a young architect; despite his name he was no relation of the great Adolf Loos, but perhaps because of the homonymy, he felt it was his duty to become acquainted with Kokoschka's brother. When sitting at a *Heurigen* with Wotruba and me, he gave an enthusiastic account of the exuberantly beautiful chimney sweep's daughter who was just the right companion for the corpulent Bohi. He told us about the ups and downs of this relationship, about Bohi's jealousy, about wild scenes and stormy reconciliations. And yet, though pursued by every man in town, the chimney sweep's daughter was strictly faithful to her Bohi, she just couldn't be seduced. As Bohi was known to be Oskar's brother, all talk about him was really about Oskar, and that is why jealousy was required of Bohi. Wotruba listened almost devoutly to all the stories about Kokoschka's brother. Young Loos, as we called him, kept provoking Wotruba with Oskar's fame. By holding Kokoschka aloft like a flag, he had gained a certain standing in our group; what he had to say apart from that didn't amount to much.

Now it was Kokoschka who spoke of his brother Bohi as matter-of-factly as if his name and circumstances were well known to all Vienna. When I went on to talk about young Loos, he seemed rather annoyed.

"An architect by that name shouldn't even exist. There can only be one Loos."

Nor did it appeal to him when I defended my friend by saying that, after all, he had been the friend of Kokoschka's brother and not, like old Loos, the friend of the real Kokoschka. This, he felt, called for a speech in praise of his brother, in the course of which I learned more about the four-volume work that no publisher would touch. Hadn't this so-called young Loos said anything about it?

No, he had only spoken of Bohi's love for the chimney sweep's daughter and described their scenes. Kokoschka, who was incredibly quick, sniffed out a connection with the famous scenes between himself and Alma Mahler and made a dismissive gesture, though I had not been so tactless as to suggest anything of the sort.

"That's pure Nestroy," he said. "It has nothing to do with Bohi's writing. Their scenes attract attention because they're both so fat. Bohi is pure. He doesn't make scenes in order to attract attention."

That sounded as if he were trying to justify his own

early scenes. When he was teaching in Dresden, he had lived with a life-sized doll, made according to his specifications to look like Alma Mahler, so perpetuating the talk about the two of them. The story was known even to people who had no use for his painting. The doll was the element of the old scenes that he still carried around with him. It sat beside him at cafés, coffee was served it, and supposedly it was put to bed with him at night. Bohi, on the other hand, quite unlike his brother, did nothing for his reputation. That is why Oskar called him "pure"; that's why he liked to talk about him; to him Bohi was his own innocence.

On one of the following days a large number of peasants paraded on Wenceslas Square. One had a good view of them from the terrace of my room at the Hotel Juliš. I invited Ludwig Hardt and a few other people to come and watch the parade. Hardt came with his wife, whom I hadn't met before. She was short like him, pretty and self-assured. When you saw the two together, you couldn't help thinking of a circus act. You expected horses to be brought in at any moment, and to see the shapely little woman leap from one to another, while he would perform no less hazardous feats at her side.

But now they were standing beside me on the terrace high over the square, where peasants from all over the country were marching past in their native costumes, some on horseback, amid music and cheers. One was reminded of a peasant wedding. A peasant stepped forward and began to dance, then others here and there in the crowd, each by himself. There was something so exhilarating about the way they burst out of the crowd and, bulky as they were, made room for themselves that tears came to my eyes. I turned away to hide them and my eyes met those of Kokoschka, who had just come out on his terrace. He too was looking down at the peasants, and our eyes met. He saw my agitation and signaled to me with as much warmth as if he had been speaking of his brother Bohi.

I could not have said at the time what moved me so in the solo dances of peasants bursting out of their groups. Their exuberance, their strength, their color left no room for sadness. This was a moment free from all dark forebodings, a moment of heartfelt happiness, though I was not included in their parade—a peasant I certainly was not. And at the same time I was moved by a recognition, a recognition of the dancing peasants in Brueghel. Paintings mold our experience. They become an essential part of us, a kind of native soil. According to the pictures we consist of, we embark on different kinds of life. My excitement over the peasants on Wenceslas Square was colorful and liberating. Two years later Prague had ceased to be Prague. But I had been allowed to experience these people's strength and heavy charm.

I had a similar feeling about the language. It was totally unknown to me. There was a large Czech population in Vienna. But no one else knew their language. Innumerable Viennese had Czech names, few knew what they meant. One of the loveliest of these was Wotruba, the name of my "twin brother," who didn't know a word of his father's language. Now I was in Prague and I went everywhere; I especially liked to stroll about in the courtyards of big apartment houses and listen to the people talking. Czech struck me as a combative language, because all the words were strongly accented on the first syllable. When you listened to people talking, you received a series of quick thrusts, which continued as long as the conversation lasted.

I had studied the history of the Hussite wars. The fifteenth century had always attracted me, and anyone trying to understand the behavior of crowds was bound to take an interest in the Hussites. I respected the history of the Czechs, and it seems likely that as an outsider trying to hear their language in all its modulations I found things in it which had no source other than my ignorance. But there could be no doubt of its vitality and some words struck me as wonderfully original. I was delighted when I heard the word for music: *hudba*.

All the other European languages I knew of had the same word for it: "music," a beautiful, resonant word— when you pronounced it in German, you felt you were leaping into the air. When you accented it more on the first syllable, it didn't seem quite so active, it hovered awhile in midair before taking off. I was almost as attached to this word as to a tangible object, but as time went on, I began to feel uneasy about its being used for every kind of music, especially as I became better acquainted with modern music. One day I plucked up the courage to speak of this to Alban Berg. Shouldn't there be other words for music? I asked him. Wasn't the Viennese public's obstinate rejection of new music somehow related to their identification with the idea evoked by the word "music," an identification so complete that they could tolerate nothing that might change the content of this word? Perhaps if modern music had a different name, they would try to get used to it. But Alban Berg wanted no truck with this idea. Like all composers before him, he said, he was interested solely in music; what he was doing derived from his forerunners, what his pupils learned from him was music, any other word would be a fraud, and hadn't I noticed that the same word had spread all over the earth? He reacted violently, almost angrily to my "suggestion," and so firmly that I never mentioned it again to anyone.

But though awareness of my musical ignorance kept me from talking about it, the idea stayed with me. And now I was fascinated in Prague when I learned by chance that the Czech word for music was *hudba*. That was the word for Stravinsky's *Les Noces*, for Bartók, Janáček and a lot more.

As though enchanted, I went from courtyard to court-yard. What sounded to me like defiance was perhaps mere communication, but if so, it was more highly charged and contained more of the speaker than we tend to reveal in our communications. Possibly the force with which Czech words hit me might be traced back to my childhood memories of Bulgarian. But those memories had vanished, I had completely forgotten Bulgarian, and how much of a forgotten language stays with us I have no way of knowing. It was certain that in those Prague days various impressions made on me by widely separate periods of my life converged. I absorbed Slavic sounds as parts of a language which touched me in some inexplicable way.

But I *spoke* German with many people, I spoke nothing else, and these were people with a conscious, sophisticated attitude toward that language. For the most part they were writers who wrote in German, and it was always evident that this language, to which they clung against the powerful ground swell of Czech, meant something different to them from what it meant to those who operated with it in Vienna.

Auto-da-Fé had been translated into Czech and recently published. That is why I had come to Prague. A young writer, now known under the name H. G. Adler, who then held a position in some public institution, had invited me to give a reading. Some five years younger than I, he belonged to a German-speaking literary group in which *Auto-da-Fé* was going the rounds. Adler, the most active of them all, did everything he could to arouse interest in my reading. He also guided me around town, making sure that none of its beauties should escape me.

He was intensely idealistic and seemed out of place in the damnable times to which he was soon to fall victim. Even in Germany it would have been hard to find a man more dominated by German literary tradition. But he was here in Prague, he spoke and read Czech with ease, respected Czech literature and music, and explained everything I did not understand in a way that made it attractive to me.

I'm not going to list the glories of Prague, which are known to all. It would strike me as almost indecent to speak of squares, churches, palaces, streets, bridges and the river, with which others have spent their whole lives and which permeate their work. I discovered none of that by myself, it was all shown to me. If anyone had a right to speak of these confrontations, it was the man who thought of them and brought them about. But he was not content with the surprises he arranged for me; he himself was full of curiosity and throughout our expeditions never tired of asking me questions. I was glad to answer him; I spoke to him of many people, many opinions, judgments and prejudices that had had a place in my life.

But he realized what it meant to me to hear all sorts of people speaking a language I did not understand, to hear them *for myself*, without anyone translating what they said. My interest in the effect of words I did not understand must have been something new to him. It was a very special sort of effect, not at all comparable to that of music, for one feels *threatened* by words one does not understand, one turns them over in one's mind in an attempt to blunt them, but they are repeated and in repetition become more menacing than ever. He was tactful enough to leave me alone for hours, though he worried about my getting lost and, I'm sure, regretted these interruptions to our talks. When we met again he would ask me about my impressions and it was a sign of my great sympathy for him that I found it hard not to tell him everything.

My Mother's Death

I found her asleep, her eyes closed. She lay there, emaciated, reduced to pale skin, with deep black holes instead of eyes, and lifeless black caverns where her magnificent wide nostrils had been. Her forehead seemed narrower, shrunken on both sides. I had expected the look of her eyes, and I had the impression that she had barred them against me. When her eyes failed me, I searched for what was most characteristic of her, her large nostrils and her vast forehead, but her forehead had lost its spaciousness, it no longer embraced anything, and the anger of her nostrils had been engulfed by their blackness.

I was startled, but still full of *her* old power; I suspected that she was hiding from me. She doesn't want to see me, she wasn't expecting me. She senses my presence and is pretending to be asleep. I asked myself what she would have thought if she had been in my shoes, because I was she, we knew each other's thoughts, hers were mine and mine were hers.

I had brought roses, she could never resist the scent of roses. She had breathed it in the garden of her childhood in Ruschuk, and when in our happy years we joked about her nostrils—no one else's were so big—she said they were so big because as a child she had dilated them smelling roses. Her earliest memory was of lying under a rosebush, and then she was crying because she had been carried into the house and the fragrance was gone. Later on, when she left her father's house and garden, she had tested the scent everywhere in search of the right one; this again had expanded her nostrils and they had stayed large.

When she opened her eyes, I said: "I've brought you these from Ruschuk." She looked at me incredulously, it wasn't my presence that she doubted but the source of the roses. "From the garden," I said; there was only one garden. She had taken me there and breathed deeply and consoled me with fruit for my grandfather's harsh treatment. Now I held out the roses to her, she breathed fragrance, the room filled with it. She said: "That's the scent. They are from the garden." She accepted my story, she accepted me too—I was included in the fragrant cloud. She didn't ask what had brought me to Paris. That was her face again with the insatiable nostrils. Her enlarged eyes rested on me. She didn't say: "I don't want to see you. What are you doing here? I didn't send for you." She recognized the scent, and I had crept into it. She asked no questions, she surrendered wholly to the smell. Her forehead seemed to widen, I fully expected her unmistakable words, hard words that I dreaded. I heard her words of bitter reproach, as though she had repeated them: You've married. You didn't tell me. You deceived me.

She hadn't wanted to see me. And when Georg, alarmed at her decline, wired and wrote, telling me to come at once, when I broke off my stay in Prague after a week, hurried back to Vienna and on to Paris, his main concern was how we could make her consent to see me. He wanted above all to disperse the obsession that tormented her and had recently become more intense, and so to avoid an outburst of rage, which was possible, he thought, even in her weakened condition.

When soon after my arrival I told him of my plan to bring her "roses from Ruschuk" and assured him that she would believe me, he said dubiously: "Would you dare? It will be your last lie." But he couldn't think of anything better, and when he realized that I not only was concerned with overcoming her resistance to my visit but really

wanted to bring her the fragrance she had been longing
for, he rather shamefacedly gave in. But he did not wish
to be present, for fear of losing her confidence in case
my plan should fail and arouse her to new anger.

She held the flowers over her face like a mask, and I
had the impression that her features grew larger and
stronger. She trusted me as before, she had dismissed her
doubts, she knew who I was, but not a hostile word crossed
her lips. She didn't say: "You've had a long trip. Is that
what you've come for?" But I remembered something she
had often told me. Before climbing the mulberry tree
where she went to read, she would stop for a moment
under the rosebush. The roses presided over her reading,
their scent stayed with her, and whatever she might be
reading was impregnated with it. Then she could bear
the worst horrors; even if she was scared out of her wits,
she did not feel threatened.

In our bad period I had held this up to her. I told her
I could attach no importance to anything she had read
while thus anesthetized. Horror that had been subjected
to such fragrance was no horror. I had never withdrawn
those hard words. And that may have put me in mind of
my stratagem.

Then after all she said: "Aren't you tired from your
journey? Rest awhile." She meant my trip to Ruschuk,
not just to Paris. I assured her that I was not at all tired,
and had no intention of parting with her so soon. She
may have thought that I had come only to bring her the
message from Ruschuk and that I would leave at once. It
might have been better if I had. It hadn't occurred to me
that once she recognized me and accepted my presence
something about me might upset her and that in her
condition she couldn't stand having anyone with her for
long. After a while she said: "Sit farther away." I moved
the chair I had just sat down on. But she said: "Farther!
Farther!" I moved again, but it still wasn't far enough for

her. I moved into the corner of the small room, realizing that she wanted to lie there in silence. When Georg came in, the position of the roses told him that she had accepted them, and he saw by her features that she felt better. But then, seeing me in the corner, he was surprised that I should be *sitting*, and sitting just there. "Wouldn't you rather stand?" he asked, but she shook her head emphatically. "Why don't you sit closer?" he added, but she answered in my stead: "Leave him where he is."

She kept him close to her; there he stayed and embarked on a series of operations, the purpose of which was not always clear to me. These were things she expected him to do, in a fixed order. She forgot everything else; she no longer knew I was there, and she wouldn't have minded if I had left. Helpless as she seemed, she anticipated certain of his operations, as though to remind him of the proper order. He moistened her hands and forehead, and moved her up a little higher on her pillows. He set a glass to her lips and she willingly took a sip. He smoothed the bedclothes and tried to take the roses out of her hands. Perhaps he wanted to relieve her of them, perhaps he meant to put them in water, but she wouldn't let go of them and gave him a sharp look, as in the old days. He felt the violence of her reaction and was glad of her energy. For weeks he had been watching and dreading the decline of her powers. He left the flowers in her hand on the bedspread; they took up a good deal of room and were as important as he was. I, on the other hand, had been relegated to the corner and doubted whether she was aware of my presence.

Suddenly I heard her say to Georg: "Your big brother is here. He has come from Ruschuk. Why don't you say something to each other?" Georg looked into my corner as if he hadn't noticed me before. He came over to me. I stood up. We embraced. We really embraced, not mechanically as when I had first come into the apartment.

But he didn't say a word, and I heard her say: "Why don't you ask him any questions?" She was expecting a conversation about my journey, about my visit to the garden. "He hadn't been there for a long time," she said, and Georg, who hated lies, went along with my story reluctantly: "Twenty-two years ago. During the First World War." He meant that I hadn't been in Ruschuk since the visit in 1915. Then our mother had once again shown me the garden of her childhood. Her father was dead, but the mulberry tree was still there, and the apricots were ripening in the orchard just behind it.

Her eyes closed, and as we stood there together she dozed off. When it seemed certain that she would go on sleeping, we withdrew to the living room. Then he spoke of her condition and told me she was past saving. Long ago, when we were children, she had thought her lungs were affected. Later, her fears had come true. Then a young doctor, aged twenty-six, he had become a lung specialist for her sake. Day and night he had spent all his free time near his mother. During his studies, he had come down with tuberculosis. His friends thought he had caught it from her. He had spent a few months in a sanatorium in the mountains near Grenoble. There he had worked as a doctor. When discharged as cured, he had resumed the care of his mother.

She had difficulty in breathing, she had suffered from asthma for years. In the last months she had declined so rapidly that he made up his mind to call me, reluctantly, because he feared the consequences of a confrontation; but the possibility of a reconciliation seemed to carry more weight. At the moment we seemed to be reconciled. Though he knew her sudden shifts of feeling and a violent outburst was still conceivable, he felt relieved at the good start. To my surprise he did not, when we were alone, reproach me for deceiving her with Paris roses and not going to her father's garden. "She still believes you," he said. "You've always believed her in the same way. That's the bond between you. You have the power to kill each other. You must have known why you protected Veza from her. I understand. But I've had to live with the effect all that has had on her. I can't forgive you for that. But that's of no importance now. She thinks you've come from the place that she never stops thinking about."

There was no room for me in the noisy little apartment on the rue de la Convention. I slept somewhere else and came to see her several times a day. She couldn't stand my presence for long, but then she couldn't stand any prolonged visits. Time and again, I had to leave the room and wait outside.

I didn't go too near her bed. Her eyes grew larger and more brilliant. Each morning when I came in, those eyes took possession of me. Her breathing grew weaker, but the power of her eyes grew stronger. She did not avert them; when she didn't want to see, she closed them. She looked at me until she hated me. Then she said: "Go!" Every day she said that several times, and each time it was to punish me. It hit me hard, though I was aware of her condition and knew I was there to be punished and humiliated; that was what she wanted of me now. Then I would wait in the next room until the nurse came in and nodded to let me know my mother had asked for me. When I went in to her, her gaze would seize hold of me with such force that I feared it would exhaust her, her eyes grew wider and brighter, she said nothing. Then suddenly would gasp: "Go!" and I felt as if I had been banished forever from her sight. I sagged a little, a convicted criminal conscious of my guilt, and left. Though I knew she would ask for me again, I took my dismissal seriously, I did not get used to it, each time I took it as a new punishment.

All the weight had gone out of her. Everything that

was still alive had gone into her eyes, which were heavy with the wrong I had done her. She looked at me to tell me so, I held her gaze fast, I bore it, I wanted to bear it. There was no anger in that gaze, only the torment of all the years in which I had not let her out of my sight. To break away from me she had felt sick, she had gone to doctors, traveled to distant places, to the mountains, the seashore, any old place as long as I was not there. There she had led her life and hidden it from me in letters, because of me she had believed herself to be sick, and years later she had fallen sick in earnest. Now she was holding it up to me; all that was in her eyes. Then she tired and said: "Go." And while waiting in the next room, a false penitent, I wrote to the woman whose name never crossed her lips, I gave Veza the trust I owed my mother.

Then she dozed and then she asked for me, as though I had just come back from a journey, and her gaze, which in sleep had taken on a new charge of the past, was fixed on me again. Wordlessly it said that I had forsaken, deceived and offended her for the sake of another woman.

And when Georg was there, all his movements showed how it should have been. He had formed no ties. He had lived only for her. In every one of his movements he served her, he could do nothing that was not good, for everything he did was done for her. When he went out, he thought of his return. For her sake he had studied medicine, for her sake he had worked in a hospital to gain the experience he needed to care for her illness. And he condemned me as she did, but of his own accord; she had not put him up to it. The youngest brother had renounced all life of his own as the eldest should have done; he had devoted himself exclusively to the service of his mother, and when it exceeded his strength, he too had fallen sick. He had gone to the mountains for the breath of life, but only in order to return to her and care for her. He had less to thank her for than I, because I was born entirely of her spirit, but I had failed her, for the sake of some chimeras I had let myself be talked into staying in Vienna, I had sold my soul to Vienna, and then, when I finally produced something worthwhile, it turned out that this something was by her, that she and not the chimeras had dictated it to me. So the whole tragedy had been unnecessary, I could have gone my way with her and arrived at the same result.

Such is the power of the dying who defend themselves against survivors, and it is well that the right of the weaker should be vindicated. Those whom we have not been able to protect are entitled to blame us for doing nothing to save them. Their reproach incorporates defiance which they pass on to us: the divine illusion that we may succeed in defeating death. He who sent out the serpent, the tempter, calls them back. There has been punishment enough. The tree of life is yours. Ye shall not die.

I seem to remember that we followed the coffin on foot, across the whole city to Père Lachaise.

I felt enormous defiance, and I wanted to communicate it to all those who were going about in that city that day. I felt proud, as though interceding for her against the whole world. No one was as good as she. I thought "good," but my meaning was not what she had never been, to my mind she was good because, though dead, she would live on. My two brothers walked to my right and left. I felt no difference between them and me. As long as we were walking, we were one, excluding everyone else. As for the others, they were too few for my liking. I wanted the procession to stretch through the whole city, to be as long as our itinerary. I cursed the blindness of those who didn't know who was being laid to rest. The traffic stopped only long enough to let the cortege through and started up again as soon as we had passed, as though no one's coffin were being driven by. It was a long march, and my feeling of defiance lasted all the way—as if I were having to fight my way through those enormous crowds. As though victims were falling to the right and left in her honor, but not enough of them to meet her claims: The more ground covered, the greater the funeral. "Look. There she is. Did you know? Do you know who is shut up in that coffin? *She* is life. Without her there's nothing. Without her your houses will cave in and your bodies shrivel."

This is what I remember of that funeral cortege. I see myself walking, defying Paris with her defiance. I'm pretty sure my two brothers are by my sides. I don't know how Georg made it all that way. Did he lean on me? Whom did he lean on? Was he sustained by some pride? Among the others in the cortege I don't see a single face. I don't know who was there. In the apartment I looked on with hatred as the coffin lid was screwed on. As long as she was in the apartment, I felt that violence was being done her. On the long way to the cemetery, I felt none of this; now the coffin was she, and nothing came between me and my admiration for her. That's how a person like her must be carried to the grave if one's admiration for her is to be free from dross. That feeling lasted, losing none of its intensity; it must have persisted for two or three hours. There wasn't a trace of resignation in it, perhaps not even of grief, for how could grief have been reconciled with my raging defiance? I could have fought for her, I could have killed. I was ready for anything. Far from feeling numb, I challenged the world. With her forehead I plowed a way for her through the city—people were reeling on all sides—waiting for the insult that would oblige me to fight.

He wanted to be alone so he could speak to her. For several days I stayed with Georg for fear he would do himself harm. Then he begged me to leave him alone for

two or three days, so he could be with her, that was what
he wanted and nothing else. I trusted him and came back
on the third day. He didn't want to leave the apartment
where she had been ill. He sat on the chair where he had
sat beside her bed in the evening and went on talking. As
long as he was saying the old words, she was alive for
him. He wouldn't admit to himself that she couldn't hear
him anymore. Her voice had grown feeble, less audible
than a breath, but he heard it and went on talking. He
talked, for she always wanted to know everything, about
his day, about the people he had seen, about teachers and
friends and passersby. He talked as he had before, when
he came home from work; at present he went nowhere,
but he still had things to talk about. He didn't feel guilt
about making things up for her, for all his invention was
a lament, a soft, monotonous, long-lasting lament, because
soon she might cease to hear him. He wanted nothing to
end; his ministrations continued in words. His words
awakened her, and she who had suffocated breathed again.
His voice was soft and full of feeling, as it had been when
he entreated her to breathe. He did not weep, he was
afraid of losing a single one of her moments; when he
sat facing her on this chair, he granted himself no relief
that might have resulted in a loss for her. His entreaty
did not cease, I heard a voice I had not known, pure and
high like an evangelist's. I wasn't supposed to hear it, for
he wished to be alone, but I did hear it because I was
worried: Should I leave him alone as he wished? And I
tested that voice a long time before making up my mind,
it has rung in my ears ever since. How does one test a
voice, what does one measure, what can one rely on? I
hear him speaking softly to the dead woman whom he
will never leave until it comes time to follow her; to whom
he speaks as if he still had the power to hold her, and
this power belongs to her, he gives it to her and she must
feel it. It sounds as if he were singing softly to her, not

about himself, no complaint, only of her, she alone has suffered, she alone has the right to complain, but he comforts her and entreats her, and assures her again and again that she is there, she alone, with him alone, no one else, everyone else upsets her, and that's why he wants me to leave him alone with her for two or three days, and although she is in her grave, there she lies where she lay ill, and in words he seizes hold of her, so that she cannot leave him.